MAKING MONEY WITH WORDS

a guidebook for writers

Clement David Hellyer

A SPECTRUM BOOK

PRENTICE-HALL, INC., Englewood Cliffs, New Jersey 07632

Library of Congress Cataloging in Publication Data

Helleyer, Clement David.
  Making money with words.

  (A Spectrum Book)
  Bibliography: p.
  Includes index.
  1. Authorship. I. Title.
PN151.H44   808.02   80–25710
ISBN 0-13-547414-0
ISBN 0-13-547406-x (pbk.)

Materials on p. 226 and pp. 236–7 were reprinted from the *Author's Handbook: Guidelines for Contributors to "Organic Gardening and Farming"* with permission from Rodale Press, Inc.

10 9 8 7 6 5 4 3 2 1

Printed in the United States of America

Editorial/production supervision and interior design by Cyndy Lyle
Manufacturing Buyer: Cathie Lenard

PRENTICE-HALL INTERNATIONAL, INC., *London*
PRENTICE-HALL OF AUSTRALIA PTY. LIMITED, *Sydney*
PRENTICE-HALL OF CANADA, LTD., *Toronto*
PRENTICE-HALL OF INDIA PRIVATE LIMITED, *New Delhi*
PRENTICE-HALL OF JAPAN, INC., *Tokyo*
PRENTICE-HALL OF SOUTHEAST ASIA PTE. LTD., *Singapore*
WHITEHALL BOOKS LIMITED, *Wellington, New Zealand*

For my wife, Gloria, who—although she did not write one word of it—was the co-author of this book.

CONTENTS

PREFACE

This is not just one more how-to book.

Making Money with Words is a *where*-to (an atlas of the writing world) and a *whether*-to . . . whether to become a writer if you aren't one already, or whether to shift to some other writing field if you already make your living as a writer.

I'll make no attempt to unravel the mysteries of short-story crafting (about which I know little), or of creating poetry (about which I know even less), or of the novelist's art—because it remains an enigma, according to Somerset Maugham. "There are three rules for the writing of a novel," he said. "Unfortunately no one knows what they are."

And although there are chapters that gingerly explore the wacky world of television and motion pictures, there's nothing here about the arcane art of scripting. The specifics of writing for this market, or that, are well covered in scores of other books, some of them long out of print, some of them still wet from the presses. Collectively, they cover the ground very well, and you will find their titles listed at appropriate places throughout the book.

The avowed mission of *Making Money with Words* is to lead the reader pleasantly and safely through that fascinating but perilous maze where we all hope to "Pass Go" and "Collect Two Hundred Dollars."

During a period spanning more than four decades, I have written and sold hundreds of articles to newspapers and magazines. I still sell most of what I write to magazine editors and book publishers. So this book is based on forty years of calluses, not merely on classroom theory.

During those four decades, I have lectured to hundreds of hopefuls in seminars, classes, and conferences on the craft of writing. Please note the verb "lectured." I do not say I have "taught" hundreds how to be writers, because that would be untrue. Neither this author nor anyone else can teach *anyone* to write who does not want most fiercely to write in the first place. The teacher-student relationship works only if (1) the teacher knows what he or she is talking about and knows how to teach it, and (2) the student really wants to learn, and will work off his or her gluteus maximus to do so.

So this book will not pretend to teach you *how* to write. It will discuss some of the things you must know if you are to succeed as a writer in any of the numerous specialties covered in the book. Learning *how* to write comes primarily from practice, like playing the tuba or blowing bubblegum.

Whenever anyone says to me, "I want to be a writer," I ask these questions:

What kind of writer, and what kind of writing?

Do you hope to become a full-time professional, or a part-time amateur?

Do you want to work for yourself (free lancing), or for someone else as a staff writer?

Do you see yourself as a novelist, a poet, a dramatist, a newspaper reporter, a writer of nonfiction books?

Would you prefer to write for children, or adults?

Are you thinking about advertising copy, or speeches, or scenarios for TV or Hollywood? Or one-liners for stand-up comics?

The response usually is a startled "I really don't know. I just want to be a *writer.*"

I will assume, perhaps unkindly, that your answer will be something like that, if you are a beginner. You are shopping—that's fine. And if you already make your living as a writer but want to know what else is available, that's also fine.

The fundamental purpose of this book is to help you with your shopping. It will challenge you to examine yourself honestly, so that you may decide whether or not you are cut out to be a writer at all, or to be a writer in some particular specialty.

If you are a beginner, this book will be worth the purchase price only if it helps you to decide:

1. that you *are* cut out to be a writer, or
2. that you are *not.*

If you already work at the craft, your purchase will justify itself if this book helps you to find a more rewarding and remunerative career in some other form of writing.

It will be worth the price especially if you are exploring the world of writing for the first time, and become convinced—by reading this book—that you are *not* cut out to be a writer. Because it will save you much pain and frustration.

There are already too many hurt and frustrated people in the world who think they are writers, and are not.

A LOOK
AT THE
BIG PICTURE

*If what you are doing is familiar and
comfortable, you probably are not
learning.*

INTRODUCTION

This book was written not only for novices and hopefuls. I had in mind, as well

- the seasoned writer, scarred and battle-fatigued, who has wearied of one form of writing and searches for other and greener pastures (and who won't mix metaphors like that);
- the literate but confined housewife, fed up with the put-out-the-garbage-change-the-baby routine, who yearns to express herself somehow (and make a little money in the process);
- the retiree who finds that you can go fishing just so many days a week without growing painfully bored, and who has something to say but doesn't know how—or to whom—to say it;
- the teacher who has written instructional materials for years, and now thinks he or she would like to take a crack at a novel,

a magazine article, or . . . at anything a little more exciting than syllabi and textbooks;

• the newspaper reporter who has honed his or her work skills and research capabilities to a fine point, and now hopes to apply those assets to something more satisfying than covering the Cave of Winds (City Hall);

• the publicity writer who thinks there must surely be something more important in this world than writing puffs for gin-guzzling movie stars or gas-guzzling automobiles (and there *is*!);

• the ship's captain, doctor, lawyer, attorney, civil servant, clergyman, librarian—just about anyone, of any age, color, or creed—who is convinced he or she can write circles around that fellow whose novel (article, short story, poem) he or she read last night in bed, and wants to give it a whirl (and *should*).

The variety of "verbal merchandise" bought and sold in today's literary marketplace truly boggles the imagination. There are one-liner jokes and fillers, and blockbuster books which sell by the pound. There are funny books and grim ones, inspirational books, and books that scare the hell out of you. Textbooks and learned tomes pour from the presses by the millions. There are hundreds of thousands of magazine articles sold and bought every year—and even a few poems.

If, then, you are to make intelligent decisions about how you should direct your talents, you should be aware, at least, of the many and varied outlets for the writer in contemporary America. Otherwise, you may be missing an almost sure bet.

WHAT'S IN IT FOR ME?

Every word in this book was bought and paid for. The same is true of virtually every word in every book you have ever read, or ever will read.

Nearly every syllable in every magazine you read and in your morning or evening paper was bought and paid for.

If you listen to radio or TV today, virtually every word you will hear was bought and paid for.

Every word you read on almost every sign or billboard you passed today was bought and paid for.

Whenever you hear the President on television, every word in his speech was bought and paid for.

The message is obvious: Somebody is being paid to write all those words you are reading or hearing. Could *you* have been that somebody?

How much—you may ask—was paid for those words? Their writer may have received sums ranging from a pittance (maybe a penny or two a word) to a bundle (like $5,000 or more for a half-hour TV script). Free lancers working for minor newspapers or trade journals may earn as little as a penny a word—the same rates paid before World War II! Hacks who churn out soaps for television may be handed weekly paychecks in the four- and even five-digit category. An Erma Bombeck or an Art Buchwald may bank a cool quarter-million or more annually, before taxes. Irving Wallace received a $1.5 million advance and a six-figure movie prepayment on his *promise* to write three more novels, which then existed only in outline form. Novelist Harold Robbins was paid $3.7 million for an idea, and a title to match it. The idea became *Dreams Die First*.

To keep the record in balance, it should be noted that the average first novel may sell fewer than 2,000 copies—not enough to pay the printer's bill. Such first books may net their authors four or five thousand dollars for one, two, or more years of hard labor. In addition, thousands of nonfiction books are published every year which make little if any money for either publisher or author.

But we don't hear about the failures. Always dangling out ahead, like the proverbial carrot on the stick, is the "Big Dream": the runaway best-seller that will bring its author instant acclaim and an advance of $100,000. There's always that "sleeper" someone in Hollywood options for $40,000, then turns into an Oscar-winning colossal starring Charlton Heston. It's the eternal lure of this gold-plated carrot that keeps most writers (of fiction at least) slaving away, day and night, at their typewriters.

But for every book writer, there are thousands of writers who churn out millions of words, every day, that will never see the covers of a book. There are armies of newspaper reporters, hordes of magazine scribes, and legions of advertising-copy writers who generate mountains of written matter every working day. There are speech-smiths, songwriters, filler writers, joke writers, report writers, learned-paper writers, training-manual writers, audio-visual writers, résumé writers, crossword puzzle creators— if there's a word involved, somewhere behind it is a man or woman banging away on a typewriter or scribbling on a notepad.

GALLIA EST OMNIS DIVISA . . .

Like Gaul of yore, today's writing world can be divided roughly into three parts:

I – Creative Writing. This is the storyteller's domain. Creative writing includes any writing—however long or short, grim or hilarious—whose primary purpose is to entertain. It may also instruct, provoke, incite, or awaken any number of emotional responses, but its overriding raison d'être is to divert. Included in this category are the novel, poetry, short stories, motion-picture scenarios, broadcast drama, plays for live theater, librettos for opera and musical comedy—all writings which draw primarily on the creative resources of the writer.

Many of these forms may be divided into sub-categories. Under novels, for example, there are novels for adults, and juvenile novels (which, in turn, may be broken into various age ranges). There are novels of mystery, detection, and suspense; espionage novels; novels based on the lives of real people told against a backdrop of real events, but with all names disguised to protect the innocent (and the author and publisher); novels centered on flesh-and-blood people whose names are used openly. There are Gothics (a very profitable genre), westerns (in which fortunes have been made ever since Zane Grey), period romances, and others.

Should you limit yourself to creative writing? Perhaps you should, if you are indeed a truly creative person.

How does one decide? What are the indicators of the creative personality? The work of Johnson O'Connor and the Human

Engineering Laboratories have provided some answers which many have found useful. Some of those answers will be found in Chapter 1.

II — Fact Writing. In terms of public demand and of sheer volume, fact writing far outdistances fictional forms in today's America. In this category are newspaper and magazine journalism, broadcast journalism, the writing of educational materials, biography, history, nonfiction writing in all its forms. Here the writer is, in one sense or another, a reporter. He or she is gathering, organizing, condensing, and presenting—in written or spoken form—information which the writer hopes will be useful to others.

Among the many types of writing which qualify in this genre are nonfiction books of all descriptions, magazine articles (for which there are thousands of markets in an astonishing variety of subject areas), research reports, learned papers, speeches, newspaper features and news stories, essays, editorials, book reviews, social commentary, columns—in short, any writings based essentially on fact, and meant to be accepted as fact. Some of these writings may be so expertly crafted that they are far more entertaining than the best of fiction. Certain forms of nonfiction writing today borrow heavily from the storyteller's bag of tricks, but they are fact writing nonetheless.

If you believe you are, by nature and training, best qualified to write nonfiction, you will want to investigate the wide variety of opportunities in this category.

III — The Great Miscellany. These are the workaday writing jobs, and there are thousands of them. They may not offer the glamour and romance of Categories I and II, but make no mistake about it: This is where the steady employment is.

I agree—there's more romance in crafting a novel or fashioning poetry than there is in writing press releases. I agree—there's much more glamour in a byline in *Harper's* than in the anonymity of bit of ad copy, or a report, or a speech for the boss. But from those less romantic and glamorous occupations there's also a steady income, money to educate the kids, and a retirement fund for the time when your typewriter goes silent.

So if security holds great attractions for you, Category III may be the place to look. Employment in writing fields listed here does not, of course, prevent you from writing novels, or articles, or poems, or anything else on the side, on your own time (unless your employer prohibits or frowns upon moonlight writing, as some do).

Some of the writing activities I have arbitrarily elected to list under "miscellany" might well have been included under the first two categories. I have chosen to group here such writing activities as public relations and publicity, and the preparation of advertising copy for print and broadcast media. Classified here also is the job market for writers in the publishing industry, both book and magazine. In this enormous industry, men and women with writing talent or proclivities may find employment in a variety of posts which do not require them to actually write, yet they deal with writers and writing every day. This category would include editors, proofreaders, and the readers in book publishing houses who review manuscripts which come in "over the transom," or unsolicited. Editors and other editorial personnel of magazines who deal with writers and their writings also would fit in this category.

I also include teachers of such subjects as creative writing, article writing, and newspaper journalism in this great family. Also listed here are literary agents. All who work in these jobs deal with writers and writing, yet may not themselves be producing writers.

Finally, under "miscellany" may be grouped a small army of people who write copy for greeting cards, song writers, creators of puzzles and jingles, those who write contest entries, and many others engaged in off-beat forms of creative and journalistic writing. (One helpful colleague wryly suggested that I might also want to include the writers of ransom notes, singing telephone messages, and obscene phone calls.)

These three major categories, then, make up the world explored in *Making Money with Words*.

Good hunting!

chapter 1

If you want *to be a writer, forget it. If you* have *to be a writer, you might just* make it.
                    SIDNEY SHELDON

WERE YOU CUT OUT TO BE A WRITER?

First things first.

Before you begin your search through these pages for a writing activity that looks right for you, take a moment to consider these fundamental questions:

First: *Were you really cut out to be a writer?*

Face the question honestly. Never mind what your mother, wife, or husband says about your writing; forget that you were the editor of your high school paper. Look honestly and penetratingly at yourself in light of the clues you will find in this and subsequent chapters.

Next question: *Assuming that you are convinced you were cut out to be a writer, which of the basic writer "types" are you: creative or nonfiction?*

If you don't know yet, that could be one reason why you are reading this book.

And finally: *Are you equipped by temperament and training to be your own boss as a writer? Or should you work for someone else?*

Translation: Do you have the intestinal fortitude (which means the patience and ability to discipline yourself) to be a freelance writer? Or are you short on this quality, and should therefore work for someone who will force you to write and regularly pay you for writing?

Here again, if you don't know the answers, read on.

HOW WOULD YOU DEFINE "WRITER"?

If you ask a man what he does for a living, and he says "I am a plumber," you know exactly what he means. He installs and fixes sinks, bathtubs, and toilets. He works with pipe and fittings. He doesn't mind getting his hands dirty and his knuckles skinned. If he isn't lazy and knows his craft, he makes a comfortable living, has two cars, a camper, a motorbike or two, a boat on a trailer, and a wife and three kids.

If someone answers, "I'm a writer," what image does that call forth from your subconscious? If the respondent is male, you may envision him sitting in his wingback before a crackling fire, pipe in hand, browsing through a bestseller (to see how the competition does it). Or walking his Irish setter through the woods while dreaming up his next plot. Now and then (you tell yourself), he sits down at his typewriter and bats out a novel, when he isn't autographing books, fleeing from nubile maidens, scuba-diving in Bermuda, or being interviewed by Johnny Carson.

If the respondent is female, you may see her sitting demurely at her quaint Victorian desk in her fluffy boudoir, writing—in Spencerian longhand—her latest (of 57) Gothics, a fluffy white poodle nestled at her feet.

Those are fantasies. They are also nonsense.

WRITERS ARE MERCHANTS

Plumbers sell washbowls and drain pipes. Druggists sell nostrums and hot-water bottles. Grocers sell Wheaties and 98-cent encyclopedias and motor oil. Writers sell words.

Wait . . . that's a half-truth. A writer sells thoughts, observations, and ideas. The words are mere blobs, physical symbols through which he or she transmits those thoughts, observations, and ideas to the reader.

Nobody—you and I included—can (or certainly shouldn't) write one single word without first taking thought. Nobody can write a phrase, sentence, paragraph, article, book, TV script, poem, or anything else without first thinking about every word in advance.

So a writer is, first and foremost, a thinker . . . not very often a profound thinker, but nonetheless a person who makes a living with brain-work. He or she is an idea merchant—a manufacturer and seller of thoughts. Words are merely the packages in which the writer wraps his or her ideas or observations, like fresh fish, for shipment to another merchant who repackages them for sale to readers, listeners, or viewers.

The book you now hold in your hand is nothing more than a shipping carton filled with small packages (words) that contain ideas, observations, or facts.

If you find it difficult to generate your own ideas, you may have trouble making it as a *creative* writer. But you may easily find a niche somewhere in the world of nonfiction writing. There you will be a reporter or translator, rather than a creator or a generator. You will be paid to describe what you see or hear, or to give form to the thoughts and observations of others.

HOW CAN YOU TELL?

How, indeed, can you tell whether you are cut out to be a writer, and what kind of writer: creative or nonfiction? And whether you have what it takes to free lance, or should you, instead, work for someone else?

There's no fail-safe method for deciding, of course. If you aspired to be a singer, you could be tested for tone-deafness. If the test proved that you can't carry a tune, this would be sufficient evidence that you'd better shift aspirations. If you hoped to be a painter, but proved to be color-blind and lacking in the slightest sense of perspective or knowledge of anatomy, any good art teacher could counsel you to take up some other endeavor.

But it seems that anyone can be—or aspire to be—a writer. All you need is a pencil and paper or a typewriter, and presto—you are a writer. You may have few if any qualifications for the calling, but who is to say that you cannot *call* yourself a writer? You can even have cards and stationery printed that say so.

There are definite hallmarks, certain identifiable characteristics which distinguish creative and nonfiction writers from one another. Here are some of them, beginning with:

Category I — The Creative Writer

> "Expressed crudely, there is only one chance in four of the wrong person's entering the business world; but three chances in four of the wrong one entering the fine arts."[1]

More than thirty years ago, Johnson O'Connor explored the personality traits which make for success in creative writing. Note the adjective *creative*. The Human Engineering Laboratories, of which O'Connor was director at the time, have since refined and enlarged upon the findings reported by O'Connor in *The Unique Individual*. But the basic premises remain the same, and they merit the study of every man and woman who is seriously attracted to creative writing as a career, or even as a pastime.

"Three quarters of all men and women belong by nature to one personality type, the remainder to another," O'Connor wrote. "From the objective multitude come prosperous business men, from the extremely subjective minority come *creative*

---

[1] Johnson O'Connor, *The Unique Individual* (New York: Human Engineering Laboratory Incorporated, 1948), p.16. Reprinted by permission.

artists, gifted writers [emphasis added], lyric poets, scrupulous surgeons, diligent scientists, and unworldly musicians."[2]

By O'Connor's criteria, gifted, that is creative, writers are definitely in the minority, outnumbered three to one by those whose personality traits mark them for success in the world of business. Are you one of those "extremely subjective" people who, in O'Connor's view, are cut out to be creative writers? Here are the criteria listed by O'Connor as "Traits of the Writer." (Note: I construe O'Connor to mean "creative writer" in every instance.)

TRAITS OF THE WRITER[3]

high	ideaphoria (creative imagination)
high	inductive reasoning
high	analytical reasoning
high	abstract visualization
extremely subjective	personality

O'Connor defines inductive reasoning as "ability to sense a common element in some heterogeneous assortment, a gift for discovering a fundamental law."

Analytical reasoning, he says, is "a gift for organizing material, for logical arrangement."

Abstract visualization, which born creative writers have in abundance, is—again according to O'Connor—the ability to deal with intangibles. By contrast, such specialists as engineers, architects, physicists, chemists, and astronomers, tend to be strong in "structural visualization," or "a mental imaging of solid forms, seeing in three dimensions."

But even those men and women who score "high" in the above cannot succeed as creative writers unless they test out very high in English vocabulary. "To apply this aptitude pattern practically in earning a living demands an exact knowledge of the nice meanings of English words," O'Connor notes. (Including, I might add, the meaning of "nice" as used in this context.)

---

[2] O'Connor, *The Unique Individual*, p. 1.
[3] O'Connor, *The Unique Individual*, p. 81.

Admittedly, the foregoing is heavy stuff (and about the only weighty stuff in this entire book). But O'Connor's findings, and results of later research by the Human Engineering Laboratories[4] throughout the nation, warrant careful study by anyone seriously contemplating a career in creative writing.

In sum, a creative writer is involved in the fine arts, just as a sculptor, painter, or musician is involved. The nonfiction writer is more apt to engage himself or herself in the everyday world of work. Fortunately, modern society needs writers from both camps.

Category II — The Nonfiction Writer

Men and women who elect nonfiction writing will find the requirements for success in this category much less demanding than those imposed on creative writers. Paul R. Reynolds, a distinguished literary agent with long experience in working with writers both creative and nonfiction, put it this way:

> If a person wants to be a painter, musician, or novelist, the first question asked is whether the person possesses the requisite talent. To a person wanting to write non-fiction the question is not germane. No special talent is necessary for the writing of non-fiction. In this respect the occupation is similar to medicine or law. Competence in these professions requires reasonable intelligence and the willingness to undertake a long learning process, a long apprenticeship. It is the same with the non-fiction writer, although the apprenticeship is shorter. Anyone with reasonable intelligence who will undergo the learning process can write publishable non-fiction.[5]

It follows, then, that the field for nonfiction writers is very much larger, very much more open, than the field for creative writers. Fortunately this is so, because the demand for nonfiction writing enormously outstrips the demand for creative forms. For example, the ratio of new nonfiction book titles to new novels published every year is in the order of eight-to-one in favor

---

[4] Called, in some states, the Johnson O'Connor Research Foundation.
[5] Paul R. Reynolds, *The Writing and Selling of Non-Fiction* (Garden City, N.Y.: Doubleday, 1963), p. xi. Reprinted by permission.

of nonfiction. In the magazine world, articles and other nonfiction forms far outweigh their fictional cousins, both in terms of the number of individual titles published and in terms of gross word count. In sheer wordage, the ratio must be in the order of tens-of-thousands-to-one in favor of nonfiction. For some types of creative writing, the demand is so miniscule as to be virtually nonexistent. Only a handful of U.S. poets, for example, have been able to live solely from their poetry.

Those who are not creative-writer types may never win a Nobel Prize or create a novel that will shake the world (à la *Uncle Tom's Cabin*). But the noncreative writer has something else going for him or her: nonfiction writing is always in high demand, and few good practitioners of the art ever starve.

SHOULD YOU BE YOUR OWN BOSS?

For any writer, of whatever category, free lancing can be a very rough row to hoe. Free lancing is the most difficult for creative writers who, paradoxically, need most the independence that free lancing implies but does not always deliver. It has now become standard procedure to warn the budding creative writer to avoid free lancing unless he or she has (1) just inherited an oil well or ten acres in downtown Dallas, or (2) had the good sense to marry a bountiful breadwinner. (James Michener once said: "The most relaxed writers I know are three who live on their wives' incomes.")

Of course, if every budding creative writer had followed such counsel, American literature would never have produced an Erskine Caldwell, who barely survived the winter in a fourth-floor walk-up bedroom ($3.50 a week) in New York City, on 50 cents a week for food, while finishing *Tobacco Road*; an Arthur Koestler (who sold lemonade in Haifa), or a Carl Sandburg (one-time barber, milkman, and janitor).

Many another fabled creative writer worked at demeaning employment while producing his or her now-famous masterpieces. William Faulkner painted houses and ran a post office. John O'Hara read gas meters. Rex Stout clerked in a cigar store. Erich Maria Remarque played the organ in an insane asylum. So there is ample and noble precedent for you to stay with that irksome job in the shipping room or that hateful post in the accounting department. In time, when your novel hits the Top Ten in *The New York Times Book Review* section, you can thumb your nose at all that ignominy. Meantime, you would be well advised to hang on to that meager but regular paycheck.

But what about the nonfiction writer who decides to quit his or her job in defiance of all this well-meaning counsel, to go into free lancing full-time? What are the ground-rules for survival?

THE THREE COMMANDMENTS FOR NONFICTION WRITERS

To succeed as a free-lance nonfiction writer, working for yourself and entirely on your own, there are three "thou shalts" which must be observed:

1. You must have (or find) something to say
2. You must know *how* to say it
3. You must know how to *sell* what you have said

Number one means that what you have to say must be of interest to a *great number of people*, and not just to your mother, your sleeping partner, or a maiden aunt in Peoria.

The second requirement means that you must know something about your mother tongue. If you did everything possible to ditch English in school, you'd better forget writing as a career *unless* you are willing to kneel contritely before *Webster's Unabridged* and pray for forgiveness. And then to work overtime on grammar and syntax to atone for your sins.

Number three means, obviously, that unless you can *sell* what you write, it doesn't matter how good it is. If you are writing for your own amusement, fine. I am assuming that you want to make money from your writing. This means you must know something about the literary marketplace, and how and where to sell your merchandise in it.

But now I see a lady in the balcony waving her hand. Yes, madam?

"That's all well and good," she protests, "if you are a creative-writing genius. I'm not. And I wish I could write magazine articles or nonfiction books, but I can't. So what's left for me?"

Madam, I'm glad you asked that question.

Category III — The Great Miscellany

Here, indeed, is an enormous marketplace for the writer's talents. In the main, this is the nine-to-five world, the world of business and industry, the classroom and the government office. It is not the free lancer's domain. Here the writer is not required to have something to say, or to know how to sell it. The writer is usually told what needs to be said, and the teller is also the seller.

However, commandment number two applies here as it does in free lancing: You must know how to *say* it. That's why you will be hired as a writer . . . because the teller and seller (that is the boss) lacks your facility with the mother tongue.

A TEST FOR PROSPECTIVE FREE LANCERS

It would be helpful if someone would invent a very sensitive machine—something like a lie detector—which could be wired to your temples and elsewhere to assess your potential as a writer, especially as a free-lance writer. Under its subtle probings, you would reveal all, while the little needle squiggled its telltale tracks on the chart. At interrogation's end, the device would whir and click, eventually spitting out a card on which would be computer-typed:

"Congratulations. You have the makings

_____ of a free-lance creative writer

_____ of a free-lance nonfiction writer."

The appropriate blank would be checked.

Or the detector, evaluating the input otherwise, would eject a card which said (curses!):

"Forget it."

As there is no such fabulous machine, I have invented a modest test which may be self-administered by anyone gullible enough to trust its results. You are invited to take this test now, and then to decide—based on your score—whether you want to continue reading this book. This may be your last chance to get your money back.

> Warning: The Attorney General has not determined that this test may be hazardous to your peace of mind. But I have.

In each category, check the space after the statement which appears most accurately to refer to you. Be fearless and forthright in your self-appraisal. Only you will know—and suffer—if you fudge.

Grade yourself as follows:

For every (A) answer — 20 points
For every (B) answer — 15 points
For every (C) answer — 10 points
For every (D) answer — 5 points

(If this is a borrowed book, please keep your records on the wallpaper or other nearby blank surface.)

On your mark . . .

TEST

Category I: Reading Habits

A. *Omnivorous*: I read whenever and wherever I can; I read anything and everything; I feel deprived when I cannot read. ____

B. *Casual*: I read now and then, but feel little or no compulsion to read. ____

C. *Light*: I read very little, and often simply because I am bored or there's nothing good on TV.   ____

D. *Zilch*: I rarely read anything except signboards, movie marquees, the funnies, and the sports page.   ____

Category II: Curiosity Quotient (CQ)

A. *Insatiable*: I am insatiably curious about the world around me, always seeking answers. I consider every new day a learning experience, and know I will never learn all there is to know.   ____

B. *Passive*: I am interested in learning new things, but feel no compulsion to do so. The learning has to come to me, not vice versa.   ____

C. *Neutral*: I am not particularly interested in new ideas or things, and wouldn't ordinarily go out of my way to acquire new knowledge. (If this is your answer, why did you buy this book?)   ____

D. *Withdrawn*: I find my own private world fascinating enough, and need little, if any, outside stimuli, including new information or knowledge.   ____

Category III: Writing Experience

A. *Consistent*: I already write professionally, or I have tried my hand many times, over the years, at self-expression—and still do.   ____

B. *Now-and-Then*: I have dabbled three or four times in writing.   ____

C. *Procrastinator*: I think a lot about writing, and how grand it would be to see my name in print and on a check in the mail . . . but I never seem to get around to making black marks on white paper.   ____

D. *Student*: If you are a student of high school or college age, you haven't had time yet to build a track record in writing. Give yourself a 20-point handicap here.   ____

Category IV: Communication Skills

A. *Above Average:* I believe I am above average in my ability to communicate, in writing or speaking. I *do* know the difference between "imply" and "infer." I *do* know the difference between past tense and passive voice. I do not misuse words like "hopefully" and "parameter." ____

B. *Average:* I would say my writing skills are average. ____

C. *Below Average:* I can communicate fairly well, but have trouble with sentence structure, paragraphing, and in saying exactly what I mean, y' know? ____

D. *Deficient:* I am seriously deficient in grammar, and have difficulty in writing correct English. ____

(**Note:** No effort has been made to test your vocabulary skills or level, as such testing is beyond the scope of this simple exercise. But the following quote from O'Connor's book should be carefully considered at this point: ". . . an English vocabulary at the 93rd percentile correlates with success in every direction and carries one over otherwise insurmountable obstacles. . . .").

Category V: Self-Discipline

A. *Organized:* I can and do organize my life, and am capable of disciplining myself to keep regular hours as a writer. ____

B. *So-So:* I am fairly good at self-discipline, with occasional to frequent lapses. ____

C. *Sidetracked:* I have the best of intentions, but am easily diverted by household chores, telephones, TV, shopping, crying offspring, lawn mowers, and so on. ____

D. *Bohemian:* I am totally incapable of self-discipline, insofar as organizing my time is concerned. I'd rather not be bothered. ____

My total score is . . . . ════

That's it. Find your score on the table below.

RANGE	PROBABILITIES OF SUCCESS
100 to 90	Outstanding to Very Good.
89 to 80	Quite Good to Fair.
79 to 70	Fair to Poor, and Dropping Rapidly.
Below 70	Finger-painting or Mushroom Culture recommended.

Caveat: This test is based on no scientific principles whatsoever. It is, however, based on knowledge, empirically derived over a writing and teaching career of some forty years by a man who would hate to tell you what his own score would be if he took the test today, and will not.

Survivors, turn the page.

II

THE "CREATIVE"
WRITING FORMS

chapter 2

I would like to write one good novel. I enormously enjoyed writing The Triumph. *There's no question but that being an ambassador—even in the rather intricate period that I was in India, even with, at one stage, a war on my hands, and dealing with such complex figures as Nehru and Krishna Menon—was infinitely easier than facing a typewriter every morning.*[1]

JOHN KENNETH GALBRAITH

FICTION: THE "DIVINE DISCONTENT"

Feast or famine.

If the prospects for fiction writers in today's America can be summarized in three words, you have just read them.

The underlying assumption, in this section, is that you are interested in writing *and selling* creative work: novels, short stories, broadcast and live-stage dramas, movie scenarios, poetry, and other forms where creativity (as opposed to reporting) is the keynote. In short, *commercial* creative writing. If your work happens also to qualify as literature, bravo.

As for feast and famine, on the "feast" side of the ledger are

---

[1] Israel Shenker, *Words and Their Masters* (Garden City, N.Y.: Doubleday, 1974), p. 180. Reprinted by permission.

such enticing entries as these, chosen at random from two recent years of publishing history:

Item: Judith Krantz, author of the best-selling novel *Scruples*, sees Bantam Books purchase paperback rights to her second novel, *Princess Daisy*, for a record $3.2 million after a fourteen-and-one-half hour auction involving eight of the nation's nine paperback houses locked in mortal combat. (To recoup its investment, Bantam would need to sell more than 7,000,000 copies of *Princess*!).

Item: *Princess Daisy* smashed the record held earlier by *Linda Goodman's Love Signs,* for which Fawcett acquired paperback rights for $2.25 million. Fawcett also negotiated, a year earlier, a package deal on Mario Puzo's books, including *The Godfather*, in which Fawcett paid Harper & Row $2.55 million for paperback rights.

Item: A movie producer and United Artists paid a record $500,000 for movie rights alone for Truman Capote's *Handcarved Coffins*, a "nonfiction account" of a crime which appeared under Capote's byline in the December 1979 issue of *Interview* magazine. The 30,000-word story was written in the style made famous by Capote in his *In Cold Blood.*

Item: In the same period, there were many other six-figure payments to authors for subsidiary rights to novels, among them $500,000 to Graham Greene for *The Human Factor*, and a like sum to Judith Richards for *Summer Lightning.*

In the "famine" column of the ledger are such sobering realities as these:

Item: many major publishing houses and consumer magazines no longer read unsolicited manuscripts. They will examine the work of unknowns only if submitted through literary agents, or if recommended by a "friend" or by one of the writers whose work they already publish. Bantam Books, a titan among paperback publishers, has announced: "We no longer accept unsolicited manuscripts. Material will be returned unread unless sent at our request." Simon & Schuster warns that "all unsolicited mss. will be returned unread. Only mss. submitted by agents or recommended to us by friends or actively solicited by us will be considered."

In some cases, the door has been shut somewhat more softly. Doubleday & Company explains its policy concerning the handling of manuscripts thus: "We return unopened and unread all complete manuscripts, accompanied by a form telling how we would like submissions made." Doubleday then notes that its editors will still read "over the transom" mysteries and science fiction. On poetry, the door is slammed peremptorily, as Doubleday has imposed "a moratorium on poetry publishing and are not accepting mss."

Similar restrictions are announced by numerous other publishers. Some major houses are, however, still doing business as usual, reading everything that comes in. (Do not take "reading" literally. An accomplished "reader" will scan a manuscript first, and usually can tell at a glance whether the ms. comes from a pro or an amateur. If a sampling indicates that the ms. may be worthy of more careful study, it may be set aside for closer scrutiny, then may be passed to other readers for evaluation.)

But the problem of unsolicited manuscripts becomes more formidable every year, and people in the industry constantly comment on its gravity. Olney Austin, editor-in-chief at Houghton Mifflin (which still reads from the slushpile), said recently:

> Trade publishers are overwhelmed by unsolicited manuscript submissions, most of them totally unsuitable for a variety of reasons. It sometimes astonishes me how many people untrained in writing expect their literary efforts to be snapped up by commercial trade publishers; surely art galleries are not swamped by the canvases of Sunday painters.

A high-ranking executive of a major New York house, whose firm also still reads mss. coming over the transom, put it this way:

> [We] receive between 5,000 and 6,000 unsolicited manuscripts a year, and it's simply impossible to comment individually on that number of submissions. In the years I have been [here], we have published exactly one unsolicited manuscript . . . that's one out of 60,000 and 70,000 submissions—not a good average.

Item: Some magazine editors will no longer read stories coming in over the transom. Among the first-line periodicals which have shut the transom are *Playboy, Cosmopolitan,* and *Ladies Home Journal.*

One *Playboy* editor, commenting on the quality (or lack of it) in unsolicited fiction, gave a clue to reasons behind the ban:

> We get stories from 15-year-olds, from elderly ladies writing about their cats, and quite a few from crazy people obsessively writing about their woes. Many are semiliterate. They couldn't write a letter to the gas company.

Item: A successful short-story author told a recent writers' conference in Denver that the short-story market has become even tighter in the past few years. Most commercial magazines, she reported, will no longer accept stories which were not written on assignment. The best opportunities for beginners in the short-story field, said this writer, are with the "little" or experimental magazines. They still read everything that comes in, but they pay little or nothing and take a long time to report, she cautioned.

The *Playboy* editor quoted earlier sounded an even more pessimistic note:

> So few magazines publish short fiction any more that it isn't possible to make a living from short stories alone.

Mark Mirsky, editor of *Fiction* magazine, told another writers' conference in New York City that his magazine paid nothing for stories. A writer in the audience promptly promised to send Mirsky a story that was worth nothing. Mirsky said that despite the rates his magazine does *not* pay, *Fiction* receives more unsolicited stories than he has time to read!

One problem constantly faced by writers who attempt to follow trends in the writing business is the fact that reports from the marketplace often conflict. Speaking at a writers' conference in Tacoma, Helen del Monte, fiction editor for *McCall's*, said her magazine *does* read unsolicited fiction, and told the delighted delegates that one-fourth of all the stories published in *McCall's* were unsolicited. Ms. del Monte informed the writers attending that agents no longer handle short stories, as a general rule, because there is not enough yield in them to justify an agent's involvement. So for *McCall's*, at least, the "slushpile" has gained added importance in recent times. This market, incidentally, was then paying a floor price of $1,250 and a ceiling of $3,000 for its stories.

PUBLISHERS' ROW, OR WALL STREET?

For nearly a century before the invasion of big business into the publishing world, the making of books was a genteel occupation, conducted in a kind of tea-and-crumpets milieu. Bourbon and Scotch have pretty well replaced the tea, and today it is difficult for an outsider to distinguish Publishers' Row from Wall Street. Now the industry which was once the preserve of ladies and gentlemen of taste and station is the arena of conglomerates, mergers, and acquisitions, with toy manufacturers bidding against television networks for the possession of some venerable old house that was publishing fine books when our grandparents were kids.

It's a world in which a credit-card giant ("don't leave home without it") moves to seize control of a powerful publishing house (which expressly thwarts it). A television network purchases an important paperback house. *TIME* magazine acquires the *Book-of-the-Month* Club, and an enormous industrial conglomerate buys a text publisher and a scientific book house.

Meantime the Justice Department and the Federal Trade Commission observe from the sidelines, eyebrows raised.

Though America's printing and publishing industry is the world's largest, it ranks very small indeed in terms of its share in the Gross National Product. The auto makers, by comparison, employ six times as many workers and contribute twenty times as much to the GNP as all printers and publishers combined. Individual titans in the book-publishing industry may gross hundreds of millions of dollars a year, yet the annual income of each may be less than General Motors (for example) collects in three or four days.[2]

Still, it is impressive—and somehow comforting—to know that book publishing in this nation was a $5.8 billion industry

[2] *U.S. Publishing Yearbook and Directory 1979-80* (White Plains, N.Y.: Knowledge Industry Publications, Inc., 1979), p. 2.

in one recent year. A modest share of those billions filtered down to authors in the form of advances and royalties.

THE PAPERBACK REVOLUTION

Although the impact of mergers and acquisitions on the book industry has been notable, the influence of "the paperback revolution" on American letters has been nothing short of colossal. The hardcover novel is still very much a part of the scene, of course. Yet the day may come—perhaps sooner than we dream—when hardcovers will be just a memory (as they have been for generations in most European and Latin American countries).

> The day of the big best-selling hard-cover novel seems to be waning. The hardcover book that attains best-sellerdom today is one that requires a hard cover for practical purposes—a cook book, juvenile, or a reference book . . . the paperback editions have virtually made enormous sales of best-selling fiction obsolete.[3]

More and more paperback houses are entering an area which earlier was closed to them: original publishing. Avon and Bantam, the two giants in the industry, are heavily into original publishing. In one year, of Avon's total of 380 books published, about 40 percent were paperback originals. In the same year, one-fourth of Bantam's output of some 375 titles was of originals.

Charles Bloch, Bantam's West Coast Editorial Representative, predicts that paperback houses eventually will become *the* original publishers in the industry. He sees the status quo reversing, with hardcover firms acquiring rights to publish hardcover editions *after* the first editions are out in paperback.

Roger Straus, of Farrar, Straus & Giroux, cites paperback publishing as one of the two great social forces (the other being television) which precipitated the decline of general-circulation magazines in the United States. Speaking to a writers' conference in California, Straus said:

[3] Alice Payne Hackett and James Henry Burke, *Eighty Years of Best Sellers, 1895-1975* (New York: R.R. Bowker, 1977), p. 21. Copyright © 1977 by Xerox Corporation. Reprinted by permission.

I'm sure you have had the experience I have had when catching a train or a plane . . . you want something to read, and it seems silly to reach down to pick up a magazine when you can pick up a mass-paperback collection of short stories by Faulkner, or a book by Hemingway, or a Malamud novel, or a Saul Bellow book . . .

The influence of the paperback on America's reading habits can readily be appreciated through a comparison of some numbers. In one recent year, one house alone (Avon) had in print nearly 20 million copies of its six top-selling titles alone. The same year, the three leading paperback sellers in the United States were:

TITLE	AUTHOR	PAPERBACKS SOLD
1. The Thorn Birds	Colleen McCullough	7,000,000
2. The Amityville Horror	Jay Anson	4,000,000
3. Jaws 2	Hank Searls	3,815,000

Contrast *Thorn Birds'* sales record against total achieved by the best-selling hardcover book for the same year: James Michener's *Chesapeake*, with 852,000 copies sold.

Of the fifteen titles on a recent best-selling paperback list, eleven were fiction. And the *bottom* entry on the list grossed twice as many sales (1,775,000) as the *top* seller on the hardcover list.

WHY WRITE?

In the face of all the hard realities, and the counsel of calloused old-timers in the field, why are men and women willing—even eager—to expend blood, sweat, and tears to write a novel or a short-story?

As Joe Gores once put it, writing chooses you, not the other way around. It's not a case of "I want." It's a case of "I must."

Phyllis Whitney, doyenne of America's mystery writers who—as queen of the Gothic novel form in this country—has won two Edgars from the Mystery Writers of America, says it simply:

Writers write because they can't help it, because it's the only thing they want to do, because it is the only way of life that satisfies them.

Yugoslavian Nobel laureate Ivo Andric suggests another reason:

> . . . could it be that the storyteller tells his own story to himself, like the child who sings in the dark in order to assuage his own fear?

Whatever his or her reasons, the successful writer will find that the capacity for hard work is one characteristic that separates winners from losers in the literary game. John D. MacDonald, one of the most popular best-selling novelists of our time, minces no words on this score:

> Most beginners think that writing is a quick ticket to some kind of celebrity status, to broads and talk shows. Those with that shallow motivation can forget it. Here's how it goes. Take a person 25 years old. If that person has not read a *minimum* of three books a week since he or she was 10 years old, or 2,340 books—comic books not counted—and if he or she is not still reading at that pace or preferably, at a greater pace, then forget it. If he or she is not willing to commit one million words to paper—ten medium long novels—without much hope of ever selling one word, in the process of learning this trade, then forget it. And if he or she can be discouraged by anyone in this world from continuing to write, write, write—then forget it.[4]

Colleen McCullough, who wrote the runaway best-seller *The Thorn Birds*, reveals that she worked on this novel for eighteen months, sometimes writing 20,000 words a day. A woman of astonishing vitality, Ms. McCullough can write all night, all the next day, and into the next night non-stop. In the course of one year, she produced two drafts of *Birds* in three months, and eight more rewrites in the next nine months.

Anthony Trollope, the 19th-century British novelist who wrote about fifty novels (some of which are still in print and selling well) attributed his success to rigid scheduling of his time. He was out of bed at 5:30 every morning, then wrote steadily for two and a half hours at the rate of 250 words every fifteen minutes. He accomplished this prodigious output while working full-time

---

[4] Ed Hirschberg, "John D. MacDonald: 'Sherlock Holmes Was a Smart-Ass' & Other Diverse Opinions," in *Writer's Yearbook '79*, ed. John Brady (Cincinnati: Writer's Digest Publications, 1979), p. 38. Reprinted by permission.

for the British Postal Service (he is remembered as the inventor of the "pillar-box," forerunner of today's corner mailbox).

Leon Uris, to write *Exodus*, conducted more than 1,200 interviews, shot more than a thousand photos, and travelled 12,000 miles in Israel. As background for his *Trinity* research, he brought back from Ireland one ton (literally) of books.

John Ehrlichman, of Watergate fame (or infamy), points also to discipline as the key to completion of his roman à clef, *The Company*.

> I came to realize the power of uninterrupted time. Never in my life have I dedicated a certain amount of hours every day to any given process. I just decided that I was going to sit down faithfully at eight-thirty in the morning and not get up again until one o'clock in the afternoon. I discovered that I could do an enormous quantity of work, and an awful lot of powerful thinking in that circumstance. I'm beginning to develop a hypothesis that maybe what's wrong with the country and the world and humanity is that we don't block out sufficient quantities of time for ourselves, but permit ourselves to be fractionalized. . . .[5]

Patience is another virtue in this business. Joyce Carol Oates believes there is an analogy between music and writing.

> I take piano lessons, and the early stages with a new piece are stumbling and disheartening. But if you keep on, it's incredible how you can build skills, how something clicks.

Ms. Oates and her husband, Raymond Smith, are members of the English Department at the University of Windsor, in Ontario, Canada. There, she says, her main task is:

> . . . to make [students] understand that you have to be patient. I give them examples of great writers who took a long time to mature. The secret is to keep going—not to give up. We live in a time where weakness is falsely extolled, as if it were sensitivity. I don't think it is.[6]

[5] Philip Nobile, "John Ehrlichman's Literary Secrets," in *Harper's Weekly*, June 28, 1976, p. 16, col. 2. Copyright © 1976 by The Minneapolis Star and Tribune Company, Inc.

[6] *Publisher's Weekly*, June 26, 1978, p. 39. Copyright © 1978 by Xerox Corporation. Reprinted by permission.

chapter 3

*It took Katherine Anne Porter seventeen
days and seventeen nights to finish her
first short story—after thinking about it
for ten years.*

WRITING & SELLING
SHORT STORIES

Many of America's contemporary novelists began their work
in the short-story medium. John O'Hara ranks as a master of both
long- and short-form fiction. John MacDonald has tried his hand at
both, and has emerged as a novelist of distinction. Kurt Vonnegut,
Jr. began with short stories in the late 1940s, moonlighting fiction
while employed in a public-relations job (at $92 a week). He
sold his first story for $750, and two weeks later sold his second
for $800. Vonnegut needed no further persuasion: he quit public
relations, and has been a free lancer ever since.

Best known today as a novelist, Vonnegut says he found the
short-story form more difficult than the novel. "You have more
room" in the novel, he comments, because the short story requires
the writer to "startle the reader in a short space."

STUDY THE MARKETS

Writers who hope to sell to mass-market consumer magazines are well advised to study these markets as a biology student dissects a frog. Under the microscope of careful study, the short story as published in today's magazines will yield up some of its secrets. Are certain themes taboo in some magazines, but not in others? What markets appear to stress characterization over plot, and vice versa? What word-lengths are required in the various markets? Does Magazine A seek, or reject, stories about old people and their problems? These and many other questions of style and technique can be answered by a painstaking survey of contemporary stories, whether they appear in the "commercial" magazines or the "little" or experimental markets.

Most commercial magazines have prepared "profiles" of their readers, and writers should study these profiles. They may sometimes be found in guidelines prepared by editors for free distribution to writers interested in their magazines. (Samples of guidelines and profiles will be found in the Appendix.) Profiles also appear in the remarkably detailed descriptions of magazines in *Consumer Magazine and Farm Publication Rates and Data*,[1] an important and valuable resource tool for writers.

Editors also release descriptions of their readership to various marketing guides, including *Writer's Market*[2] and *The Writer's Handbook*.[3] *Mademoiselle*, for example, discloses that their audience consists largely of college-educated women between the ages of 18 and 30. *Redbook*, widely (and almost reverently) regarded as the last great stronghold of fiction in the U.S. consumer-magazine market, says its readership is made up primarily of women aged 18 to 34. *Redbook's* editors are quite specific about their "target" reader, describing her thus:

Our "target" reader is a young woman in her twenties who is probably

---

[1] *Consumer Magazine and Farm Publication Rates and Data*, revised monthly (Skokie, Ill.: Standard Rate & Data Service, Inc.).

[2] *Writer's Market*, issued annually (Cincinnati: Writer's Digest Publications) Marketing information cited in this chapter and at many other points throughout this book is drawn primarily from *Writer's Market*.

[3] *The Writer's Handbook*, issued annually (Boston: The Writer, Inc.).

married or expects to marry; her child or children are almost certainly under ten. She has had some higher education, has probably traveled and held a job that required special skills, and if she is not working now, she probably expects to return to work when her children are older. She has curiosity, a sense of humor, a strong sense of realism, and a well-informed concern about the world. Her attitude toward the women's liberation movement is favorable. Her tastes, attitudes, lifestyle and problems reflect the overriding fact that she is young.

In *Redbook's* case, there is an example of the taboos mentioned earlier. Because of the "target" readers' favorable view of the women's liberation movement, *Redbook* makes it clear—in its market note—that "supposedly humorous fiction with 'women's libbers' as its target is not welcomed here."

No-nos of various types are cited in market notes covering many publications, and these should be carefully heeded. For example, *Seventeen* (which will read unsolicited manuscripts) does not like photocopied manuscripts, or stories typed on so-called erasable bond paper. But *McCall's* has no objection to either photocopies or erasable papers. *Redbook* does not publish short mysteries, but will look at novel-length mysteries. The *Atlantic Monthly* publishes mainstream fiction, but "no concrete or haiku poetry." *Mademoiselle* abhors formula stories, and says so flatly in its market note.

(*Tip for writers*: It is probably safe to assume that most magazine editors and publishing house readers prefer manuscripts *not* typed on erasable bond. The slick surfaces of these papers will not retain inks from certain types of pens, and the type tends to smear on some of them if inadvertently rubbed.)

So much for the bad news. There is still music from some sectors of the magazine chorus to offset the sour notes from others. There are handsome inducements from such giants as *The New Yorker*, where a byline can launch an unknown into fame overnight. Widely respected for the general excellence of its prose, *The New Yorker* each year buys about 50 stories both "serious and light," and with lengths running between 1,000 and 6,000 words. *Good Housekeeping* wants romance, mainstream, and suspense fiction averaging 4,000 words, and condensed novels (10,000 words). *Mademoiselle* states it is "particularly interested in encouraging young talent," and annually offers a $500 prize for each of two winning stories in its college fiction contest. *The Atlantic Monthly* awards cash prizes for the first major unpublished pieces of fiction by unestablished authors, and publishes these. As *The Atlantic Monthly* is regarded as one of perhaps half-a-dozen of the best showplaces in the nation for intellectual fiction and nonfiction, publication in this magazine assures an unknown writer immediate professional recognition.

Other major markets also offer opportunities for free lancers, but the truly wide-open territories for beginners (especially) lie in two areas: the "little" or experimental magazines, and the religious periodicals. The so-called confession magazines also offer inducements to new writers and veterans alike. However, some professionals who have written for the confessions for many years now say that these once-thriving publications are on the decline and are not long for this world.

The "write your wrongs" books have long suffered a bad reputation among writers on several counts. First, they are POP (Pay on Publication) markets. This policy is anathema to pros, who regard it (rightly) as unprofessional and unethical. Second, the "confessions" pay no more today than they paid a decade ago—generally in the three-to-five-cents-a-word range.

The "target" reader of these magazines is likely to be under 30 years of age, with a high school education or less. The family breadwinner is probably a blue-collar worker. It is important to grasp these concepts in preparing to write for the confessions, just as it is important to know—in writing for *Mademoiselle*—that the "target" reader is from 18 to 30, and is college-educated.

One former confessions writer, Lois Duncan, sold a string of these tales in her early writing days to pay the rent and buy groceries. She ground them out week after week. In time, however, Ms. Duncan was forced to stop writing these lurid (but largely phony) first-person narratives.

"I ran out of sins!" she confesses.

There are so-called "clean" confessions, and some that are not so sanitized. A perusal of samples on any well-stocked newsrack should give a prospective confessions writer a good idea about which markets hold the most promise for him or her.

FAITH IN FICTION

You will never bump your taxable income into a higher bracket by writing stories for religious publications. But you may gain much valuable experience—and the confidence that comes from seeing your name in print—by writing for this large family of second-echelon publications.

The dominant aim of all these magazines is, quite obviously, to inculcate religious principles in the readership. For example, *Aspire* will read "anything illustrating spiritual laws at work" (maximum, one cent per published word). *Christian Herald* seeks religious fiction 400 to 1,500 words in length, and will pay three cents a word. *Columbia* is looking for stories "written from a thoroughly Christian viewpoint," for which it pays a surprising (and atypical) $300 maximum. *Columbia* is directed to "the Catholic layman and his family." *Insight* calls for "humorous, mainstream, and religious" fiction, and the editor is quite specific in his requirements:

> I'm looking for short stories that are not preachy but that lead our readers to a better understanding of how their Christian beliefs apply to their daily living. They must do more than entertain—they must make the reader think something in a new light.

Rates at *Insight* are $45 to $100 for from 1,000 to 3,000 words.

There are dozens of these magazines, directed to the full spectrum of religious beliefs and faiths. One advantage of writing for religious magazines is that, in general, they are non-competitive. Hence a writer may ethically offer the same merchandise to several of them. It is considered good practice to let an editor know that you intend to make "multiple submissions" of a given manuscript, and that you will protect the editor by sending it only to markets which do not compete with his or her magazine.

An outstanding example of editor-writer cooperation and collaboration may be seen in the guidelines for writers published by *Home Life*, one of the religious magazines. This periodical, a monthly publication of The Sunday School Board of the Southern Baptist Convention, Nashville, Tennessee, makes available to prospective contributors an elaborate kit which describes the magazine and its needs and requirements. The kit includes a pocket-size folder called "Tips for Writers" which shows how the magazine likes its manuscripts prepared, and explains the periodical's policies. The kit also features a two-page statement, "How We Evaluate Manuscripts," and lists nineteen "high-priority subjects" for articles and short stories. (This magazine's guidelines appear in the Appendix.)

Many magazines, in all categories of the marketplace including trades, consumers, house organs, mystery, and others, publish such guidelines. (Guidelines issued by Alfred Hitchcock's *Mystery Magazine* and *Ellery Queen's Mystery Magazine* and other periodicals appear in the Appendix.) It is well worth any writer's time to request some of these, and to study them with care. Magazines which make guidelines available usually mention, in their market notes, that they may be obtained by writing the editors.

If your fiction is avant-garde, experimental, or mainstream, and does not conform somehow to the requirements of consumer magazines, you may wish to submit your work to one or more of the thousand or so "little" literary magazines which thrive throughout the Republic. The mortality rate among these labor-of-love publications is about 25 percent annually, but so is the birthrate, so the gross population about balances out from year to year.

Some of the "littles" are husky, slick-paper productions. Others may appear on the cheapest of paper, sometimes in tabloid format. Many are distributed free, and those which are sold fall in the $2.50-to-$3.00 per issue range. Many are quarterlies.

Nearly all of these experimental efforts are money-losers, and are grubstaked by friends, subscribers, and editors. Some enjoy subsidies from The National Endowment for the Arts, the Ford Foundation, and other funding sources.

chapter 4

. . . could the aim of these stories be to throw some light on the dark paths into which life hurls us at times and to tell us about this life which we live blindly and unconsciously . . . ?

IVO ANDRIC

THE GREAT AMERICAN NOVEL

Defying the expert counsel of editors, publishers, and other writers, every year thousands of unpublished authors write first novels. And every year, thousands of them are rejected. A few hundred survive as published first novels. Now and then, one of these astounds the experts and becomes a best seller.

Case in point: *Scruples*, by Judith Krantz (see Chapter 2). In her case, lightning struck two years in a row, and struck with sufficient force to propel her second novel, *Princess Daisy*, to a new record in publishing history.

Why does one novel attain best-seller status while another may barely pay the printer? Why does one horse win while another fades on the back stretch? No one knows with absolute certainty.

But there are clues when it comes to novels. Anyone with

the time, curiosity, and literacy can probe for these clues in the best-seller lists published every year. Here is the list for one sample year. Study the titles. Read the reviews which praised (or panned) these novels. Better yet, read the books themselves, then decide why one ranked first and another came in tenth, or twentieth. Your informed opinion will be as good as the next fellow's.

RANK	TITLE	AUTHOR	COPIES SOLD
1	*Chesapeake*	James Michener	852,000
2	*War and Remembrance*	Herman Wouk	275,000
3	*Fools Die*	Mario Puzo	274,084
4	*Bloodline*	Sidney Sheldon	210,000
5	*Scruples*	Judith Krantz	210,000
6	*Evergreen*	Belva Plain	182,738
7	*Illusions*	Richard Bach	162,688
8	*The Holcroft Covenant*	Robert Ludlum	153,820
9	*Second Generation*	Howard Fast	145,800
10	*Eye of the Needle*	Ken Follett	122,000
11	*The Human Factor*	Graham Greene	119,000
12	*The Far Pavilions*	M. M. Kaye	114,843
13	*Prelude to Terror*	Helen MacInnes	114,433
14	*The World According to Garp*	John Irving	103,000
15	*Whistle*	James Jones	102,413
16	*The Last Convertible*	Anton Myrer	98,000
17	*Stained Glass*	William Buckley	96,877
18	*The Empty Copper Sea*	John D. MacDonald	95,000
19	*Bright Flows the River*	Taylor Caldwell	93,161
20	*Metropolitan Life*	Fran Lebowitz	92,000

Some of these writers were riding the crest of a wave of popular acceptance created by earlier successes, among them Michener, Wouk, Puzo, Sheldon, Bach (*Seagull*), Fast, Greene, MacInnes, MacDonald, and Caldwell. But why Krantz? Or, for that matter, Buckley?

ARE YOU A BORN STORYTELLER?

Before worrying too much about the mechanics, anyone contemplating the gargantuan task of writing a novel should indulge in a little introspection, asking such questions of himself or herself as these:

1. Does the human character fascinate me? Do I believe, with Lamb, that the proper study of man is himself?
2. Am I involved with my fellow men and with mankind? Do I agree with John Donne that the bell tolls for *me*? Are people important to me?
3. Am I a natural storyteller, active or latent? Would I, in another age, another clime, have been a bearer of tales, wandering from tent to tent? Have I ever told a story to others, inventing it as I went along?

If the answer is "yes" in most or all cases, chances are that you may be equipped by nature to attack a novel. Whether you have the word skills and the other attributes needed for the task is a question which only you and time can answer.

WHAT KIND OF NOVEL?

Novels come in a variety of shapes, sizes, and types. Will yours be a big-screen story—a *War and Remembrance, Thorn Birds,* or *Gone with the Wind*? These are among the great panoramics, in which the author paints an enormous mural to depict some epic event (World War II or the Civil War) or to chronicle a family through several generations (*Thorn Birds*). This genre of novel, by the way, is one which many publishers constantly look for—because these king-sized novels really *sell*.

Will yours be a *roman à clef* (à la *The Company*), a novel based on real history but with fictitious characters? Or do you favor science fiction, the mystery, the love story, the hard-boiled detective yarn, espionage, Westerns, Gothics, fantasy?

Assuming you have selected a category, you should examine

the lists of many publishers before submitting a proposal or finished manuscript to any house. Catalogs of the various publishers can be found in *Publishers' Trade List Annual,*[1] which is available in any well-stocked public or university library. Catalogs of individual houses also may be obtained by writing to the publishers for copies. You may also find much important information about the likes and dislikes of the various houses by *studying* (not merely reading) publishers' market notes in *The Writer's Market* and *The Writer's Handbook.*

You will find, for example, that some houses do not publish mysteries, while others may stress them. Some feature science fiction, others abhor the genre. One publisher notes that his house wants no collections of short stories, or books with a heavy regional flavor. In many cases, the houses spell out the word lengths within which they expect writers to work. It would be folly to ignore these readily available guidelines. Under the best of circumstances, it may take weeks, and sometimes months, to receive a reaction of a publisher on your manuscript or proposal. If you send it to the wrong house simply because you failed to do your homework, you have wasted much valuable time.

WRITING A PROPOSAL

Which, you may ask, should I submit: a completed novel manuscript, or a query? First, consult the market notes or guidelines issued by the house or houses to which you plan to submit. In some instances, the house rules are quite plain: One may state flatly it will read queries only, and no completed manuscripts. Another will inform you, just as bluntly, that it will read no manuscripts at all from unknowns, and that you must go through an agent. Still another will leave the door open, allowing you to submit query or manuscript, as you wish. In any case, you must know the rules at a particular house.

If you submit a completed manuscript, you are—of course—truly speculating. You have invested your time and energy on an

---

[1] *Publishers' Trade List Annual,* revised annually (New York: R.R. Bowker).

idea without, before the fact, having tested the marketability of the idea. In some instances, the very nature of your idea or theme demands that you write the novel first and then try to place it. In other cases, the style of your writing may be the key to the novel's success or failure, and a finished manuscript may be required to showcase your style.

Commercial novelists, however, generally sell their novels as ideas first, and then deliver the finished manuscript after they have obtained a commitment from a publisher. How do they write their proposals?

The minimum elements in a proposal for a novel are:

1. A brief, tight statement of the central idea of the book. This can be part of a letter of transmittal.
2. One or more sample chapters of the book. (One house's rule-of-thumb is "at least 50 pages").
3. An outline or synopsis of the rest of the book, perhaps by chapters, with possibly a précis of each chapter.
4. A résumé of your writing experience and your publishing record, if any, to give the editor some measure of your commitment to writing.

If you have special qualifications for writing the particular novel you are proposing, these can be included in your letter of transmittal. For example, John Ehrlichman would certainly mention his White House experience in proposing a novel like *The Company* if he believed the editor to whom he was making the proposal had not read newspapers or watched television during the Watergate debacle.

You should include the famous SASE (self-addressed stamped envelope or mailing carton) with sufficient postage affixed to insure the safe return of your proposal or manuscript should it be rejected. This is mandatory, except in the case of authors who have already done business with a publisher and are considered members of the family.

A success story involving a full-time free-lance writer named Jory Sherman will show how proposals work. Sherman was reading the catalog of a publisher, Pinnacle Books, and became fascinated with the "series" novels advertised by this house. He was impressed to note that one of their writers alone (Don Pendleton) had something like 33,000,000 books in print in his "Mack Bolan" series. Sherman decided to try his hand at writing a series of novels. He wrote to a vice president of Pinnacle, setting forth his writing background, and stating that he would like to write a series based on a character he would call "Chill." This was to be the nickname of his central character, Russell V. Chillders. Chill would leave investigations of homicides and routine street crimes to others. He would become, instead, the Sherlock Holmes of the occult and supernatural. Sherman sketched a brief word-picture of Chill, and mentioned in passing that he (Sherman) had assembled a sizeable library of occult literature. Sherman was obviously enthusiastic about the project.

Two months later, Sherman received an interested reply asking for more details. He submitted three chapters of the first in the series (*Satan's Seed*), and outlines of half a dozen plots for as many more titles, plus additional notes for a total of 26 titles. His prospectus covered 60 pages.

Pinnacle was sold. Sherman was offered an initial contract for four books of 75,000 words each, a $2,000 advance on each book, and an option on up to six more titles. Jory Sherman was in the series-writing business.

The "series" novel has meant long-lived success and prosperity to many other writers, among them John Jakes. For many years, Jakes was a moonlight free lancer, writing on the side while holding down a job in the advertising business. By the time he began his now-famous American Bicentennial Series, Jakes had already written some 200 short stories and about 50 books, including six historical novels. These books, under the pen name Jay Scotland, "sank like a stone," Jakes recalls wryly.

Then he conceived the idea for the series which would tie in with the celebration of the nation's 200th birthday. These novels would trace a family's history through two centuries, up to present-day America. In 1973, with the help of a $15,000 advance, he began the series. Jakes worked in a makeshift office in the basement of his home on a typewriter he had bought for $35 in 1955.

Jakes found he could produce a 500-page book in about eight months—four for research (he does all his own), four for writing. His titles (among them *The Bastard*, *The Rebels*, *The Seekers*, and some half-dozen others to date) have enjoyed enormous success. In one year, his first five books were all on the list of the nation's top 20 best-selling paperbacks.

GENRE NOVELS

Many writers concentrate on a specific genre, finding that they do best as specialists. Erle Stanley Gardner, who wrote something like 90 of his Perry Mason "case" books, is a prime example. Louis L'Amour is another. L'Amour, who is unquestionably the world's best-selling writer of Westerns, has published nearly 75 novels, most of which are in print. More than 55 million copies of his work, in 17 languages, have grossed more than $32 million. At least 31 movies have been based on L'Amour books, including *Hondo*. The average sale of his Bantam Books' titles is around 750,000 copies, and Bantam keeps 50 of his titles in paperback at all times.

With the demise of *Gunsmoke* and other TV favorites, the Western has all but disappeared from television. But it is enjoying something of a renaissance in print. However, warns one publisher, public fancies are cyclical—it may be Westerns today, something else next week. Gothics, which for many years were sure-fire sellers in the paperback market, seem to be on a down swing. Mysteries, however, are holding their own.

The contemporary detective story mirrors the times in which we live, times Sherlock Holmes and Miss Marple might find unnerving. Dylis Winn, author of *Murder Ink*, a charming miscellany of things criminous, explains:

> Today the detective story has come down out of the upper classes in its setting and gotten down into the lives of ordinary people. Realism is a big thing. I don't know anything about pouring sherry in the afternoon, and I don't own a big country estate. What I do know about is getting mugged. So crime stories have not only come down to

earth, they've gone into the streets. Nowadays, the poison isn't dropped into the sherry, it's put in the pizza.[2]

The romantic novel is also alive and well, especially in England, where Barbara Cartland—undisputed queen of the genre—was still (at last reports) writing 70,000 words a week, and publishing 24 books a year. Ms. Cartland, who keeps ten secretaries and research persons busy, had written more than 230 novels by 1980.

For writers who can handle the genre, juvenile novels offer enormous attractions. In general, they are a safer investment of one's writing time than adult novels. Here also, series books are great favorites, and some series juveniles have sold well generation after generation. Among these are the Nancy Drew books (60 million sold to 1975), the Bobbsey Twins (15 million) and Tom Swift (7 million). Five of Dr. Seuss's books sold more than five million copies each between 1957 and 1975. L. Frank Baum's *Wonderful Wizard of Oz* also sold an estimated five million copies in the period 1900–1975, but it took the *Wizard* 75 years to accumulate the same sales record which each of five Dr. Seuss's books garnered in less than a generation.

THE BUSINESS SIDE

According to surveys conducted by the Authors Guild, royalty provisions today are based primarily on publishers' list prices. For novels, the most common royalty clause provides 10 percent for the first 5,000, 12½ percent for the next 5,000, and 15 percent thereafter.

Advances vary widely, but—says the Guild survey—the majority of contracts provide advances of more than $5,000, with one in three contracts providing lower advances. Only 3.4 percent paid no advance in the group sampled.

On proceeds from mass-market paperback licensing by hardcover publishers, the conventional split was 50 percent to

---

[2]Herbert Kupferberg, "Murder Ink," in *Parade*, November 11, 1973, pp. 20–21. (New York: Parade Publications). Reprinted by permission.

the author, 50 percent to the publisher. The same split was conventional when reprint licenses were negotiated with book clubs, according to the Guild.

In the all-time history of American best sellers, how does fiction fare as compared with nonfiction? Of the fifteen titles listed below (combined hardcover and paperback sales), eight are fiction. The all-time best-selling novel for the period (eighty years, from 1895 to 1975) was an upstart named *The Godfather*, which achieved this spectacular sales record in barely six years (and the book was rejected by at least one New York publisher!). Perhaps significantly, however, not one of the top five is a novel. All of the five leaders in the eighty-year period are reference-type books, and two of the five are cookbooks.

Here are the 15 leaders, nonfiction and fiction, in 80 years of publishing:[3]

TITLE	AUTHOR	COPIES SOLD
Pocket Book of Baby and Child Care	Benjamin Spock	23,285,000
Better Homes and Gardens Cook Book		18,684,976
Webster's New World Dictionary of the American Language		18,500,000
The Guiness Book of World Records		16,457,000
Betty Crocker's Cookbook		13,000,000
The Godfather (1969)	Mario Puzo	12,140,000
The Exorcist	William Blatty	11,702,097
To Kill a Mockingbird (1960)	Harper Lee	11,113,909
Pocket Atlas, Hammond		11,000,000
Peyton Place, (1956)	Grace Metalious	10,672,302
English-Spanish, Spanish-English Dictionary (1948)	Carlos Castillo and Otto F. Bond	10,187,000
Love Story	Erich Segal	9,905,627

[3] Alice Payne Hackett and James Henry Burke, *Eighty Years of Best Sellers 1895–1975* (New York: R. R. Bowker, 1977), p. 10. Copyright © 1977 by Xerox Corporation. Reprinted by permission.

Valley of the Dolls (1966)	Jacqueline Susann	9,500,000
Jaws (1974)	Peter Benchley	9,475,418
Jonathan Livingston Seagull (1970)	Richard Bach	9,055,000

LEARN TO SAY "NO" TO A "NO"

One lesson which may be derived from a study of this fascinating parade of best sellers relates to rejections: Don't take them too seriously. At least three of the titles listed (including *The Godfather*) were rejected at least once.

An executive of a major publishing house once remarked that 90 percent of a publisher's business is saying "no." One senior editor estimated that, as a reader in a major house, he had said "no" on some 2,500 manuscripts. The unrelenting pressure of making so many negative decisions drove him to a physical breakdown.

As a measure of the fallibility of human judgment, examine this list of novels which were turned down by publishers—some of them several times—before they finally found a home, and best-seller status:

TITLE	AUTHOR
The Naked and the Dead	Norman Mailer
Topaz	Leon Uris
Lord of the Flies	William Golding
The Sand Pebbles	Richard McKenna
The Ginger Man	James P. Donleavy
The Lost Weekend	Charles Reginald Jackson
Day of the Jackal	Frederick Forsyth
Look Homeward, Angel	Thomas Wolfe
A Separate Peace	John Knowles
No Time for Sergeants	Mac Hyman
Lolita	Vladimir Nabakov
Deer Park	Norman Mailer
Sister Carrie	Theodore Dreiser
Auntie Mame	Patrick Dennis
Tropic of Cancer	Henry Miller

Contrary to myth, *Gone with the Wind* was not rejected by anyone. It was purchased by the first publisher to which it was shown: Macmillan. Harold Latham, then editor of Macmillan, while visiting Atlanta met Margaret Mitchell. He had been told by others in Atlanta about her compelling narrative of the Civil War. Latham asked Ms. Mitchell about the manuscript, and she at first denied its existence. However, Ms. Mitchell later took her great stack of mss. to the lobby of Latham's hotel in Atlanta, and turned it over to him. The rest is history.

Would anyone believe that Eudora Welty ever collected rejection slips? She did, many of them, as a young writer fresh out of the University of Wisconsin. Now, with a Pulitzer Prize and other laurels behind her, she can smile when she says of her early efforts: "They always came straight back!"

Why do editors reject "naturals" like these (and perhaps yours)? A clue may lie in something once said by a senior editor of a New York house:

> Any intelligent, well-educated person can tell if a book has quality. What's hard to tell is if the book is going to sell.

So, an editor may regard your brainchild highly, as a book. He may not view it so highly as merchandise. And that, dear scribe, is the much-touted bottom line.

chapter 5

. . . here, you see, it takes all the running
you can do, to keep in the same place.

LEWIS CARROLL

WRITING FOR
MOVIES & TELEVISION

If it's fortune alone you seek (not fame, not fulfillment), go west, young writer . . . to Hollywood.

Tinselville on the Pacific is the Mecca of Mucho Dinero for writers who can make the grade in TV and movie scripting. It's also the land of cutthroat competition, blasted hopes, duodenal ulcers, and heart-wrenching unemployment. So unless you were born with armorplate for skin and copper tubing for intestines, take Horace Greeley's classic advice *cum grano salis*.

For an unknown and inexperienced newcomer, the odds of crashing the world of film or television scripting are just slightly better than of finding the Lost Dutchman Mine. There is not really much point in discussing these highly specialized media in this book, except for the fun of it.

The best way to learn about writing for the tube and the screen is to talk shop with people already involved—actors, producers, electricians, grips, script girls, and of course writers. The next best is to read everything ever written by and about writers and writing in Hollywood (see Suggested Readings in Appendix). If you hope to write for the screen, you should be an incurable movie buff. Writer Eric Roth (*Concorde: Airport '79* and others) advises hopefuls to "go see millions of movies." Roth, before moving from New York to the West Coast, saw as many as nine movies every week. Whenever he visits Los Angeles (from his home in Del Mar) he sees at least two a day. If it's TV that lures you, you should have been—like teleplay writer Ann Collins—a TV freak since age six.

An inkling of the odds against the newcomer can be gained from a statistic: The Screen Writers Guild (which includes a TV Division) boasts some 5,000 members. One veteran script writer guesses that there must be at least three times as many hard-breathing hopefuls who are *not* Guild members, waiting in the wings. And while the writer population appears to be multiplying year after year, the number of script-writing openings appears to be decreasing.

The craftsmen who qualify as Kings of the Mountain—the six- and seven-figure earners—may well be content with their hibiscus-draped villas in San Fernando Valley or Malibu, complete with kidney-shaped pools and kidneys that don't work very well. But for many a sensitive writer-soul, Tinselville falls somewhat short of paradise. Novelists who have done well in their craft often find, for example, that the skills of the novelist are not necessarily interchangeable with those of the scriptwriter.

Old hands know, from years of gall and wormwood, that every movie script and teleplay—no matter how superbly and honestly crafted—will be rewritten countless times until the original becomes totally emasculated. Writing is by committee, with businessmen collaborating with artists in the final product. Any resemblance to real life in a movie script is, as a rule, sheer accident.

Eric Roth, for example, called *Airport '79*'s story line "insanity." As a veteran teleplay writer put it, "you've got to be incredibly bright to write beautifully about nothing at all."

The Inevitable Agent

Question, heard everywhere: How do I get a foothold as a writer?

Answer, heard everywhere: Get a good agent.

Next question: But how do I get a good agent?

Answer: That's a good question.

In Hollywood (or, if you prefer, Los Angeles), producers simply do not read unsolicited screen plays or teleplays. They return nearly all of them unopened. Occasionally, if a writer will sign a release guaranteeing the producer against all harm including warts and flat feet, a producer will read an offering. But the rule is "no unsolicited mss." Reasons: (1) they are too busy producing films or teleplays or getting a tan, and (2) they live in mortal fear of nuisance suits charging plagiarism, piracy, or paternity.

Ergo, just shy of 100 percent of all scripts must be routed through Hollywood Shylocks. OK, says the lady in the balcony, I'll send my material to an agent. It isn't that simple, because newcomers will find it almost as hard to sell their work to an agent as to a producer. Agents are besieged day and night by newcomers, most of whom are pathetically unequipped to write for movies or television, or even for soup-can labels.

However, madam, if you insist, you may write for a list of agents to the Writers Guild of America, 8955 Beverly Boulevard, Los Angeles 90048. Then you may select an agent from this list, and mail him or her several samples of your work. If these samples are good enough, you will probably hear from the agent. But be sure to enclose the required SASE.

These samples can be teleplays (if TV is your thing) aimed at any series show you enjoy on the tube, or "film concepts" if the screen is your love. Dave Balsiger, co-author of *In Search of Noah's Ark*, made it to the Big Time that way. He wrote a film concept (a several-paragraph statement describing an idea for a movie), and sent it to Sunn Classics (*Life and Times of Grizzly Adams, Chariot of the Gods*, and others). Balsiger was working at the time for an advertising agency, and didn't know a screen play from a laundry list. Sunn called Balsiger and said "we want to see you." They saw, and he conquered and ended up as an executive with Sunn Classics.

TV writer Peggy Elliott had no idea about how one becomes a teleplay writer when she spurned a journalism scholarship in El Paso to seek her fortune in Los Angeles. She knew no one in show business, but serendipity was her salvation. Ms. Elliott took a job with a marketing research firm whose offices were located on the Columbia Studio lot. There she met the right people, and wound up writing a documentary. When the documentary market began to fade, she switched to comedy writing. After more than a dozen successful years in comedy (*The Odd Couple, Petticoat Junction*, and others), she broke away from her writing-team relationship with another pro and began writing solo. Now she earns as much as $25,000 per teleplay, plus another seven or eight big ones for each first rerun. Ms. Elliott likes the freedom this kind of money buys, including the freedom to garden, play tennis, and read eight books a week.

If you aspire to write for TV, say the long-time pros, you can't do it in Minnesota or Vermont. Because all but a few teleplays are produced in Smogsville, you must uproot and move to California. Producers will not travel to you.

One sure clue to making it in television is getting inside. No matter how you do it, somehow get a foot in the door. One enterprising writer, realizing he would never get inside through sheer talent alone, devised a brilliant ploy: He took a job as a lowly page in a network studio, a job in television roughly equivalent to bagboy in a supermarket. Soon he became acquainted, on a nodding basis, with actors, cameramen, grips, electricians and—most important—producers. In his network uniform, he was constantly identified as a member of the family. So one day, after he had become a name rather than just another face, he walked up to a producer and said: "Mr. (so-and-so), I've written an episode for this show, and would appreciate it if you'd glance at it when you have a moment." The producer glanced, was impressed, and the page soon traded his uniform for a typewriter.

Ann Collins, a TV writer (*Hawaii Five-O*) describes teleplay crafting as formula writing and highly structured. She remembers

Jack Lord (McGarrett of *Hawaii Five-O*) once commenting that a teleplay is like a sonnet: each is structured to achieve a certain effect. The structure shows up in these ground rules for a one-hour show: 52 minutes of teleplay, eight minutes of commercials, four commercial breaks. Before each break, the suspense must rise to such an unbearable level that the viewer will resist every temptation to switch channels. The writer must follow this formula, or else.

About stage plays: Old hands in the business say that most plays are sold on a person-to-person basis. Here again—as in television and motion pictures—friendships and acquaintances are very important. Through these contacts, the playwright learns who is buying what, and where.

The talents of movie scripters and teleplay writers are interchangeable with those of playwrights, as the career of Neil Simon amply demonstrates. Simon's record—before he abandoned Hollywood for Broadway—included 16 movies, 17 plays, and success as a television gag writer. Simon once had four of his plays running simultaneously in New York. He remembers his days as a TV writer as exhausting.

> Then, I used to work six days a week, late into the night, which is what all the TV writers (in Hollywood) still do. These guys have breakdowns because they're working so hard.

RIDE A CYCLE

Television and motion pictures are cyclical industries. One year it's the Big Disaster movie—*Titanic, The Poseidon Adventure, Airport, Earthquake, Towering Inferno*. (One wag threatened to write a sequel to *Earthquake* and *Towering Inferno* and to title it *Shake-and-Bake*). Then public fancy shifts from cataclysms to the supernatural and occult—*The Exorcist, Chariot of the Gods, The Omen, In Search of. . .*This novelty wears off, and a jaded public looks for new thrills in science fiction—*Star Wars, The Black Hole*. Westerns and police films are eclipsed, but will one day return when the industry runs out of catastrophes, spooks, and space. Suspense films, like Tennyson's brook, go on and on forever.

Writers must remain sensitive to these trends and cycles, ever ready to shift with them. Or even to create them.

As for plots, it's forever *Bad Day at Black Rock*. TV and screen writers tirelessly rework old veins in the plot mine, just as standup comedians constantly rewrite *Joe Miller's Joke Book*. One screenwriter admits to borrowing at least two of his movie themes from Walter Van Tilburg Clark's *The Track of the Cat*, with different protagonists in each case wounding the mountain lion, then tracking down the hapless beast for the kill to prove the hero's machoism. In one version of a Western, the trail boss contracts a disease and the townfolk won't let him drive the cattle through. In another, it's the cows that fall victim to some mysterious malady.

WHAT PRICE CREATIVITY?

Hollywood is brutally hard on novelists who take pride in their work (and many have fled, screaming, back to the hinterlands). Creative writers know that network and studio executives—some of whom cannot write anything except checks—always contribute their own ideas to a story. Studio people insist that *they* know what the public wants and the writer *doesn't*. So writers write for executives, not for the public. One seasoned scripter estimates that at least two out of every three original ideas die aborning in Hollywood.

William Goldman, a novelist for a decade before he began to write for the screen, still practices the novelist's craft. Goldman knows that whatever he writes for the movies has little chance of surviving in the form in which he wrote it. So now and then he plays hooky from films to write a novel. He knows his novels will survive and will become his own personal statement with all the original vices and virtues intact.

Goldman is also a realist. He knows that one Hollywood movie script (examples: *Butch Cassidy and the Sundance Kid, All the President's Men*) can yield more hard cash than some novelists earn in an entire career. In a way, he has the best of both worlds.

Footnote: Goldman writes in New York. Why not Hollywood, surrounded by flaming bougainvillaea and orange blossoms?

"I couldn't possibly work (there)," he admits.

chapter 6

Few poets achieve best-sellerdom, and nearly all who do, reflect popular rather than intellectual American taste.

EIGHTY YEARS OF BEST SELLERS[1]

POETRY

Someone once remarked that only four American poets in the history of the Republic had made a living exclusively from their poetry.

I don't have the roster, but perhaps it would include Kahlil Gibran, whose *The Prophet* had by 1975 sold six million copies in the United States (but who really doesn't qualify, because he was Lebanese). Maybe it would include Rod McKuen, whose *Listen to the Warm* sold more than two million copies between 1967 and 1975. The roll also might list Robert Frost, Archibald Macleish, Emily Dickinson, Robert Hillyer, and Carl Sandburg

---

[1] Alice Payne Hackett and James Henry Burke, *Eighty Years of Best Sellers* (New York: R.R. Bowker, 1977), p. 53. Copyright © 1977 by Xerox Corporation. Reprinted by permission.

(though his nonfiction books may have grossed more than his poems). And in a more popular vein, Edgar Guest (about whom Dorothy Parker was somewhat less than complimentary).

Whichever poets made the list notwithstanding, there weren't many of them. As any student of U.S. literary history will attest, there never has been, there is not now, and there may never be a genuine market for poetry in this country.

Judson Jerome, a teacher and poet of long experience, lays facts on the line:

> A poet would be an idiot to be in it for money. . . . My rough guess
> is that U.S. magazines pay little more than $10,000 per year for about
> 500 poems, out of at least half a million poems submitted. If my
> estimates are anywhere near accurate, your latest poem, launched in
> that sea, stands about one chance in a thousand of earning $20. There
> is no such thing as an average poet, but suppose there were one, who
> wrote and sent out 20 new poems a year—an output too large to be
> consistent with quality. He or she might, at those odds, expect to
> be paid $20 for one every 50 years.[2]

Fortunately for mankind, Samuel Johnson was dead wrong in declaring that "no man but a blockhead ever wrote except for money." Most poets are not blockheads, and most poets do not write for money. And neither, for that matter, do true painters, novelists, sculptors, or musicians create and compose primarily for financial gain. Creative people create because they would be miserable if they didn't. If their efforts bring cash dividends, true artists feel doubly rewarded: first by the fruits of their labors, second because their efforts have brought material as well as spiritual remuneration.

The world would be a sorry place indeed without its poets— the "painters of the soul," as someone so aptly described them. We all need the Millays and the Tennysons, Brownings and Frosts, the Hillyers, Lowells, Dickinsons, and Sandburgs. *And* the Kilmers, Guests, Richard Armours and Dr. Seusses. Not to mention the weavers of limericks both proper and profane and the confectioners

---

[2]Jerome Judson, "Why the Poetry Game Resembles Russian Roulette," *Writer's Yearbook 1980* (Cincinnati: Writer's Digest Publications), pp. 30–32.

of Burma-Shave doggerel. Even if we don't read them, their poems form part of our culture and our heritage.

Where would America be if there were no poems which begin thus:

" 'Twas the night before Christmas . . ."

"This is the forest primeval."

"Listen, my children, and you shall hear . . ."

"O beautiful for spacious skies . . ."

or even

"There was a young lady from Dallas . . ."

How impoverished our life would be without them, and a thousand others.

The message seems clear, however: If you must write poetry, do not write it for money. Do not expect to make a living from poetry alone, or even a side income of any consequence.

To paraphrase Kirk Polking, director of the Writer's Digest School:

I just sold a poem.
The payment was nifty:
A check for three figures—
One dollar fifty.

III

NONFICTION WRITING FORMS

chapter 7

The magazine article has become the characteristic literary medium of our generation.
  ROBERT KIRSCH, LITERARY CRITIC
            LOS ANGELES TIMES

WRITING ARTICLES FOR CONSUMER MAGAZINES

Name six well-known magazine-article writers.

(Silence)

O.K. . . . name *three*.

(More silence)

Well . . . can you name just *one*?

Chances are you cannot, unless you are (1) one of the six writers, or (2) an editor who buys their material. Yet most schoolboys can name six big-league ballplayers, or TV stars, or rock singers, or. . . .

Magazine-article writing is no freeway to fame. Or, for that matter, to fortune. The men and women who write those frothy pieces that entertain us in *Reader's Digest,* or *Playboy,* or *Woman's Day,* or *The Rotarian,* or *Harper's* are—in the main—little-known scribes whose bylines are as ephemeral as mayflies. Their writings may stir nation-wide shock waves or unseat scoundrels from high places, but the writers themselves remain—with rare exceptions—faceless and next-to-anonymous.

Why, then, do hundreds—even thousands—of hopefuls try to join their ranks every year? Why do legions of apprentice authors sign up every season for courses in article-writing? What is the fascination this special branch of writing holds for so many novices? And why do so many seasoned pros remain in its service, year after year?

One attraction of article writing lies in a very significant statistic:

Ninety percent or more of all editorial copy in today's big consumer magazines is nonfiction. A bare ten percent of total space is reserved for the storyteller.

This breakdown is a startling contrast to percentages of three or four decades ago, when short stories outnumbered articles in virtually every issue of the big magazines. Today, the American public looks to television and the movies for most of its fantasies. They expect magazines to supply them information on a vast array of subjects, month after month.

Fledgling writers, hearing about that great, hungry market for fact writing, naturally think of article writing as a way to break into print, and to make money. But many of these beginners are laboring under the false assumption, at the outset at least, that writing articles for magazines must be much easier than novel writing, or movie scripting, or creating poetry. Magazines (they may think) are markets for which one may "dash off" something before lunch, or to which they may sell a piece or two "on the side" to grubstake themselves while they do some "serious" writing.

Few novices who leave the starting gate in this frame of mind ever cross the finish line; most of them drop out at the first turn. However, beginners who approach magazine-article writing maturely and soberly, and filled with zeal to learn their craft, go on to become tomorrow's pros. These zealous ones may account for five percent of the total who try. The other ninety-five in a hundred fall away, being too lazy, too undisciplined, too unwilling to learn, to make it in this exacting marketplace. That is precisely why there is always room at the top in the writing business, and why the old pros do not fear that competition will drive them out. It is also why the veterans will share their secrets with newcomers: they know that many will make a start, but few will persevere.

Professionals who labor at article writing full-time keep doggedly at it—flushed with victory and paychecks one season, poor as churchmice the next—because (1) they love the work, (2) they can't bear the thought of retreating to the world of time clocks and executive washrooms, (3) they get stuck in the trade and feel ill-equipped to do anything else after two or three decades in the business, or (4) they are really good at article writing and never lack for assignments and money. Or combinations of these.

There are a few (hold up some fingers) who make a handsome living, year after year, by writing for mass-circulation magazines. One echelon down from these superstars are a larger number who sell occasionally to the biggies, more often to the middle- and lower-level periodicals, and thus manage somehow to pay the bills while retaining a form of independence. A still larger number manage by producing quantity for the lower-paying markets, including the trades (discussed later).

And nobody knows how many are moonlight scribes. These are men and women who work a normal nine-to-five, then write at night or on weekends or vacations, or even at brown-bag lunchtime— one hand holding the ham-on-rye while the other pecks at the typewriter. One moonlighter earned between $15,000 and $30,000 a year while working a 40-hour week. He accomplished this astonishing feat by showing up at his downtown Manhattan office every morning at 7:00, and working at his typewriter until his regular day began at 9:30. He must have been the inspiration for the fellow who wrote: "One thing common to most success stories is the alarm clock."

FACTS VERSUS FANCIES

This chapter will explore some of the facts, and some of the fictions, about magazine-article writing. It will deal exclusively

with "consumer" magazines—and there are some 1600 of them—
a term which the publishing industry applies to periodicals which
show up on newsstands or are bought by subscription.

The consumer "books" (people in the trade sometimes refer
to magazines as "books") are divisible into three broad categories:

1. the majors, or "slicks" (because they are printed on slick
   paper), including giants like *National Geographic, McCall's,
   Cosmopolitan, Playboy, Ladies Home Journal*;
2. the secondaries, which includes hundreds of publications
   aimed at special-interest readerships (hobbies, sports, political
   beliefs or affiliations, religious convictions, fraternal ties,
   and so forth); and
3. the so-called "little" magazines, without which much of the
   nation's mainstream and avant-garde writing would have no
   place to go.

There are two other broad categories, covered elsewhere in
this book:

- The business-paper press, more commonly called "trade
journals" or simply "trades," including something in excess of
4,000 publications, and
- Company publications, also called "house organs," published
by businesses, associations, and industries to serve their employees,
stockholders, customers and, in some cases, the general public.
One expert estimates their number at around 4,000.

These thousands of periodicals collectively form an enormous
marketplace for literary merchandise, purchasing millions of
words annually from free-lance writers. People who hope to make
money with words should, therefore, study the marketplace with
great care.

Included in this vast wonderland of print are magazines
aimed at every conceivable sector of the reading populace, from
the kinkiest to the most conservative, from the near-moronic to
the most cerebral. If you have a special interest, occupation,
hobby, profession, sport, or other activity which engrosses you,

there is probably a magazine out there to serve you. The range includes innumerable off-beat, regional, and highly specialized periodicals which go to very small but demanding readerships. Examples, chosen at random, would be *Turkey Call* (for wild-turkey enthusiasts), with 31,000 subscribers; *Pickin' Magazine* (for fans of old-time bluegrass, country, folk, jazz and other specialty music), whose followers number 40,000; *Omaha Magazine*, which goes to some 10,000 "upper-income (or those who aspire to be), educated Omahans"; and a host of others.

Best known of all are "general interest" books like *The New Yorker, Reader's Digest, Harper's, National Geographic, Atlantic, The Saturday Evening Post* (a pale shadow of its former glorious self), *Saturday Review*, and the like. Then comes a veritable army of publications which zero in on much narrower targets: those concentrating on travel, home and garden, finance, the senior citizen, theater, movies and TV, detective and mystery (mostly fiction), confessions (fiction pretending to be fact), aviation, automobiles, fraternal groups (Elks, Rotarians, Lions, et al), and dozens of other categories.

Somewhere in the mix are the so-called "in-flights," those breezy little magazines tucked in the pocket of the airliner seat ahead of you, which you remove by inching back your knees.

IT WASN'T ALWAYS THUS

The consumer-magazine world of today bears little resemblance to its ancestor of 30 or 40 years ago. To writers of younger generations, the point may seem academic. Yet it is, I believe, useful to know why so many magazines have folded in the years since World War II, and why the periodicals of today are what they are.

In pre-TV America, magazines provided some services which they no longer provide, at least to the same degree. Before the Big Eye, magazines were important escape mechanisms for Americans. The pulps—Westerns, mysteries, romances, and others—were the forerunners of today's TV soaps and serials. When there was no longer a need for them, the pulps simply vanished. The confessions, in which free lancers write their wrongs, have long been staples in the reading diets of distaff Americans. They have survived the changes which decimated or destroyed the Western, mystery, and detective pulps, and persist today. But there is evidence that even the hardy confessions are suffering syndromes of senility, and their days may be numbered.

Similarly, many of the great general-interest magazines, *The Saturday Evening Post* and *Collier's* among them, were viewed as entertainment media, publishing quantities of fiction along with much smaller diets of fact. These giants began to suffer from years of subscription obesity and hardening of the editorial arteries soon after World War II, and eventually expired. They found, to everyone's astonishment, that bigger and bigger circulations were not necessarily better for business. As their readerships grew by leaps and bounds, so did their dollar losses. Tied to this economic phenomenon was the advent of television, which made inroads on advertising revenues on which magazines had long enjoyed a virtual monopoly.

As some of the titans began to fold, newcomers moved in. Some succeeded, and are still around. Others—many more than the successes—folded after a few issues, bankrupt. The key factor in the success of those which prevailed was (and continues to be) a magic ingredient called "reader identification." John H. Allen, a McGraw-Hill executive, put it this way:

> I believe that magazines generally achieve closer, far stronger audience attachments than television does. Today, no magazine can live very long without it (reader identification), no magazine can continue to earn its reader's time, unless it speaks to him personally, individually, and intimately about activities that vitally interest him. And so, magazines have been shifting their approach to readership, seeking out and appealing to specialized needs in specialized markets. A stage has been reached today where a whopping general-circulation magazine is somewhat suspect.[1]

Mr. Allen, speaking of "specialized needs," is referring to the phenomenon noted in detail in the table on page 70. Witness

---

[1] San Diego Union, October 12, 1971. Reprinted by permission.

there the number of magazines serving special categories of readers, among them:

boxing, wrestling, karate	65
car and van	138
fishing, hunting, camping	62
skiing, boating, aviation	61
sports	99
women's interest	80
and so forth	

To be sure, there were 74 "general-interest" publications listed in the survey cited. But 30 or 40 years ago, one would have looked in vain for anything like 138 "car and van" publications, or 28 ethnic magazines. And who would have dreamed, three decades ago, of a magazine named *Mother Jones*? Today, fire-breathing *Mother Jones*, described by one of its editors as a kind of "reverse *Fortune*," boasts a readership approaching one quarter of a million. *Prevention*, viewed in the 1950s as a kind of editorial odd-ball, now is hailed as an outstanding spokesman for the cause of ecology, with a circulation topping one and a half million—nearly doubling in a decade.

Nor could anyone in World War II years have forecast success for a magazine called *Runner's World*. A young fellow named Bob Anderson (then 17) started it under the title *Distance Running News*, with a $100 bankroll. At first, fellow-runners wrote articles for him free, and Anderson hand-stapled, folded, and mailed the first 28-page issue to 300 subscribers. This grew into *Runner's World*, now the flagship of a fleet of profitable publishing and athletic-supply enterprises with more than a hundred employees, and annual revenues approaching five million dollars. *Runner's World*, and the jogging binge that inspired it, would have been unthought of in the forties, and probably even in the fifties.

U.S. consumer tastes as the 1970s drew to a close were reflected in the following table of magazine categories:[2]

[2]*CPDA News, Journal of the Council for Periodical Distributors Associations,* 1977. Reprinted by permission.

SUBJECT CATEGORY	NUMBER OF TITLES IN PRINT
Almanacs	8
Astrology	26
Boxing, wrestling, and karate	65
Business and commentary	20
Calendars	11
Car and van	138
CB	23
Children's	25
Crossword	146
Cycle	61
Detective and westerns	48
Diet	26
Ethnic	28
Fishing, hunting, camping, guns	62
General interest	74
Girlie	164
Home, garden and building	83
Mechanics, electronics, science	17
Men's adventure	16
Monster	15
Movie	30
Photography	21
Romance	43
Science fiction, U.F.O., weird	36
Sewing and craft	51
Skiing, boating, aviation	61
Sports	99
Stereo hi-fi and audio	18
Teenage and music	62
Tax	8
T.V.	58
Weekly and bi-weekly	36
Women's interest	80
Total	1,659

CONTENT "STYLES"

"Styles" in magazine-article content naturally mirror trends of the times. The hot subject of today may well be the dodo of tomorrow. Twenty years ago, you probably could not have sold an article on ecology, dual-career marriages, or women's liberation to any major publication. Today, these are among the commonplace "must" items in a table of contents.

Not only must a successful magazine writer be acutely attuned to what *is* trendy; he or she must also know what is *not* in vogue. In the late sixties and early seventies, pieces on higher education—especially student unrest—were a dime-a-dozen, as were articles on civil rights. But by 1973, these subjects, along with heavy stuff on international affairs, simply were not finding the welcome that had greeted them earlier. Books were still being written in these fields—commissioned when their subjects were flooding the print media—but the magazines had, in the main, dropped them.

Any writer who expects to sell to major markets must, therefore, keep eyes and ears sensitive to the slightest change in public sentiment. And once he or she senses a shift, or some new trend, the writer must begin immediately to capitalize on the change. To wait until a trend is in full bloom may be fatal, for by then other writers may have seized the initiative. Or worse, the trend may weaken and die.

If you are gifted with prescience, and can sense trends or shifts long before they materialize, you will also need to learn to sit on certain ideas until their time comes. To try to capitalize on a subject before it takes root in the "mass mind" is to invite rejection slips. I will cite two examples from my own experience:

1. In the late 1940s, I wrote what I believe was the first slick-paper article on skin-diving ever published in the United States. The piece sold to *National Geographic*, and later appeared in their *Book of Fishes* (1952 edition). At the time I was living in Southern California, and enjoying "goggle-diving" in the surf off La Jolla. ("Goggle-diving" was the granddaddy of today's SCUBA diving.) Enthusiastic about this new sport, I wrote to a major

New York publishing house which specialized (and still does) in sporting books. Would they consider a book on this new, under-water recreation? No, wrote the editor. He did not think very many people would be interested in playing around under water, wearing a faceplate and snorkel. I abandoned the project. Within a decade or so, a small library of books on the subject had been published. I foolishly allowed myself to be discouraged by the opinion of one short-sighted editor, and did not follow up on my idea. My notes languished in my files, and I lost out.

2. In the mid-forties, I knew a man who had undergone a then-rare operation called a vasectomy to protect his wife's health, after doctors told her that another pregnancy might prove fatal. After making some inquiries, I found that vasectomies were much more common, even then, than was supposed. I proposed an article on the subject to *Reader's Digest*. No, wrote the editor. They did not believe many people would be interested in an article on such an off-beat and unpleasant subject. Since then, a rash of pieces on vasectomies has broken out in general-interest publications.

Both of these ideas (and others) were ahead of schedule. I should have placed them in a tickler file, marked for resubmission in a year or two—or whenever the time seemed propitious—rather than consigning them to the dead file.

So do not abandon a good idea. You might be in the vanguard, and may have to wait for the world to catch up with you.

WHERE THE MONEY IS

Consumer-magazine pay scales for articles range from a low of around five cents to a dollar or more per word. In exceptional cases, paychecks for articles have hit legendary peaks. One of these super-checks went to a writer contracted by NASA to prepare a 6,000 word piece on the Viking Mars Landing program. His fee was $24,000, or four dollars a word. Perhaps the all-time high (until now) was the $50,000 reportedly paid to Harrison Salisbury for an *Esquire* piece. (Lest you are tempted to rush off a batch of manuscripts to *Esquire,* Xerox Corporation, according to *The New*

York Times, paid Salisbury's fee, and also is said to have paid *Esquire* for the space in which it ran.)

Such astronomical sums are, of course, exceptions. Established "generalists," who write on anything that looks saleable and catches their fancy, may receive as little as $100 for an article, and now and then $3,000 or more, plus expenses in many instances. For a blockbuster assignment worthy of mention on the magazine's cover, the rate will climb well beyond $3,000, especially if the writer is well-known in his or her special field (an astronaut, for example, or an outstanding sports or entertainment personality).

The biggest producers, according to one informed estimate, may gross between $20,000 and $50,000 a year. If such a writer also authors books, his or her annual income may hit the six-figure level. And if the writer is truly versatile, he or she may accept other sideline assignments far afield from article writing. One long-time pro has also written a syndicated newspaper column, campaign speeches, publicity copy, and television scripts—all while carrying on his article-writing career.

So there *is* money to be made in the business. The trick is to learn how to make it.

WHAT PRICE SUCCESS?

What does it take to succeed as a writer of big-time consumer-magazine articles? A number of qualities and qualifications go into the mix:

First, a genuine flair for communicating ideas in written form. You *must* know the English language well enough to abuse it now and then, and to know the difference between use and abuse. You must enjoy using the language, and show proper reverence for the mother tongue. You must be impatient with shoddy constructions, tautologies, clichés, buzz words, and other monstrosities.

Second, you should be blessed (or afflicted) with an un-quenchable thirst for new knowledge, and an insatiable curiosity about the world around you.

Third, you should genuinely enjoy research. This means you should love books and things bookish. Libraries should be your second home (even your first), and you should feel happiest when surrounded by books. If books make you uneasy, you should either avoid this profession, or concentrate on some facet of it which demands little from the world of books (straight reporting, for example). You must respect facts, and be able to pursue them as a bull terrier pursues rats. James Michener—whose worldly and literary success few will challenge—once said that he would go anywhere on the globe to correct a mistake in his research, even if only one person in the world would ever know he had made that mistake!

Editors expect you to adhere to the facts, and will prove unforgiving if you short-change accuracy. Veteran magazine writer Joseph Bell—who managed to get in trouble in spite of adhering to the facts—tells a charming true story about an article idea he once sold to the editors of *Reader's Digest*. During World War II, a student pilot in training for his wings was taking his first solo flight in an advanced trainer. All went well until clouds closed in, and the pilot—suddenly above the overcast with no experience in instrument flying—radioed the tower that he was lost.

"Keep cool," replied the flight officer in the tower. "We'll talk you down. Just follow my instructions."

The tower proceeded to radio careful orders, telling the young pilot when to change headings, when to descend to a lower altitude, and so on, until the tower was convinced that the pilot was on his final approach. The somewhat shaken airman acknowledged all these orders, and said he was complying. At last the tower told the pilot he was right on target, and instructed him to touch down. The pilot landed.

Good story? Not really . . . until you learn that the pilot, following these detailed orders while flying blind, landed at *another airport*!

Reader's Digest encouraged Joe Bell to go ahead on the story. Joe did, and sent his finished copy to Pleasantville. The editors liked it, and told Joe it was a great yarn. But, they said, there were one or two things they would need to know before publishing the piece. First, the name of the pilot. And the name of the control-tower operator. And some other details that—years after the event—everyone had long since forgotten.

Joe Bell was unable to provide the required details, so Pleasantville regretfully rejected the article.

(Epilogue: Joe, being a very enterprising fellow, put the piece in a fresh envelope and sold it to *The Saturday Evening Post* as a short story that later appeared in hardcover as one of the *Best Post Stories of 1956.*)

Fourth, you should be endowed with sound health and a more-than-average supply of raw physical energy and endurance. Walter B. Pitkin, who made a small fortune on his book *Life Begins at Forty*, and who was himself a mountain of vitality, would tell his Columbia University students that raw physical energy was the Number One requisite for success in free-lance writing.

One very successful husband-and-wife writing team living in Florida read 60 magazines between them every month, gutting them for their clipping files and plundering them for new article ideas. They also read dozens of press releases, bulletins, and everything else they could lay hands on. The mere act of *reading* so many words, apart from their research and writing chores, placed enormous demands on their physical strength.

Fifth, this is a business demanding a larger-than-usual stock of intestinal fortitude. One young San Diego newsman, disenchanted with deadlines and city editors, broke away to free lance. He locked himself in his bungalow to crank out thousands of words of fiction, week after week. He didn't sell one word.

Months passed, and still no sales. Then one day he hit upon a specialty which grossed him $16,000 his first year. He followed up on bizarre crime stories, interviewing the detectives and other principals in a case, and wrote "true crime" stories for magazines and tabloids. These "stories" are, of course, really articles dressed up to read like fiction. This kind of "new journalism" has been around for a long time, reaching a high point in Truman Capote's best-selling *In Cold Blood* (which took Capote five years to research and write).

Another example: A young couple, fed up with running a

retail business, abandoned commerce to free lance full-time. Both are avid backyard gardeners and staunch champions of the organic method of raising crops. Both now contribute regularly to a range of gardening and natural-living magazines, grossing together between $700 and $1100 a month. They admit they will never grow rich this way, but this is the life they prefer and they intend to stick with it.

Finally, you must have good "story" sense. That is, you must be able to recognize a good article idea when you see one, and to understand the difference between an article and an essay, editorial, or commentary.

MISTAKES BEGINNERS MAKE

Most amateurs really do not understand the magazine article, and cannot define what an article really is. In a recent contest for article writers, *Writer's Digest* received almost 1,000 entries. Said *Writer's Digest* Associate Editor Rose Adkins, who read them all:

> Two kinds of manuscripts made up the majority of the entries: Failing attempts at humor, and all-too-personal essays. There were many good topics, but many poor treatments of those topics. The leads were weak in most of the entries.[3]

Said another way, the majority of the entries were (it appears) what pros and editors would call "nonresearch" pieces. That is, they were written off the top of the writers' heads, without any legwork or strain. This is the lazy way to write magazine articles, and the way which usually insures receipt of a rejection slip. In rare instances, you may produce a nonresearch piece, and sell it. Examples are seen in the "Drama in Real Life" contributions in *Reader's Digest*, which are derived from true-life experiences.

Pro-writer Jerome E. Kelley tells of writing a nonresearch piece for *Reader's Digest's* "First Person Award Story" department in three hours—which netted him $3000! But he comments that

---

[3] Art Spikol, "The Winnahs," *Writer's Digest*, November 1979, p. 56.

such a top-of-the-head piece is a rarity, adding that most articles will require a lot of research.

Many "inspirational" pieces sold to such magazines as *Guideposts* also might qualify as nonresearch articles. But such pieces must be exceptionally well done to sell.

In sum, you cannot depend on nonresearch writing in the long pull. You may have one or two of these pieces in your system, but you will soon be "written out." One professional estimate says that nonresearch articles comprise about five percent of the total article sales to consumer magazines. So they are—at best—a 20-to-1 shot.

Many beginners confuse the personal essay with the contemporary magazine article. Such essays are also, as a rule, nonresearch pieces in which the writer dips into his memory, or his prejudices, or convictions, for material. In most instances, the result is more an editorial than an article. Or it becomes an essay— a literary form which, 50 to 75 years ago, was much in vogue, but which today goes begging for markets.

The unpleasant truth is, no one—least of all the hard-bitten editor of a mass-circulation magazine—really cares a tinker's dam what you or I think about any given subject. They might, if your name were Teddy Kennedy or Jackie Onassis or Elizabeth Taylor. But under the average writer's byline, personal-opinion stuff is largely unsaleable. Exceptions: the so-called Op-Ed (opinion-editorial) pages of certain major dailies will buy the views of the man or woman in the street, if they are phrased in graceful English and touch on some subject of consuming importance.

Writers who see the magazine article as a forum for carrying their ideas and views to the public should concentrate on the intellectual journals. Of these, Landon Y. Jones wrote in *The Chronicle of Higher Education*:

> A couple of years ago, a group of Columbia University educators (tried) to identify the most influential intellectual journals in the country. In their view, the real marketplace of ideas was not the university, but rather those magazines in which ideas were tested, sifted, and finally either approved or rejected by the intellectuals. Magazine editors, they argued, served as intellectual gatekeepers or salon hostesses, "deciding who can say what about what subject."

The researchers conducted a poll and came up with a list of eight leading intellectual journals: *The New York Review of Books, The New Republic, The New York Times Book Review, The New Yorker, Saturday Review, Partisan Review, Commentary,* and *Harper's.*[4]

Mr. Jones, then editor of the *Princeton Alumni Weekly,* pointed out that such studies need to be updated frequently due to the mercurial nature of some magazines. *Saturday Review,* he noted, had "shed two editorial skins" since the survey was made, *Harper's* had survived "a top-to-bottom change in editorship," and two intellectually influential magazines which should have been listed were not on the list at all: *Rolling Stone,* and *Atlantic.*

However, the central point is clear: if you aspire to write essays or commentaries, or articles which pass for these, you must search out and familiarize yourself with the magazines which buy and print such material. Do not send a piece to *Woman's Day* or *Esquire* which should have gone to *Partisan Review,* or vice versa.

As anyone who has ever taught a class on article writing can testify, an astonishing number of beginners consider themselves natural humorists. The same teachers will attest also that very few amateurs really understand what written humor is, and even fewer can write it. That is why, of course, the truly funny writers, at any given period in history, can be counted on the digits of one hand. And why, as well, they are paid such fabulous sums for their writings. For every Art Buchwald or Erma Bombeck, there are thousands of unsuccessful imitators.

In sum, unless you were born with a native genius for humor, don't waste your time trying to make it in the laugh department.

WHAT TICKS OFF THE EDITORS?

The most common complaint heard from editors about free-lance contributions can be condensed into five words:

You haven't read my magazine!

[4] Landon Y. Jones, "The September Magazines," *Chronicle of Higher Education,* 8, no. 1, September 24, 1973, p. 16. Reprinted by permission.

Worse yet, you haven't *studied* their magazines. To read is not necessarily to study.

Every month thousands of manuscripts pour into magazine offices unsolicited. The overwhelming majority of these "over-the-transom" or "slushpile" offerings should never have been sent to the magazines to which they were addressed. For some reason which defies all logic, hopeful beginners send manuscripts to markets about which they know nothing—except their addresses. Manuscripts about skateboarding go to journals published for macramé fans . . . articles about women's lib go to *macho* men's books . . . pieces concerning Baptists are sent to Congregational organs, and so forth. And manuscripts of 6,000 words are dispatched to magazines which never, never buy anything longer than 2,500, as their market notes carefully emphasize.

Rule number one, which every beginner (or pro, for that matter) violates at his or her peril is: Read, read, read. Study magazines to which you hope to sell. Study them as writers, not merely as readers. Read their articles analytically. Dissect them as a medical student dissects a cadaver. How long are the articles in Magazine A? What kinds of leads does the editor appear to prefer—anecdote, question, quotation, dialogue, straight exposition, and so forth? Does the editor like flashes of humor? How about the endings—what techniques are used there? Study the magazine's ads. Try to envision the "average" reader of Magazine A as you scan its advertisements. What kinds of merchandise are offered? High-quality, expensive stuff? Or courses in "how to increase your biceps?"

In this business, detail is important (like forgetting to enclose a self-addressed, stamped envelope). Here are a few of the common peccadilloes (some of them not so trifling) that really irk editors:

- o enclosing insufficient postage for return of a manuscript or a reply to a query
- o wrapping manuscripts with tape, requiring a ten-minute session with shears, scissors, and old razor blades to open the package
- o using onion-skin tissue instead of 20 lb. manuscript bond
- o submitting manuscripts loaded with typographical errors and misspelled words

○ using typewriter ribbons purchased in 1957 and maybe dipped a couple of time in black Shinola in the meantime

○ enclosing, as a return envelope, a tiny envelope left over from last Christmas' mailing of cards, and into which no letter or manuscript could ever be shoehorned

○ submitting dozens of poems at one time (one editor said she had received one batch of 90 from one free lancer in the same envelope)

○ submitting photocopies which are barely legible (assuming the magazine will even read *good*, legible copies)

Commission of any or all of these sins will most certainly prejudice your chances with any editor, and can prove fatal.

PAY ATTENTION TO THE GROUND RULES

Editors who take the trouble to formulate their ground rules for manuscript acceptance (and most of them do) expect you, the writer, to pay attention to the dos and don'ts they have taken pains to formulate. Pay special attention to the no-nos. Here are a few recent examples:

TRAVEL & LEISURE

○ No unsolicited manuscripts. Queries only. Keep them short.

○ Don't send a list of places you'd like to visit and write about. Know something about a place already and query about it.

○ Query about one idea at a time. The editor doesn't like letters proposing 15 article ideas at once.

○ The magazine wants quality writing on topics never before covered or at least not covered recently.

If you follow this editor's mandate, you won't (1) tell him you're about to depart on a swing through South America, and offer to write a piece on every city touched; (2) send him a transcript of your travel diary, made on that trip to Fiji, which your Aunt Mabel told you was sure-fire *Travel & Leisure* copy; (3) send him an article about your perfectly routine trip to England, where you did perfectly routine things (Tower of London, trip on the Thames, and so on) in a perfectly routine way.

One of my students, understanding this principle, made it her business to acquaint herself thoroughly and intimately with the pubs of New Zealand. She had no trouble at all selling that one.

READER'S NUTSHELL

○ Articles on sex or drinking are taboo.

○ Send seasonal material (Christmas, Thanksgiving, for example) eight months in advance. Not five, six, or seven—*eight*.

MIDNIGHT/GLOBE

○ No violence.

○ No sex.

○ Material must be fresh.

○ Don't pad your copy with unessentials. Keep writing tight.

LADIES' HOME JOURNAL

○ No personal essays (sound familiar?).

○ No travel pieces.

○ No unsolicited manuscripts. Will accept mss. through literary agents only.

Note that the editors, in the cited instances, have given you a clue to some of their pet phobias. It would be insane not to heed these guidelines. It would be idiotic *not* to check the market notes for any given periodical before submitting a query or a manuscript, precisely to be warned of any such in-house ground rules.

CUTTING YOUR TEETH ON FILLERS

One place to cut your editorial teeth in preparing for a career as a magazine-article writer is the filler market. Louise Boggess, an experienced author and teacher who has written a book on the subject, tells how fillers sometimes are born.

> At a luncheon the woman sitting beside me pointed to her overweight friend at the end of the table and remarked, "She bought a reducing machine last week for a ridiculous price." The comment kept cropping up in my mind all during the luncheon as a possible filler. Before I arrived home several hours later, I had written in my notebook: "Substitute *figure* for *price*. . . ." Here was a salable filler.[5]

As the name implies, the original function of fillers was to fill blank space, usually at the bottom of a column of type. They still serve this function in newspapers and magazines throughout the land, of course. But readers have become so enamored of these morsels that many magazines have built entire departments around them, including *Reader's Digest, The New Yorker*, and *Playboy*. *The New Yorker's* bottom-of-column items are avidly awaited by the magazine's fans, who often turn to these shorties before reading the longer, more cerebral pieces, or even before viewing the cartoons for which *The New Yorker* is world-famous.

Fillers come in all shapes and sizes, beginning with a few words in length and topping off at around 500. Fillers also can be artwork—reproductions of old steel engravings, woodcuts, or maps, with the writing limited to captions.

Fillers may be puns, silly definitions, want ads with weird or thigh-slapping typographical errors, anecdotes about people or animals, printers' errors (*The New Yorker* delights in featuring these), quotations from people famed and infamous, jokes, helpful hints for housewives and do-it-yourselfers—anything that will fill space while entertaining or informing, or both.

No one can make a living by writing fillers, but many do pad out their incomes by keeping a stock of these short takes in the mails. One Ohio filler expert is said to have as many as 200 in transit at all times. Pay may range from a mere $1 to the posh rates paid by *Reader's Digest*, which actively solicits short items.

[5] Louise Boggess, *Writing Fillers That Sell* (New York: Funk & Wagnalls, Inc., 1978), a division of Harper & Row, Pub., Inc., p. 1. Reprinted by permission.

Reader's Digest's rates, certainly among the highest in the industry for short items, are:

- o $300 for up to 300 words, for "Life in These United States."
- o $300 for up to 300 words, for "Humor in Uniform," "Campus Comedy," "All in a Day's Work."
- o $35 for "Toward More Picturesque Speech."
- o $35 for items used in "An Encouraging Word," "Laughter, the Best Medicine,""Notes From All Over," "Personal Glimpses," "Points to Ponder," "Quotable Quotes," and "Time Out for Sports."

Competition for acceptances in these high-ticket *Reader's Digest* departments is formidable. According to a *Digest* senior editor, the magazine receives more than 400,000 submissions annually for its Excerpt and Filler Department, and another 172,000 for the "Life in These United States" feature.

Students of the filler format may profitably study and analyze several issues of the *Digest* to see how the real pros put these items together.

Writing fillers is a knack, like wiggling your ears. It comes naturally to some writers, but can be cultivated by the less gifted. Ideas for these mini's are all around you—in snatches of conversation overheard in the supermarket, elevator, or at a cocktail party; on funny signs in shop windows or along the highways; on TV or radio shows; in the books, magazines, or newspapers you read. Parents are fond of relaying the witticisms of their offspring in filler form, and a few of these are worth enshrining. In the course of research for a full-length piece, you may stumble upon some delectable tidbit which has all the earmarks of a good filler. (How about the origins of the terms "croissant" and "mariachi"? I spotted these recently, and will build fillers around them.)

Today's fillers must do more than merely fill space. They must match the overall editorial tone of the magazine to which they are submitted. A paragraph best suited to *Playboy's Party Jokes* columns would certainly bomb at *Guideposts*, or vice versa. And a shortie on golfing would find no home at *Skateboarder*.

Some magazines insist that fillers be based on actual events, or—in the phrasing of a *U.S. Naval Institute Proceedings'* market note—"at least plausible ones."

Though funny fillers are probably the most avidly sought, informative fillers are also in constant demand. *Alternative Sources of Energy* wants fillers that "cover events and inventions related to energy." *Trails*, aimed at elementary or junior high girls, can use fillers about crafts, nature, or party and holiday items. And so on, endlessly. The market notes in *Writer's Market, The Writer's Handbook,* and other sources are loaded with requests for fillers.

The editors of *Reader's Digest* and other blockbusters take pride in ferreting out and rejecting "repeaters"—old jokes whose lineage can be traced to *Joe Miller's Joke Book* or beyond, anecdotes about famous people which are purely apocryphal, and hackneyed material of all genre. But once in a while they goof. *Reader's Digest* once printed a joke from the *Toledo Blade* in a January edition which had appeared in *The Saturday Evening Post* the previous November—and each magazine attributed the funny to a different writer. A recent issue of *Reader's Digest* carried a joke which I first heard during World War II, and have heard repeatedly since.

What are your chances of acceptance in the filler market? The more material you keep in circulation, the better your odds (assuming the material is good to begin with, and written properly). One pro in the filler business has found he will sell three in every ten submissions.

Caveat: Keep a copy of every filler you send to market. You may never see it again, as many editors will not return fillers— even if they are accompanied by an SASE. There are simply too many of them to cope with.

A STRANGE AND WONDROUS TONGUE

Marketing notes often include exotic terms which, for the novice, require translation. Examples:

○ *Kill fee.* If an editor *assigns* you to a story, the editor may agree (or offer) to pay you a "kill fee" if the story is not used. The fee may equal an arbitrary percentage of the total which would have been paid had the story been published—say 20 or 25 percent. Or it may be based on the number of hours you spent researching and writing the piece. In some cases, the full fee is paid as a kill fee if the story is cancelled for reasons beyond the writer's control. Negotiate the terms.

o *Book.* When applied to a magazine, a synonym used in the business meaning "magazine."

o *SASE.* The most important four-letter word in the trade. It means "Self-Addressed Stamped Envelope." To submit a query or an unsolicited manuscript without enclosing an SASE is considered not only a breach of professional ethics, but downright bad business. Without an SASE, you may never receive a reply. Many of the giant consumer magazines receive hundreds, even thousands, of unsolicited manuscripts and queries every month. Postage costs have become major budgetary concerns, so many publications simply will not return unsolicited material at their own expense.

o *No byline.* Precisely what it says. Your piece may be purchased, but the magazine does not use by-lines on its articles. This is a minus, as publishing credits help to build your image in the business. And they look good in your clipping file.

o *Piece.* Synonym for "article," used by writers and editors, and by authors of books about writing.

o *Phone queries OK.* Many editors don't want to be bothered by phone calls from writers who have article ideas. They want queries in writing. Other editors don't mind phone calls, and may say so in their market notes. If an editor does not specifically invite phone inquiries, assume he or she doesn't want them, and write. Exception: If you have a really hot article idea which is highly perishable, on which the time element is critical, you might risk a phone call. But it had better be truly hot. Otherwise a mailgram or letter is advised.

o *Simultaneous, photocopied, and previously published submissions OK.* This means the editor will not mind if you send the same story, or a rewrite of it, to a non-competitive journal. It also means that he will read photocopied (Xeroxed, for example) manuscripts. Some editors still insist on reading only original manuscripts, but their number is declining. It means, also, that the editor doesn't care if the piece has already appeared elsewhere, but only so long as the earlier appearance was not in a journal in direct competition with his. (One enterprising free lancer sold one piece 276 times for a total of $7,000—probably the all-time high in the business.)

○ *Study recent issues.* Translation: "Don't be a ninny and send me something without knowing my magazine inside and out. Nobody can write for us without reading and studying us first."

○ *Free sample copy and writer's guidelines.* If an editor has reason to believe that you are serious and competent, he or she will have a free sample copy of the magazine shipped to you, along with guidelines for writers if these are available. Many magazines offer such guidelines, and several of these are reproduced in the Appendix to this book. If you ask for guidelines, it is courteous to enclose an SASE.

○ *Captions required.* Captions are short explanatory texts appearing under or alongside photographs. If people appear in the photo, and their identities are important, be sure to identify each person correctly and completely (name, initials, and titles where appropriate), reading from left to right as the editor views the photograph.

○ *Model release.* Subjects whose faces are clearly shown in photos usually are required to sign "model releases" by most magazines. A sample model release is found in the Appendix.

○ *Payment negotiable.* Probably bad news. An editor who will not publicize his word or photo rates is saying he wants to bargain with you, to get his merchandise as cheaply as possible. Pin the editor down before committing one word to paper.

○ *No payment.* Do you work for no payment? A handful of magazines with starvation budgets may offer payment in free copies containing your article. The all-time champ in this department was the bakery which solicited short stories to print on its pie boxes. It would pay—in pies (50 per 1,200 words)!

○ *POP.* Pays on Publication. POP magazines (most of them in the trade-journal category) are anathema to veteran writers. (Perhaps the best definition of POP came from one of my students who was asked to define the acronym in her final exam. Nonplussed, she wrote: "Poop on Publishers?")

○ *On spec.* Or "on speculation." When an editor says he or she will be glad to read something you write if you will submit it "on spec," this means the editor is making no prior commitment whatsoever. If he or she likes what you send, a sale may be in the offing. However, if an editor invites you to send something "on spec," you have taken a giant step toward publication. No editor will extend such an invitation unless he or she genuinely likes your idea, and thinks your proposed article would be appropriate for his or her book. Take such an invitation as definite encouragement, and a compliment. Until you have sold numerous articles and have established a name in editorial offices, most of the material you send to editors will be submitted "on spec."

ARE MAGAZINES IMPORTANT?

Some social critics tend to pooh-pooh the importance of the magazine in American culture. But periodicals do exert enormous influence on the way Americans think and act, whether for good or bad.

Landon Jones, writing in *The Chronicle of Higher Education,* put it this way:

> Magazines have never received much respect in this country. They get written on, wrapped around fish, thrown away, and even left in doctors' offices. They are treated like the most ephemeral products of our culture—which is nearly what they are.
>
> Yet there is also evidence that magazines have a considerable impact on the way literate people think. Many new ideas received their first airing in magazines; old ideas are deflated; trends are spotted; institutions are dissected. More people read magazines each week than go to to the movies or read novels.[6]

---

[6] Jones, *Chronicle of Higher Education,* September 24, 1973, p. 16.

chapter 8

A classic is something that everybody wants to have read and nobody wants to read.

MARK TWAIN
THE DISAPPEARANCE OF LITERATURE

WRITING & SELLING THE NONFICTION BOOK

There's a book in nearly everyone, says an old adage.

Probably true. Anyone who has lived a full life (to whatever age) doubtless has at least the embryo of a book within himself or herself. However, as in the generating of progeny, conception is the easiest and most pleasant part. It's those months of gestation and the final birth-pangs that eliminate the fainthearted. If this were not so, mankind would be deluged with books.

There is a corollary to the "book in everyone" truism: Most men and women are one-bookers. Publishers will talk to one-book authors, of course, provided that that one book is marketable. However, people in the publishing industry—especially agents— take more kindly to the steady producers, the writers who can generate one successful book after another. In short, the professionals.

This should not discourage you if you have only one book in mind. Yours might well become the Book of the Year (or, better yet, of the Month). After all, Margaret Mitchell was a one-novel author, and the world is still reeling from her *Gone With the Wind*. Even if you don't aspire to be a word-factory like Isaac Asimov, read on. You'll find much useful data ahead.

YOUR CHANCES ARE GOOD HERE

Of all the many opportunities open to writers, the nonfiction book ranks highest in terms of challenge and potential yield. Fiction in all its forms, especially fiction which qualifies as "literature," calls for special talents which few possess. Article writing can be practiced by the same men and women who can write nonfiction books, but the competition in article writing is frighteningly fierce and the yields are relatively low.

By contrast, a well-written book of nonfiction on a subject with strong buyer appeal can bring a measure of fame to its author, plus monetary returns which may range from "break even" to phenomenal. A blockbuster nonfiction book (and there are many of these every season) can literally make its writer independently wealthy.

Nonfiction book manuscripts are sought and bought by publishing houses in the following categories:

○ *"Trade" publishers.* So called because they sell to the "trade," that is, to bookstores, book distributors, and others who deal with the book-buying public. Paperback houses also deal with newsstands and magazine distributors. Most general-run nonfiction books are published by "trade" houses.

○ *University presses.* As the name implies, these are enterprises linked to and controlled by universities or colleges. Their output is largely centered on scholarly works aimed at the academic community, although occasionally a university press will produce a work with wide popular appeal.

○ *Textbook publishers.* These supply texts to elementary, high school, and university-level markets.

- ○ *Mail-order book publishers.* These sell books primarily through direct-mail advertising, as opposed to bookstore sales. Subscription book publishers also fall into this category.
- ○ *Publishers of promotional books.* Their titles promote a business, company, individual, or product. Publishing costs are underwritten by the beneficiary, and the books customarily are distributed free.
- ○ *Self-publishing enterprises.* See Chapter 22 on self-publishing.
- ○ *Vanity presses.* These are author-subsidized houses, with the writer paying all or a substantial portion of the costs of producing his or her book. (See Chapter 22 for detailed discussion.)

Until recent years, the conventional scenario called for publication of a book first in hardcover, then in paperback. In many cases, the roles are now reversed, with paperback houses publishing the first edition, then selling hardcover rights to the old-line hardcover houses. Charles Bloch, West Coast Editorial Representative for Bantam Books, is one executive who believes that—eventually—paperback publishers will emerge as the dominant original publishers.

THE MONEY SIDE

One can only generalize about advances and royalties. Practices vary widely in the industry, and there are no fixed norms. Each contract is an individual document, and should be examined with great care—preferably by a lawyer, agent, or veteran writer who has learned how the big print giveth and the small print taketh away.

In general, the industry-wide royalty on a adult-level hardcover book of fiction or nonfiction is 10 percent on the first 5,000 copies sold, then 12½ percent to the 7,500-to-10,000 level, and 15 percent thereafter. Royalties on textbooks may start as low as 8 percent and round off at 19 percent for college-level material, and may range from 3 to 5 percent on elementary and high school texts. Juvenile royalties compare with those paid for adult books, except that royalties may be shared by author and illustrator if the book is not illustrated by the writer.

If you are offered a contract, note whether royalties are paid on "income received" or "net receipts" of the publisher, or on the retail price of your book. If the contract specifies payment on "net receipts," this means you will receive a percentage of the wholesale price of your book, in which case you should try for a higher percentage than if royalties are based on retail prices.

Advances may be as little as $500, depending on the project, the experience level of the writer, and the publishing house. The basic minimum for a full-length nonfiction book (or a novel) appears to be in the $1,000 to $2,000 range, half of which usually is paid on signing of the contract, the balance on delivery of a finished manuscript. But advances on a trade book often fall in the $5,000 to $15,000 range. Negotiate, remembering that you will incur expenses in the production of your book which you may not, in the first blush of your enthusiasm, anticipate. Examples: secretarial fees for typing your final manuscript, the cost of acquiring permissions to quote passages from other works or to use illustrations from other books, payment to a lawyer to examine your contract (if you feel uneasy about it), and—of course—your living expenses while writing the book (if you are free lancing).

If your publisher decides to produce his own paperback edition of your book, you will probably be offered a royalty of 7½ percent on paperback sales, although the figure could be as low as 5 or 6 percent (based on retail prices, in all cases). If your publisher makes a deal with another house for the production of a paperback edition, your contract probably will call for you to share paperback income with your publisher, fifty-fifty.

If you sell your book to a university press, expect little if any advance, as these presses are subsidized and rarely make much (if any) profit from their operations. Some of the more aggressive academic presses do offer royalties, perhaps as high as 15 percent.

For a discussion of the opportunities and yield in writing textbooks and other educational materials, see Chapter 19.

The costs and returns involved in self-publishing, and in vanity-press arrangements, are discussed in Chapter 22.

THAT SPECIAL SOMETHING

What do editors and publishers look for in a nonfiction book idea? Are they searching for some special subject, some unique quality? These are questions which always surface at writers' conferences, and whenever budding writers meet an experienced editor or publisher over cocktails or lunch.

Charles Bloch, West Coast Editorial Representative for Bantam Books, a man with long experience in the publishing industry, once answered these questions at a writers' conference as follows:

> In nonfiction, we are buying either (1) information or (2) a celebrity. Every book should have a revelation of some kind. The reader is spending more time with you—the writer—than nearly anyone else. He or she wants to come out of that experience with something—a revelation, maybe a personal adventure . . . something new, something the reader cannot experience in any other way.

In sum, even if your book covers a subject which already has been treated in many earlier titles, your book may be bought and published *if* it has some unique quality, or makes some special contribution to the subject, some "revelation" which the reader will enjoy, or benefit from, or both.

One key to producing book ideas that will attract publishers is to try to see things from the publisher's point of view. He, or she, is a business person. Publishers are not in the business solely for prestige, or for their health. They are there to make money, and they are looking constantly for ideas which they can package as books, and sell for a profit.

Book publishing is Big Business. According to *U.S. Book Publishing Yearbook and Directory,* total revenues for the industry in 1978 were 5.8 billion dollars.[1] That's *billion.* The figure is impressive, but when viewed in the context of American industry as a whole it loses some of its awesome stature. Xerox alone grossed more than the entire publishing industry in that same year—and on *Fortune's* list of the big 500 U.S. companies, Xerox ranked 36th.

Nonetheless, important money is being made in publishing, and substantial quantities of those dollars do filter down to the writers who keep the publishers in business. Witness, for example, the nonfiction record figure paid for paperback rights alone for

---

[1] *U.S. Book Publishing Yearbook and Directory 1979-80* (White Plains, N.Y.: Knowledge Industry Publications, 1979), p. 25. Reprinted by permission.

Linda Goodman's Love Signs: $2.25 million. This eclipsed by nearly three quarters of a million dollars the amount paid to Carl Bernstein and Robert Woodward for paperback rights to *The Final Days*.

In terms of gross numbers, how do the various book categories compare in a given year? Take, as an example, the statistics for new books published in one recent year.[2] They show:

SUBJECT FIELD	NEW BOOKS PUBLISHED
Agriculture	340
Art	1,369
Biography	1,281
Business	912
Education	802
Fiction	2,065
General Works	953
History	1,245
Home Economics	607
Juveniles	2,337
Language	333
Law	726
Literature	1,084
Medicine	2,123
Music	173
Philosophy, Psychology	899
Poetry, Drama	875
Religion	1,555
Science	2,082
Sociology, Economics	5,165
Sports, Recreation	780
Technology	1,530
Travel	421
Total new titles	29,657

[2] *The Bowker Annual of Library & Book Trade Information,* 25th ed. (New York: R.R. Bowker, 1980), p. 447. Copyright © by Xerox Corporation. Reprinted by permission.

In addition, there were 7,565 new editions of previously published books, for a grand total of books published in that year of 37,222 (down from the previous year, when the grand total for the year was 41,216).

WHAT MAKES A BEST-SELLER?

What do best-sellers have in common? Very little, it would appear, if the 1978 list is any criterion. Topping the 15 titles which achieved "best-seller" status in that year was Erma Bombeck's *If Life Is A Bowl of Cherries—What Am I Doing in the Pits?* Counting hardcover and paperback sales, *Cherries* led the pack with more than 700,000 sold. This lighthearted entry shared the spotlight with a serious work, *In Search of History: A Personal Adventure*, by Theodore H. White. *In Search* briefly displaced Ms. Bombeck's book at the head of the list, only to be dislodged by yet another heavy title, *A Distant Mirror: The Calamitous Fourteenth Century*, by Barbara Tuchman. Other serious works in the top 15 were William Manchester's biography of Douglas MacArthur (No. 13), Richard Nixon's memoirs (No. 6), H.R. Haldeman's *The Ends of Power* (No. 11), and *A Time for Truth*, by former treasury secretary William E. Simon.

The No. 3 spot, with 543,449 sales, went to James Fixx's *The Complete Book of Running.* The Number Two book in terms of gross sales, outranked only by *Cherries*, was Wil Huygen's *Gnomes*, which found 650,000 buyers.

(Demonstrating the chain-reaction effect which often hits the publishing world, *Gnomes* spawned faeries, and faeries in turn spawned dragons, complete with dungeons. On the heels of the dragon books came dragon calendars, dragon songs, dragon jewelry, dragon toys, dragon games and—of course—dragon movies. The cult even gave rise to a University of the Dragon in San Diego, where the faithful might study the arcane secrets of dragonry.)

Several other 1978 nonfiction titles passed the 100,000 mark in sales, but still did not rate mention on either the top 15 best-seller list or in the 10 title "runner-up" category.

Prospective nonfiction book writers should note carefully

the diversity of the top-seller titles, ranging from jogging and gnomes through national politics and medieval history. Subject matter, it is obvious, is important, especially "topical" subject matter tied to current history (Nixon, Haldeman, Simon, and others). But how, then, explain the overwhelming success of *Cherries*? or *Gnomes*? Or (good Lord!) jogging? There are a thousand theories to explain why these strangers became bed-fellows on the list, and yours is as good as anyone else's. Quality of writing comes high on the list of reasons, of course.

IS ANYTHING "SURE FIRE"?

If there is any such critter as a "sure-fire" subject in book publishing, the "how-to" book would be a strong contender for the title. Why is this?

First, we live in times when nearly everyone needs to know at least a little about a variety of things just to survive. People need to know how to cook, sew, repair plumbing, refinish furniture, keep accounts, write, prepare income-tax returns, fix cars, start a business, install electrical fixtures, mow lawns, plant and maintain gardens, remove spots, make friends, raise kids, and—you name it—somebody wants or needs to know about it.

The how-to book offers beginning writers their best opportunity to break into print. Why? How-to books are relatively simple in structure, and can be outlined and written with less skill and experience than other, more complicated forms such as history, biography, criticism, and so on. A writer with a how-to book in mind usually has some knowledge in the field to be covered, or may even be an authority in that field.

How-to books now make up close to one-third of the trade-book market. With the housing crunch reaching crisis proportions, the number of new home-repair and build-it-yourself titles has doubled every year for several years. And with the cost of labor for virtually every kind of service on the continual rise, books for do-it-yourselfers are constantly in demand. One publisher, asked by a beginning writer if he believed anyone would ever write The Great American Novel, replied: "Forget The Great American

Novel. What this country needs is a good book on how to repair your own car."

DON'T TAKE REJECTIONS TOO SERIOUSLY

Never be discouraged by rejections, either of book ideas or of finished manuscripts, if you have real faith in your idea and have produced a manuscript of professional quality. Publishing history is filled with dramatic examples of poor judgment on the part of editors and publishers. Here are a few sorry samples:

• At least 16 houses rejected *The Peter Principle* before it found a home. A McGraw-Hill editor, rejecting it, said: "I can foresee no commercial possibilities for such a book and consequently can offer no encouragement." The book was an instant success, launching its author—Laurence J. Peter—into fame and fortune overnight.

• Harper & Row looked at a manuscript about a seagull learning to fly. The reader decided it was not an adult book, and sent it to the house's juvenile department, which declined it. *Jonathan Livingston Seagull* nonetheless flew to the top of the best-seller list, and author Richard Bach laughed all the way to the bank.

• Simon & Schuster said "no" to *The Lost Weekend*. Doubleday saw no future for *Up the Organization*. *Lord of the Flies* failed to turn on a Lippincott editor. Four titles which any publisher would today welcome (hindsight being 20/20) were passed over by Harcourt Brace: *No Time for Sergeants*, *Lolita*, *Deer Park*, and *The Godfather*.

• The same editor who, at Dell, turned down *The Diary of Anne Frank* also said "no" to *Love Story*, according to *Writer's Digest*.

• Farrar, Straus and Giroux was the thirteenth house to read (buying it) *Tell Me That You Love Me, Junie Moon*, which was to make author Marjorie Kellogg independently wealthy.

And if your book's subject has been done before, don't necessarily take that as a negative sign. Subject-matter repeats, as you may readily prove to yourself by checking that invaluable source book, *Subject Guide to Books in Print.*[3] If a given house already has published three or four titles on your theme, chances are strong it might welcome another manuscript on the same theme provided the angle is somewhat different and the writing is competent.

DOES YOUR MANUSCRIPT HAVE "HEFT"?

How long should a nonfiction manuscript be? Ideally, it should conform to the classic definition of a proper length for a woman's skirt: long enough to cover the subject. There are limits, upper and lower. The minimum hovers around 60,000 words. Below that count, a book doesn't have much "heft," and customers—perhaps unconsciously—tend to buy books by weight. If the subject is so arresting and so commercial that a publisher may feel justified in producing a book containing fewer than 60,000 words, its weight can be padded out by the use of large type, wider-than-usual margins, heavier paper, and other devices.

There's no stated upper word limit, but it may well exceed half a million words, as it did in William Shirer's *Rise and Fall of the Third Reich.* If you plan, then, for between 60,000 and 100,000 words (between 240 and 400 manuscript pages, at 250 words to a page), you probably will be safe. But if your book concept will not support at least 60,000 words (assuming it is a routine adult nonfiction book), you probably do not have a marketable book idea.

THE WELLSPRINGS OF IDEAS

Where do ideas come from for nonfiction books? Sometimes from the oddest places—academic theses, for example. A. Scott Berg's best-selling biography *Max Perkins: Editor of Genius* grew out of

---

[3] *Subject Guide to Books in Print*, issued annually (New York: R.R. Bowker).

his senior thesis in history at Princeton. It won a grade of A⁺, the Princeton Thesis Prize, and advice from his professors to expand the paper into a book. Berg did, though it took him seven years.

Ben Bradlee, while a general-assignment reporter for the Riverside (California) *Press-Enterprise*, was assigned to cover the trial of three black men accused of shooting two Riverside policemen. He became intrigued with the story, resigned his reporting job, and spent a year and a half writing *The Ambush Murders* for Dodd, Mead & Company. He interviewed 158 people in the process.

Two best-sellers of some years ago started life as doctoral dissertations, written for Columbia University's Graduate Department of English and Comparative Literature: *Sexual Politics*, by Kate Millett, and *Zelda*, by Nancy Milford.

Eric Weber was painfully shy as a young man in New York, and "absolutely terrified" of starting a conversation with a strange girl. He confronted his problem head on, overcame it, and wrote *How To Pick Up Girls*. No publisher would buy it, even when Weber rewrote the manuscript to make it more "popular." So Weber decided to print and sell it himself. He advertised in such high-quality outlets as the book-review sections of *The New York Times* and the *Los Angeles Times*, and from these ads sold 7,000 hardcover copies at $7.95 each. His profit, before taxes, was $25,000. About then, publishers woke up, and Bantam Books bought the paperback rights.

Another success story—a most heartwarming one—concerns St. Martin's Press and a (then) unknown Scottish veterinarian named James Herriott (his pen name). Thomas J. McCormack, president of St. Martin's, while on a buying trip in London stopped in for a chat with a literary agent. Did the agent have any interesting books or manuscripts? The agent handed Mr. McCormack a copy of an "animal book" titled *If They Could Only Talk* which one of his clients (Herriott) had recently published. Without much enthusiasm, Mr. McCormack agreed to read the book. He packed it in his luggage and . . . but let Mr. McCormack tell the story:

> I headed back to America, where the book lay on my bedside radio at home for a full three months, constantly elbowed aside by more likely manuscripts. One night it was, in fact, my wife who read the

book first, and she said to me in the soft-spoken way I've learned to listen to, "You've got to read this, and if you don't publish it—you booby—I'll kill you." So I read it. And I loved it.

Herriott's name was totally unknown. He was a foreigner and he'd never written a book before. As an author, he was about as scratch as you can get. As for the subejct: When I first gathered round me the sympathetic faithful at St. Martin's to tell them what this wonderful new book I'd bought was about, the first thing I said was, "It's the memoirs of a doctor!" and everyone beamed. And then I added, "Of course, ah, he's not a people doctor, he's an animal doctor," and their looks began to change. And then I added, "Of course, it's not really the memoirs, it's only two years." And I added that the two years weren't current really—they were the years 1937 and 1938. And when I added by final subtraction that the setting was not Kansas or Connecticut or someplace lovable like that, but Yorkshire, England, I was confronted by a sight I hope none of you has to behold, and that is a dozen of your closest friends walking away from you sideways. "Come back!" I shouted to them. "It's going to be a best seller! My wife says so!"

That is the subject of the book. It's the first two years in the practice of a young Scottish veterinarian.[4]

The rest is publishing history. James Herriott's *All Creatures Great and Small* became a runaway best-seller, was picked up by the Book-of-the-Month Club, selected by Better Homes & Gardens Club, and purchased for serialization in a number of major consumer magazines. Bantam bought the paperback rights, and Hollywood purchased movie rights. The book also became the basis of a television series.

All Creatures was followed by *All Things Bright and Beautiful* and *All Things Wise and Wonderful*, titles adapted from a hymn:

All things bright and beautiful,
All creatures great and small,
All things wise and wonderful,
The Lord God made them all.

---

[4] Excerpt from remarks before an annual meeting of the Association of American Publishers, Inc. Reprinted by permission.

(Fans of Herriott everywhere owe Mr. McCormack another debt: He dissuaded Dr. Herriott from the temptation to name his first book "Ill Creatures Great and Small.")

ROLL UP YOUR SLEEVES

Setting aside the "flukes" which seem to write themselves, writing a nonfiction book usually involves blood, sweat, and tears. Louis Shaeffer labored for 17 years (and spent $90,000) in compiling his Pulitzer-winning biography of Eugene O'Neill. Shaeffer said he sometimes rewrote a paragraph 15 or 20 times. The "meaty" quality of works like Shaeffer's derives from deep research. The author estimated he had collected 50 times as much material as went into the two-volume, 600,000-word-biography.

A Denver writer, Bill Hosokawa, author of several nonfiction books, counsels writers to collect five to ten times as much material as they will be able to use in a given book. Hosokawa wrote one book which totalled 150,000 words, and later said he had enough raw material to produce a manuscript three times that long.

Isaac Asimov, who thrives on hard work and is a compulsive writer, produced his first 100 books in a 20-year period. He began writing at age 11, works every day (Sundays included) beginning about 8:30 a.m., and keeps a spare electric typewriter on stand-by in case the one he's using suffers heart failure. His incredible work habits have, of course, paid off. Dr. Asimov's hardcover book sales average something like 250,000 a year, not counting foreign sales and translations.

A. Scott Berg, in writing his prize-winning biography of Max Perkins, plowed through a file of some 50,000 letters at Scribner's (where Perkins shepherded the works of such greats as Ernest Hemingway). He also read more than 500 books in the creative process.

BOOKS FOR BODY AND SOUL

If you have a sweet tooth or a gourmet's tastes, check into the cookbook field. Since 1895, cookbooks have been the most sure-fire of all nonfiction titles. In the ten-year period ending 1975, more than 3,000 new cookbooks were published. The *Better Homes & Garden Cook Book*, first published in 1930 (Meredith), was outclassed by only one title in the list of all-time best-sellers (for combined hardcover and paperback sales): Benjamin Spock's *Pocket Book of Baby and Child Care*, with 23,285,000 copies, outsold the *BH&G Cook Book*, which sold 18,684,976 copies to 1975. The cookbook even outran *Webster's New World Dictionary of the American Language*, which came in third with gross sales of 18,500,000. Number Five on the all-time leader list was another kitchen companion, the *Betty Crocker Cookbook*, with 13 million sales. Significantly, these four body-food books outsold such fiction blockbusters as *The Godfather, The Exorcist, To Kill a Mockingbird, Peyton Place, Love Story, Valley of the Dolls, Jaws,* and *Jonathan Livingston Seagull.*

Even more impressive is the record turned in by cookbooks on the all-time best-seller list for *hardcover* books alone during the same period. The top three were all cookbooks: *BH&G, Betty Crocker's New Picture Cookbook,* and *The Joy of Cooking.* These were followed by *The Prophet,* by Kahlil Gibran, then five juveniles by Dr. Seuss, with still another cookbook bringing up the rear: *The Good Housekeeping Cookbook,* with sales topping five million.

Study that record. It tells you that America travels on its stomach, and that American readers seek food for the soul and body before anything else when it comes to books.

Beverly Anderson Nemiro provides a good case history of the way in which a creative, enterprising wife and mother can become a cookbook writer to win fame and a measure of fortune. Mrs. Nemiro and her husband travelled extensively throughout the world, and Mrs. Nemiro collected recipes wherever they went. Eventually these recipes found their way into published cookbooks—eight of them to date.

Using her imagination, Mrs. Nemiro noted that one-third of the continental United States lies at altitudes exceeding 2,000 feet. So she wrote *The Complete Book of High Altitude Baking.* This unique work found a warm welcome not only in high-altitude America, but in embassies throughout the world where heights pose culinary problems. Her book has achieved classic status, and has paid the same level of royalties year after year.

Mrs. Nemiro classifies all cookbooks into four categories:

- ○ Basic, or general
- ○ Specialty (an all-fish cookbook would be an example)
- ○ Status ("beautiful people" creations)
- ○ Public-relations cookbooks, written to promote some product or enterprise

She warns that cookbook writing requires hard and sustained work, and the resources to underwrite testing and other expenses while writing. During the production of her high-altitude cookbook, Mrs. Nemiro and her collaborator tested some 2,000 recipes—and printed only 300. Shoddy research simply will not do, she cautions. "Print one faulty recipe and you've lost your readers forever."

If you are tempted to write a cookbook, be sure it is a good one covering a subject which has not yet been exhausted. The cookbook editor for one major New York house put it this way:

> To write a cookbook you have to have more than a love of cooking. You have to be able to provide something that's fresh. I do think there will always be room for something that is valid and makes a real contribution. What we don't need is more unnecessary cookbooks.[5]

Jean Anne Vincent, of Doubleday, sounded a further caution.

> The cookbook market peaked several years ago . . . maybe as early as 1969. At that point there was just a big glut on the market. A lot of people wrote cookbooks who probably shouldn't have . . . they were mainly collections of recipes by women who had cooked all their lives or had learned to cook in recent years and received lots of compliments.

But the books were published anyhow, said Ms. Vincent, because:

> . . . there is this myth that all cookbooks sell a million copies . . . (the truth is) that the average cookbook sells between 1800 and 3500 copies in the first year to 18 months, then sinks without a trace.[6]

---

[5] Jean Anderson, "Is the Cookbook Market Simmering Down?" *Publisher's Weekly,* 206, no. 8 (August 19, 1974), pp. 42–48. *Publisher's Weekly* is published by R.R. Bowker Company, a Xerox company. Copyright © 1974 by Xerox Corporation.
[6] Ibid., p. 42.

Cookbook writers appear to have strained a bit in their zeal to specialize. The editor of a cookbook club noted that she had received three published cookbooks on how to cook for your dog! Unnecessary books certainly are not needed ". . . in a market that has already given us the definitive works on peanut butter, coffee and tea, not to mention the best collected recipes of the Mafia, the hip and the gay."[7]

Religious and inspirational books have long been best-selling perennials which establish new sales records year after year. The Holy Bible ranks, of course, as the number-one best seller of all time. Norman Vincent Peale's *Power of Positive Thinking,* first published in 1952, sold 5,205,000 copies by 1975, while Fulton Oursler's *The Greatest Story Ever Told* (1949) sold 3,858,938 in the same span of years.

THE BRASS TACKS

Two elements come together to produce a book:

First—the author's compulsive desire to write. Not necessarily to write a specific book, just the desire to write.

Second—a book theme or idea which comes to the writer.

If the compulsive desire is strong enough, and the theme is logical enough, these two forces meld and a book is written.

The fact that you are reading this book is evidence that you have at least some desire to write. Perhaps it is not compulsive, but the desire is sufficiently strong to have led you to this book. Eventually you may conceptualize an idea for a nonfiction book, if you don't have one now.

At that point, you should exercise great caution and sound judgment. For if the book idea you generate is not feasible in the *marketing* sense ("put yourself in the publisher's place"), your project is foredoomed. At this point also remember: just as many hours and days and months can be taken from your writing life by a flop as by a success. You cannot recoup that lost time. So you should assess with consummate care any book idea that comes

[7]Anderson, *Cookbook Market,* p. 42.

to you before you commit yourself to it, especially if you decide to write the book without first receiving any encouragement, or any commitment, from a publishing house. In other words, you decide to write the book first, and sell it as a finished product. This approach is defensible for a novel, and for certain exceptional types of nonfiction books (humor, for example); generally, it is unwise for a nonfiction book.

Assume, then, that you are driven by the desire to write a book, and that a feasible idea has occurred to you around which you believe you can produce a full-length manuscript of 60,000 words or more. What's next?

Step Number One. Scout out the competition. This is doing your homework, which any publisher will expect you to do. Find out what book, or books, have been published already on your theme or subject. Most importantly, find out what books of this description are presently in print by consulting the *Subject Guide to Books in Print*, the index cards in your public or university library, and your local booksellers. These titles (if there are any) are your competitors. You must know about these books, in some detail, before you can intelligently proceed to the next step.

Step Number Two. Write a brief, condensed description of your book idea. It will help, perhaps, to pretend that you have been asked by a stranger, or a relative, what your proposed book is about. Answer the question, tightly but thoroughly. You should be able to describe the "nut" of the idea in one sentence. And you should be able to discuss the entire book, in some detail, in one page or less of single-spaced typing. If you cannot, you probably don't know enough about the idea, or have not thought it out clearly enough, to justify tackling the writing phase.

You may not, as yet, have done much research on your theme or idea. That's understandable. You don't want to waste time on legwork if the idea is not basically sound. But you will need to do enough preliminary digging to at least permit you to write a convincing query letter, which is the next step.

Step Number Three. Compose a letter of inquiry, or query letter, to a publishing house. Select the publisher from

Writer's Market, The Writer's Handbook, Literary Market Place, or any other reliable source (including, perhaps, the recommendations of a writer friend or a teacher). The selection should not be a random one. You should try to single out, from the lists of scores of publishing houses, those whose current lists and past publishing records indicate that your book would be a logical addition to their inventory. You would not, for example, send a book on dog breeding to a house which has published nothing but avant-garde fiction, or vice versa. In the selection process, choose five or six publishers' names, listing them in the order of priority (strongest possibility first, next strongest second, and so forth). If the first house rejects your idea, send it immediately to number two, and so forth until you either strike gold or strike out.

Your query letter should contain the germ of your book idea, tightly stated (perhaps a paragraph). The letter should also list your earlier publishing credits, if any. If you are just beginning, don't make an issue of the fact; just say nothing, period. This query letter also should show that you have done your homework by discussing, briefly, any competitive titles, and explaining how *your* book will be different and what it will do for the reader that the competitors' books will not. Don't bad-mouth the competition; just state, dispassionately, how they fall short or differ from yours, if they do.

The letter should also set forth any special qualifications you may have for writing this particular book. If it is to be a book about furniture refinishing, for example, and you have been refinishing furniture for 20 years, by all means make this point strongly. If the book describes the people and customs of Paraguay, and you lived for five years in the city of Asunción, stress the fact. No one will be interested in your book if you underscore the fact that you know nothing about the subject, but intend to do a lot of research to compensate for your ignorance.

Your letter should not exceed two pages of ordinary letter-sized bond paper, single-spaced. A single page is better, if you can do justice to the project in one. Don't be coy. Be very businesslike. Eschew the temptation to draw cute figures on the margins, or to tie the whole prospectus with ribbon. Nonsense like this spells "a-m-a-t-e-u-r," and is guaranteed to turn off editors and publishers. Also, avoid offbeat salutations in your letter, like "Hi," or "Dear

Mr. Publisher." Just say "Dear Sir" or "Dear Ms." and state the addressee's last name. Many editors are acutely allergic to such forms as "Hi," especially right after a three-martini lunch.

To this query letter, append a tightly written outline of your book. It will be understood by all hands that an outline can only be tentative at the project's beginning. This outline should occupy perhaps a page of manuscript, single-spaced. Outline in any way most comfortable to you. If you have chapter headings in mind, use them as your major categories, followed in each instance by a short description of the chapter in question.

Finally, attach a sample chapter from the proposed book. It need not be chapter one, or the final chapter. The idea is to give the prospective publisher some idea of your writing style and capabilities. This chapter might run, say, three to five thousand words—enough text, in sum, to convince the publisher to offer you a contract.

In your query letter, which is also a letter of transmittal, you will refer to the fact that the outline and sample chapter are attached.

Step Number Four. Mail the whole package, *flat,* in a large kraft envelope. Enclose another kraft envelope of the same size, folded double, addressed to yourself with adequate postage affixed. This is the famous SASE (self-addressed stamped envelope) without which the entire publishing industry would grind to a halt. If you are a Ring Lardner fan, you may be tempted to disregard the SASE protocol. Lardner once wrote:

> A good many young writers make the mistake of enclosing a self-addressed stamped envelope, big enough for the manuscript to come back in. This is too much of a temptation to the editor.

You can listen to Lardner's advice and enjoy it, but it would be extreme folly to heed it. Nothing is more certain to raise an editor's hackles than the absence of an SASE.

Mail the whole mess, and drop in at the nearest church, temple, tabernacle, or bar for a moment of silent prayer. Then forget it. Move on to something else—preferably a second book project. If you hold your breath until the reply (at least three or four weeks), you will never survive to write the book.

chapter 9

GHOST WRITING

If behind every successful man there stands a woman (or vice versa), behind many a successful author there lurks a ghost. The average reader would be surprised, no doubt, to learn how often a ghost writer can make, or break, a book. Or an article, speech, or any other piece of writing, for that matter. Ghosts are the unsung heroes of publishing in America.

If you have acquired a substantial measure of skill with the mother tongue, and are searching for new sources of revenue, you might consider ghost writing.

But this is not a job for novice writers. A client hires a ghost because the client lacks the necessary skills (or sometimes merely the time) to bring a book, speech, article or other piece of writing into being. One famous sports figure, commenting on a new book bearing his byline, noted wryly that it was the first book he had ever written—or had ever read!

Ghosting requires the writer to submerge his or her identity—and ego—by agreeing to forego, or at least to downplay, his or her role in a writing project. If you are unwilling to play the part of a faceless, anonymous scribe, surrendering most or all of the limelight to a client, then ghosting is not for you.

Some ghosts help their clients to craft and market novels and short stories. Others specialize in speeches, autobiographies, family histories, memoirs, or first-person accounts drawn from the client's experiences. If your forte is creative writing, you might concentrate on helping less talented people to put their novels, short stories, poems, dramas or whatnot into marketable form. If your strength lies in nonfiction, you will probably be well advised to avoid prospective novelists or short-story writers, and to stick with biography, speeches, and other nonfiction forms.

Some clients will insist, as a condition of a contract, that you keep your collaborative role a secret. In a way, your relationship with the client parallels that of a doctor to patient, or lawyer to client, and you are honor-bound to promise—and maintain—confidentiality. In other instances, your role will be openly acknowledged by the client, perhaps in the form of a shared byline such as "with (your name)" or "as told to (your name)." Or perhaps you will rate mention among the bylined author's listed acknowledgements.

Many professional writers have ghosted books for well-known public figures—movie or television personalities, politicians, government individuals, sports figures, or individuals thrown suddenly into the spotlight by the course of events. In such cases, the professional writers usually are contracted by the house which is publishing and marketing the book, or by an agent. Payment is negotiated, and may be an outright flat payment (often very substantial), or a payment plus a percentage of royalties, or—in cases where the ghost believes the book may achieve bestseller status—a larger share of the royalties and no fee at all. Where the author shares the credits on the title page, the percentage may be less than if he or she remains anonymous, a byline being considered a form of payment.

Perhaps the easiest starting point for fledgling ghosts, especially those who live in smaller communities, is in speech writing for politicians about to hit the campaign trail. Or for business or professional men and women who want or need to make speeches, but lack the ability or time, or both, to prepare them.

Speech-writing season usually peaks in those weeks and months prior to elections, when small armies of political hopefuls hit the hustings. Many budding politicos hire advertising or public-relations firms to handle their campaigns, or retain professional campaign managers. If you have the necessary qualifications to offer yourself as a speechwriter (and a strong enough stomach), you can contact these PR or managerial types to ask that you be considered for ghosting work. If the firm has no one on the staff qualified to do the job, you may be hired on the spot. After all, every U.S. president of recent vintage has had his battery of speech-ghosts squirreled away in the White House, so a local politico would be following sound tradition.

You can also advertise in the classifieds or with small display ads in your local newspapers or magazines, offering to ghost speeches, articles, books, or anything else for clients. Such ads can be productive, although in general it is unwise to expect your first ad to give you all the business you can handle. Budget enough cash to run a series of such ads over a period of weeks or months. People who might be potential clients six weeks or two months down the pike will clip and save your announcement, intending to contact you when the occasion arises. So don't give up if your first ad or two does not excite a rash of responses.

A year-round source of ghost-writing clientele in every city of any size is the business and professional community. Many of the business and professional leaders (corporation officers, doctors, lawyers, dentists, and so on) are—or aspire to be—civic leaders. Some of them are in constant demand as luncheon or dinner speakers, but very few of them are born speakers or competent writers. If your fees are reasonable, you may well build a stable of clients in the business and professional community which will draw on your talents the year round. If you are good at your work, your fame will spread by word of mouth as one satisfied customer recommends you to another prospect (assuming the customer will admit, to anyone, that his material is somewhat less than original).

As for fees, there is no set schedule or rule. Decide what your time is worth on an hourly or project basis. If you are ghosting part-time, and have other regular sources of income, you can perhaps afford to work for somewhat less than if you are ghosting as a full-time occupation. If you decide that your time is worth, say, $15 an hour (an arbitrary figure here, as an example only), try to estimate how many hours a given speech-writing job will require, or how many work-days a nonfiction book will involve. Multiply your hourly rate by the time required, and set your fee (or your estimate) accordingly. You may request an advance, against which you will chalk up hours of actual performance until it is exhausted, then ask for another advance. Or you may bill your client for hours actually worked on some periodic basis— daily, weekly, monthly, and so forth. Your business expenses can, of course, be charged against your gross income for tax purposes.

If your strength lies in editing rather than writing, you should offer your services as an editor. Many people have manuscripts of one kind or another which sorely need a competent editor's firm and informed touch, but which do not need a total rewrite. You also may advertise your services as an editor, setting your fees according to your own realistic assessment of your worth. (See also Chapter 21.)

One area in which ghost-writers may find interesting and remunerative activity is in the writing of corporate and family histories. This form of writing is discussed in the following chapter.

chapter 10

There is no heroic poem in the world but is at bottom a biography, the life of a man; also, it may be said, there is no life of a man, faithfully recorded, but is a heroic poem. . . .

SIR WALTER SCOTT

WRITING FAMILY & CORPORATE HISTORIES

If you enjoy research, have a sense of history, and work easily with people, look into a new and growing field for free lancers: the writing of family and corporate histories.

In this field, as in ghost writing, an advanced level of writing competence is required. And here, as in ghosting, the writer must bring to bear a more-than-average skill in interviewing people, especially in eliciting information from sources who can, at times, prove reluctant, or who may not realize that what they have to say may be important.

Two major groups in every community will comprise most of your potential clientele: influential citizens (many of them elderly) who—in the words of one biographer—may seek to "gain a moment of immortality" by retaining your services, and successful businessmen or corporation executives who want to tell their own or their corporations' stories in book form.

A resourceful writer can also work other rich veins in his community for prospective clients. Civic, fraternal, and patriotic organizations may have a proud history to record and preserve in print. Local churches constitute another target of opportunity, as do private schools, and even municipalities and other governmental units.

One successful free lancer built a lucrative business by working primarily with senior citizens. He reached prospective clients through mailing lists obtained from senior-citizen centers, labor-union rosters of retired workers, church organizations which work with the elderly, and—showing true imagination—by watching the newspapers for stories about wedding anniversaries.

He also recruited prospects by making himself available as a speaker on family history at senior-citizen and family reunions. Advertisements placed in newsletters circulated among the elderly and notes on bulletin boards in senior-citizen centers also produced leads for him.

This writer's *modus operandi* calls for extensive interviewing, and the collecting from the client of every possible clipping, diary, and letter which might provide helpful data. In some cases he has found it necessary to interview others in the community who have known, or known about, his client over a period of years, or to mail questionnaires to sources living outside the community. He has also consulted records in historical societies, churches, courthouses, and other sources where personal data is customarily deposited.

One of the most active and successful free lancers in this field is Richard Sawyer of Seattle, Washington. Sawyer, a veteran writer with more than thirty years of experience in magazine and newspaper journalism, has written numerous individual and corporate histories since deciding, in 1974, to concentrate on this area.

Sawyer's experience has been that senior citizens are not, as a general rule, able to afford the services of a professional biographer—or at least to pay the writer what his or her services are really worth in today's job market. He has found that it is no more difficult to gain entree into the monied circles of the community than into the less affluent. This is not elitism or snobbery, Sawyer points out. It is reality.

Sawyer obtains the membership rolls of the community's more prestigious clubs, and lists of sponsors of art museums, the symphony, local theater groups, and the ballet. Through these, plus word-of-mouth recommendation, he has been able to "gain access to that spectrum of society most likely to appreciate the services I offer, and most able to provide me with the kind of income I feel my experience warrants."[1]

This Seattle writer has some very concrete counsel for prospective writers of family and corporate biographies and histories:

1. When prospecting for clients, go where the money is.

2. Coordinate all the work necessary for the production of the end product, or do all the work yourself. (Sawyer follows his own advice: he and his wife produce their own camera-ready copy on an IBM Selectric II typewriter, and prepare their own layouts, bluelines, and camera-ready flats.)

3. Charge fees more comparable to those of attorneys (and plumbers) than of haberdashery salesmen. And don't be apologetic about fees. The writer (if he is worth his weight in typewriter ribbons) has served a long and difficult apprenticeship. His is an exacting craft, and he possesses skills not shared by one in a thousand of our population.

Sawyer makes many of his contacts through personalized form letters to corporate executives (usually board chairmen or presidents) and to individuals. On dignified letterheads bearing his name, address, and phone number, Sawyer spells out his services, and makes compelling arguments for the preparation of these histories. In his letters to business executives he stresses that "time is the enemy . . . Facts and figures about the early days of the business are probably already recorded, but the human stories of struggle, humor and triumph—the very elements which will guarantee that your company book will be read and used—may be lost for all time if measures are not taken to assure their preservation."

In sales literature sent to individuals, Sawyer stresses that

---

[1] Letter to the author.

people seldom think of leaving a *legacy* of experience and ideas to their heirs when they pass away. They think, instead, of leaving securities and *things*. Yet a family's history has enormous social value, he points out.

> To leave only the physical evidence of our having lived is to deprive our grandchildren and great-grandchildren of an important and integral part of their birthright. The true heritage of America and of òur families cannot be accurately measured and assessed only by the number and variety of objects we owned.

This branch of specialized writing, still in its infancy, offers immeasurable opportunities to free lancers who have the writing skills, the personalities, and the imagination to capitalize upon it.

chapter 11

*My own experience (with writing) has
been that there is no field where one who
is in earnest about learning to do good
work can make such enormous strides in
so short a time.*

DOROTHEA BRANDE,
BECOMING A WRITER

THIS ONE'S ON
THE HOUSE

What family of American magazines carries no ads, collects no
subscription fees, yet boasts of a collective readership exceeding
160 million?

Members of this special group are known variously as "house
organs," "house magazines," and "company publications." They
are published in every state of the Union, and come clothed in a
variety of shapes, sizes, lengths, typefaces, and colors.

Many beginning writers—and even a few pros—do not com-
prehend what a fertile sector of the marketplace this is for writers
who understand the particular needs of house organs, and know
how to fill them. Numbering in the thousands (no one really
knows how many), these special-purpose publications are sponsored
by businesses, industries, clubs, associations, government agencies,

and other organizations throughout the nation. With rare exceptions, they are distributed free and do not solicit advertising.

Some are pocket-sized, some are tabloids. A few are *LIFE*-sized titans with sumptuous four-color covers. Some are in newsletter format. Nearly half of the company publications listed in the *Internal Publications Directory*[1] measure 8½"x11", or *TIME*-sized.

The *Directory* lists some 3,000 U.S. and Canadian titles, and estimates that their total readership tops 160 million. A sizeable percentage of the 3,000 are not interested in free-lance material, and many of those which are in the market "seldom buy," "buy only a few articles," or "rarely buy." However, many house magazines not in the market for text do indicate they will buy "product-related" photos.

In a recent edition *Writer's Market* listed 55 titles under their "Company Publications" heading, including many of the most active and best-paying markets in the field.

Rates paid by house organs are generally attractive, starting at around five cents a word. Several will pay fifty cents a word or more—astonishingly good rates, comparable with top-level rates in the consumer field. For example, *Buckeye Monitor*, an organ of the Buckeye Pipe Line Company in Radnor, Pennsylvania, will pay $300 to $500 for pieces ranging from 600 to 1,200 words, and buys about a dozen manuscripts a year. *Exxon USA* also solicits free-lance material, and declares it pays fifty cents a word. *Bristol-Myers New York* is another high-pay book, in the thirty-to-fifty-cent range, though it buys "less than one manuscript per issue."

What's the key to success in writing for company magazines? The secret word is "company." Writers who sell to these markets never forget that the purpose of every house periodical is to serve the company or organization which sponsors it by improving the sponsor's image, increasing sales, or otherwise benefitting the publisher.

A substantial percentage of these magazines are staff written.

---

[1] *The Working Press of the Nation*, Volume 5, *Internal Publications Directory*, Janice B. Lewis, ed. director (Burlington, Iowa: The National Research Bureau, Incorporated, 1980).

But a formidable number of them look to outside writers for professionally written, sparkling pieces to brighten their pages.

What kinds of articles do these organs seek, and how should they be written? An examination of writers' guidelines issued by three of the nation's most attractive house magazines will provide all the answers the average writer will need. They were obtained from *Seventy Six Magazine, Ford Times,* and *Small World.*

The following excerpts from these guidelines are quoted with permissions from their editors.

First, *Seventy Six,* an excellent example of the house-organ publishing art, published by Union Oil Company of California:

SEVENTY SIX MAGAZINE
EDITORIAL POLICY

Seventy Six magazine is a corporate magazine. We usually publish articles about employees, their problems and how they solve them. Most articles are anecdotal.

Topics we write about: exploration and production (acquisition of land, geology, drilling, production), refining and marketing and petrochemicals. We prefer to write about these subjects through the people who accomplish these jobs—we are a people-oriented publication.

Topics we generally don't write about (and almost never buy): dealers (service stations), product utilization, travel, jokes. . . .

Note. We are not a dealer publication. (There is a publication for dealers.) When we do publish an article about a dealer, it must have some news hook. For instance, we have done dealer profiles on Jack Russell, Ernie Banks and Bronko Nagurski—because they were sports names.

As a freelancer, your best bet might be a profile on a commercial salesman who saved 15 heavy duty engines for a customer, a landman who succeeded in signing a wealthy recluse to a land contract, a tank truck driver who saved the lives of a couple injured in an auto accident, or a geologist whose hunch paid off in finding a billion-barrel oil field.

We write about people, their problems and their successes.

EDITORIAL PREFERENCES:	750, 1000 words.
EDITORIAL RATES:	Payment on acceptance upon factual confirmation by our researchers.
	Basic rates: 10¢ a word, plus bonus for quality work. Higher rates to established writers.

Comment: If you had not read these guidelines, you might logically assume that *Seventy Six* would welcome pieces about your neighborhood Union Oil stations. Not so. Like its counterparts in the consumer-magazine field, *Seventy Six* is looking for pieces "about people, their problems, and their successes."

One representative issue of *Seventy Six* contained the following articles:

○ "Tapping the Gulf's Reserves"—about natural gas, and Union Oil's natural-gas wells in the Gulf region.

○ "Smiles Are Deaf Teens' Camp Payoff"—concerns a weekend summer sports camp in San Diego for deaf and hearing-impaired teenagers, which Union Oil Foundation co-sponsored.

○ "Popcorn Sulphur Enhances Farmlands"—about a Union Chemicals product which looks like popcorn and is used to neutralize alkalinity in Southwest farmlands.

○ "Dealer Tech Turns Out Pros"—a piece about Union Oil's training centers in Illinois and California for prospective dealers.

○ "Darkness Cloaks a Childhood Landmark"—a bit of nostalgia about a Southern California landmark—a huge Union Oil neon sign no longer lit at night because of a company energy-saving policy.

○ "Meet San Diego's Seagoing Seiners"—the title says it all. There are neat and subtle tie-ins to Union Oil in the text and the photos.

○ "Industrial Hygienists at Work"—describes Union Oil's work in protecting employees' health and safety.

○ "Museum in Motion"—a visit to Chicago's Museum of Science and Industry. Mentions contributions of the Union Oil Foundation to the museum's long-range repair, renovation, and improvement program.

○ "New Employees Tour Union Facilities"—self-explanatory.

118

All articles except the nostalgia piece were unsigned. Dramatic color photos (combined with black-and-whites) were used throughout, including on the cover.

Next, *Ford Times*, which some writers think of as a general-interest publication, but which is in reality a company magazine.

FORD TIMES

Published monthly by Ford Motor Company
Editorial Office: P.O. Box 1509-B, Dearborn, Michigan 48121

General Information for Contributors

FORD TIMES is a monthly magazine for motoring Americans. Generally speaking, it can be said to view America through the windshield, but we interpret this very liberally. Some of our most successful stories have had no connection with the automobile but were published because they interested us and because we thought, therefore, they would interest our readers.

The magazine strives to be colorful, lively and engaging. We believe a story that entertains is as valuable as a story that informs. We are particularly attracted to material that presents humor, anecdote, dialog, first-person discourse, intelligent observation and superior writing. Over the years we have published original work by some of the most celebrated and gifted writers in the English language. However, many of our best articles have been written by people of no special fame who succeeded with us because of an excellent editorial idea and an enthusiastic belief in it.

Subject matter: Almost anything relating to American life, both past and present, that is in good taste and is cheerful rather than gloomy, joyous rather than sad. Topics include motor travel, sports, fashion, where and what to eat along the road, vacation ideas, reminiscence, portraits of big cities and small towns, the arts, Americana, nostalgia, the outdoors.

We have a commitment to originality and try as much as possible to avoid stories that have appeared in other publications. However, a fresh point of view and/or superior writing on an old subject will be welcomed.

(Reports on Ford products and material for the Famous Restaurants feature are prepared exclusively by staff members.)

Locale: The 50 states, Canada, and, to a lesser extent, Mexico and the Caribbean. At present we are not considering material based on other foreign countries but will look with interest on articles about the United States by foreign writers.

Length: A maximum of 1,500 words. We prefer to be queried in advance, but will review speculative submissions.

Rates: $250 and up for full-length stories. Payment on acceptance.

Illustrations: Speculative submission of high-quality color transparencies and black and white photos *with manuscripts* is welcomed. We want bright, lively photographs showing people in happy circumstances. We need publicity releases for people whose identity is readily apparent in photos. Writers may send snapshots, postcards, brochures, etc., to suggest how illustration may be accomplished. Paintings are normally done on assignment.

THE EDITORS

Reprinted by permission of *Ford Times*, a Ford Motor Company publication.

Like many another high-quality company magazine, *Ford Times* avoids overt puffery. Even though the book tends to "view America through the windshield," the writer is not pressured to drag a Ford into every story. This *Reader's Digest*-sized publication (although much thinner) goes to more than two million readers—customers, potential customers, and friends of Ford. The magazine is so attractive, and so well written, that many of its fans preserve—and even bind—their copies. Back issues are avidly sought by collectors.

One issue of *Ford Times* included the following pieces:

○ "Several Reasons for Liking Camden"—a visit to a "salty, shipshape Maine coastal town."

○ "Fallingwater"—"a testament to America's greatest and most controversial architect," Frank Lloyd Wright, centering around his home, Fallingwater.

○ "Virginia's Haunted House Highway"—"175 miles of unexcelled haunting," with some fine, spooky artwork.

○ "Three Free Minutes in Paris"—a light, frothy description of the writer's first overseas telephone call and the problems encountered.

○ "Adopt a Wild Horse"—a story and photos by the writer. "Not all mustangs, pintos, and broncos are Fords. In many sections of the American West there are magnificent wild horses roaming the range."

○ "Edison's Better Ideas"—"Henry Ford admired Thomas Edison so much that he named the now famous museum-village complex after him."

○ "Feasting on the Church-Supper Circuit"—a church-supper aficionado tells how he uses bulletin boards in supermarkets, drugstores and churches as his restaurant guides to good eating.

○ "Small Miracles in a Chicken Coop"—In the old building where she used to gather eggs, Margaret Burke of Americus, Kansas, turns out her famous Marlow Woodcuts.

○ "Things That Go Whoosh in the Night"—about bats.

Sprinkled discreetly among these handsomely illustrated articles are house pieces on the latest Ford passenger-car products.

All the above articles except the house pieces are signed, probably by free lancers who sold them after querying or who were assigned to write them.

Finally, *Small World,* an attractive and highly professional publication mailed to Volkswagen owners throughout the United States:

A GUIDE FOR SMALL WORLD WRITERS AND PHOTOGRAPHERS

General Guidelines

1. *Editorial needs*—SMALL WORLD is the magazine for Volkswagen owners in the United States, and all stories must have a VW tie-in. Our approach is subtle, however, and we try to avoid obvious product puffery since SMALL WORLD is not an advertising medium. In most cases, we prefer a first-person, people-oriented handling.

2. *How to submit manuscripts*—All text should be typewritten, double-spaced, on good-quality white bond, with pages numbered consecutively. Every story must have the name, address and telephone number of the author on the first page. Please include a return envelope with postage. Although we take special care with all free-lance material, we cannot be held responsible for lost manuscripts. It is good practice to keep a carbon of all submitted material. Send manuscripts to: Editor, SMALL WORLD Magazine, Volkswagen of America, Inc., Englewood Cliffs, New Jersey 07632. You will usually hear from us within six weeks of our receipt of your material.

3. *Article length*—SMALL WORLD articles seldom exceed 1,500 words in length. Shorter pieces (some as short as 500 words) often receive closer attention.

Queries

If you have a long feature possibility in mind, please query first. That will save time for both of us. Though queries should be no longer than two pages, they ought to include a working title, a short, general summary of the article and an outline of the specific points to be covered. Where possible, please include a sample of the photography available. (See Appendix for sample Model Release Forms necessary for any photos.)

Specific Article Needs

The following list of our article needs is intended to give direction to writers. However, we are always looking for fresh ideas, and stories need not fall under these categories. Ultimately, the best way to learn a magazine market is to read the magazine. We strongly advise writers to read at least two past issues of SMALL WORLD before working on a story. These may be obtained from SMALL WORLD on request.

1. *"Volkswagenmania" stories*—Volkswagens and VW owners have a knack for finding themselves in unusual—sometimes whimsical —situations. Accounts of these incidents must be true, and, where possible, we would like documentation. *Sample:* "A Mouse in the House," about a mouse who tenaciously lodges in a VW Campmobile.

2. *Travel stories*—We are *not* interested in general travel stories ("first we went here, then we went there"); we need a *specific* slant, usually one revolving around a particular person, or of particular interest to VW owners. Good-quality color transparencies are a must. *Samples:* "Ghost Towns," exploring ruins in a VW; "Holland's Small World," on a miniature city—with a few miniature VWs—in the Netherlands.

3. *Human-interest stories*—We need stories on colorful people with unusual jobs or avocations. *Sample:* "In Love With Puppets," about a lady who brings joy to children by staging puppet shows. She travels in a VW.

4. *Personality pieces*—We'd like stories about well-known people who drive VWs. *Sample:* "Running to Olympus," a profile of Francie Larrieu, America's top female distance runner, a VW owner.

5. *"How-to" stories*—We're always interested in how readers have adapted their VWs for specific needs. *Sample:* "Room for Haul," how to get the maximum cargo capacity in a Beetle.

6. *"Public Service" articles*—Fact or opinion pieces on topics of interest to automobile owners. *Sample:* "Is There a Cow in Our Future?" on how methanol may become increasingly important as an automotive fuel.

7. *General "service" articles*—General "how-to" stores interest us too, if they have a VW slant. *Sample:* "Photographing Kids," tips from a child photographer—who uses a Volkswagen.

8. *True adventure*—We're basically a family magazine, and we're not looking for "hairy-chested" articles. However, we do use adventure pieces—so long as they are actual and documented. *Sample:* "Rescue in the Andes," about how stranded American tourists are rescued with the aid of a VW Bus—in a remote section of Bolivia.

9. *Humorous articles*—These should be short. If they're about children, all the better. *Sample:* "Gregory's Love Affair," the saga of a goose who falls in love with a VW Beetle.

10. *VW arts and crafts*—VW owners have come up with numerous pieces on VW-related projects. *Sample:* "Fold Your Own Rabbit," about the paper-folding arts of Origami.

11. *Miscellaneous stories*—*Sample:* "Soccer—American Style," how the world's most popular sport is finally catching on in the U.S.A.

Assignments

In rare cases we will assign a writer whom we know to a particular story. Our normal policy, however, is to work on speculation. That is, we examine all material before deciding whether or not to purchase it.

Fillers

We are in the market for short humorous anecdotes about VWs; we're also looking for pictures of humorous or unusual VW situations. For a sample of what we need, see the magazine.

Cartoons

Cartoons should deal with situations or characteristics peculiar to VWs or VW drivers; they should be original and humorous.

SMALL WORLD
PUBLICATION RELEASE FORM

Please complete the form below in duplicate and return both copies with your material.

———————————————————————————————————

I, _____, for $_____ or an amount to be determined on publication by the editor of Small World, do hereby transfer, sell, assign and release the following material and any and all rights therein to Volkswagen of America, Inc.:

_____

_____

☐ have

I   taken out a copyright on the above mentioned material.

☐ have not

Rate of Payment: Minimum payment for individual cartoons, fillers and photographs is $15. For feature articles we pay $100 per printed page for photographs and text; otherwise, a portion of that amount, depending on the space allotted. Payment for cover photographs is $250.

Date:_____   Signature:_____

Address:_____

City, State, Zip:_____

A sample issue of *Small World* contains nine signed articles, all apparently by free lancers. These are:

- ○ "Fastest Feet in the West"— an account of the Fourth Annual Human Power Speed Championships "where competitors must power their vehicles through a timed course of 200 meters without any motors or stored energy of any kind."
- ○ "Music for a Special Audience"—describes how "music therapists use their skills to treat a wide variety of disorders."

Reproduced by permission of Volkswagen of America, Inc.

○ "How Not to Enjoy Camping"—describes how the author, in his Volkswagen Campmobile, enjoyed a weekend despite the crowds in the parks.

○ "How to Keep Your Camper Secure"—a service feature including "tips for cutting your risks."

○ "Sailing Ships and Maine Memories"—about old sailing ships which lie rotting in small coves and seaports on the Maine coast.

○ "Pacific Coast au Naturel"—a journey along California's coastline.

○ "Rabbit in the Ruins"—a tour of ancient Indian ruins of the Southwest in a Volkswagen Rabbit.

○ "Camping the Klondike"—a trip up the Alaska Highway to Whitehorse ("rough and dusty").

○ "Mt. McKinley: Photographer's Paradise"—"America's highest peak is a magnet that draws wild-life photographers."

In several cases, the writer was also the photographer, shooting in color as well as in black-and-white.

Many major U.S. firms publish several house magazines, each with its own editor and staff. Exxon Company U.S.A. publishes more than twenty, at least half a dozen of which solicit free-lance material. Armco Steel Corporation sponsors five house organs, all of which will review free-lance queries and manuscripts.

Quality Inns International Incorporated will buy "articles on industries that seek to supply products to hotels or motels" for its *Reporter*, along with photos at $50 to $100 each. There are many other firms which publish strings of magazines.

In contrast, Sherwin-Williams Company has nine magazines, none of which buys from free lancers (or, at least, does not list itself in the *Internal Publications Directory* as a market). Only one of Western Electric's 22 organs appears to be interested in buying articles. And, as might be expected, the U.S. Navy's ten in-house organs have no budget for articles by outsiders.

As with the trades and, to a somewhat reduced degree, with the consumer magazines, this is a marketplace where resourceful writers may ethically pyramid their sales by re-slanting the same basic raw stuff to a variety of periodicals.

Make a call on the Big House. And when you knock on the door, remember the password: "Company!"

chapter 12

*And the wise man said, when asked by
what means he had attained so high a
degree of knowledge: "What I did not
know, I was not ashamed to inquire about.
I inquire about everything."*
OLD PERSIAN PROVERB

THE WEIRD &
WONDERFUL WORLD
OF THE TRADES

You've probably never curled up by the fire with a copy of
Chain Saw Age, or read yourself to sleep with the latest *Archery
Retailer* or *Computer Decisions*. If you've never even heard of
these trade publications, don't feel put down—neither have millions
of other Americans.

These are but three of the thousands of highly specialized
journals called "trades" which collectively serve every conceivable
sector of U.S. business, industrial, and professional life. To people
not involved in their narrow subject fields, these magazines are of
zero interest. But to thousands of readers who make their living
in these fields, the trades are virtually indispensable.

Every merchant, manufacturer, doctor, lawyer, dentist,
tradesman—whatever his or her calling—forever seeks the answer
to one simple question:

How can I show more profit in my business?

The business press exists primarily to answer this query one way or another. They tell the reader how others in his field are doing some certain thing better and more economically, thus making more profit.

Trades make up the hungriest segment of the manuscript marketplace, buying and publishing thousands of articles and photos every month. Many writers—even some with long experience in the business—know little or nothing about the trades, the *terra incognita* of the writing world.

As used here, "trade journal" or "trade" applies to some 3500 or more publications. A trade may be a weekly or a monthly, a bi-monthly or semi-weekly, or it may appear on some other less conventional schedule. In appearance, these journals range from newsletters to standard magazine formats of the conventional sizes. Their circulation may range from mere hundreds per issue to well in excess of 100,000. (House organs are not included in this chapter; they are discussed at length in Chapter 11.)

Nobody knows how many writers make all or part of their living in trade-journal writing. For some, it is a precarious occupation, with sales few and far between. For others—probably a handful—writing for the trades can produce five-digit incomes, in some cases topping the $20,000-per-year mark.

Any man or woman with a modicum of news sense and modest mastery of the English language can work successfully in this field. A hard-working, persistent trade writer, by practicing rigid self-discipline, can—in time—sell virtually every word he or she writes.

IS THIS YOUR CUP OF TEA?

Before taking the plunge into this weird and wonderful world, you should acquaint yourself with its basic ground rules, and hear both the good news and the bad.

These are the most important requirements:

Writing skill. Moderate. Not nearly so exacting as the level of skill required for success in the "consumer magazine" market.

Style. High level of tolerance for the boring, the mediocre, and the trivial. The patience of Job and the persistence of a ferret. Better-than-average ability to interview, and to extract bright answers from dull people. A well-honed sense of humor—the ability to laugh at human foibles, including your own—will make it all seem worthwhile.

Hardware. A healthy typewriter of post-diluvian vintage, and the ability to make it sing. A 35mm single-reflex (SLR) camera, with appropriate lenses and filters, and a flair for dial-reading and button-pushing. A tape recorder unless, perversely, you are driven by some masochistic urge to record everything in longhand, or even in shorthand.

THE GOOD NEWS, AND THE BAD

The Pluses (and there are many).

+ You will find the trades to be an enormous, incredibly diversified, and endlessly hungry market for your output.

+ You may pick and choose the subject fields which interest you, and for which you believe you can write, from a mind-boggling range of categories, including:

advertising and public relations	chemical
amusements	churches and ecclesiastical
architecture	cleaning, dyeing, and laundry
automotive	college engineering
aviation and aerospace	confectionery
baking	dairy products
banking and finance	dental
beauty, barber, and cosmetic	department stores and merchandising
beverages and bottling	drugs
book trade, journalism, and publishing	electrical and electronics
building	engineering—civil and construction
ceramics and glassware	export and import
chain stores	

farm equipment
fertilizers and farm chemicals
florists, horticulture, and nursery
food processing
furniture manufacturing and house furnishings
fur trade and animal breeding
gas
gifts, antiques, and novelties
grocery and food marketing
hardware
home economics
hospitals and nursing
hotels, motels, restaurants, and clubs
industrial
instrumentation, automation and data processing
insurance
jewelry
legal
lumber and forestry
machinery
marine
meat packing and merchandising
medical and health
metalworking and metallurgy
military
milling, feed, and grain
mining and coal
mortuary and cemetery
municipal and county
music and music trade
office equipment and stationery

optical
packaging
paint, painting, and decorating
paper and paper products
petroleum and energy
pets and pet supplies
photography and microfilm
plastics
plumbing, heating and air conditioning
power
printing, graphics, and commercial arts
produce
purchasing
radio, television, and recording
railroad
real estate and building maintenance
refrigeration
rock and cement products
schools and education
selling and marketing
shoes and leather goods
textile
tires and rubber
tobacco
toys, crafts, arts, and hobbies
travel and tourism
vending and automatic merchandising
wearing apparel
welding
woodworking

If there is a make-money activity known to man which is not covered somewhere in this list, it must be obscure indeed. Chimney-sweeping? Not yet, but they'll get around to it! Blacksmithing? Believe it or not, the *American Farriers' Journal* wants how-to pieces, interviews with shoers or manufacturers, and nostalgia bits about yesteryear methods of shoeing Old Dobbin. They'll pay $1 a column inch (maybe one or two cents a word, depending on type size).

+ The level of writing skill expected by trade editors is relatively modest. Obviously this does not mean that trade papers are the playground of illiterates. Editors neither expect nor condone sloppy writing. You must spell correctly, and organize your thoughts into sound sentences and paragraphs. But the editors are not paying you for deathless prose, lofty thoughts, or exceptional gifts of imagery. Just the facts, m'am. If you have written for dailies or weeklies (however humble or great), or even for your school newspaper, you have already survived your bootcamp training in trade writing.

+ You can write for trades full-time or on days off while keeping a steady job (recommended), or merely now and then. It's up to you—there's no time-clock to punch, though perhaps there should be. Once you master the tricks and techniques, you can apply them any time, any place.

+ A free-lance trade writer, especially one with correspondent status with one or more journals, can "guesstimate" probable income from month to month, assuming that a certain level of productivity is maintained. A writer free-lancing for "big" article markets cannot plan like this; writing for consumer magazines is much more iffy.

+ Opportunities for newcomers in the trade-writing field seem to be ever-present. This is no doubt due, at least in part, to the fact that some writers who begin in the trades each year move into other forms of writing, or abandon writing altogether, leaving a void which newcomers can fill.

+ The more advanced writer who is working on The Big Novel, or on an article for a major consumer magazine, can flesh out his or her income by writing for trades on the side. The income from such part-time writing might be modest, but the extra dollars can make the difference between making it alone, and retreat to the timeclock world.

+ Trade-journal writing can lead to other writing activities which may prove more remunerative and interesting. For example, a source interviewed by an enterprising free lancer, impressed with his or her personality and skill, may invite the writer to perform special writing chores: brochures, press releases, ad copy—yes, even speeches. The writer sets his own prices for such services.

+ Once you have sold an article or two, you have what amounts to a press credential. Without stretching the truth, you can then say to an editor, or a story source, that you are a writer for this journal or that. In time, you might even be given a press card by a magazine or chain of magazines. Such a card is to be coveted more than a key to the Playboy Club.

+ Writers who become known among editors as steady, reliable producers may be named regional correspondents, stringers, or even "bureau chiefs" for the magazine, or for the chain to which it belongs. McGraw-Hill, Inc., for which I once was a regional stringer, publishes more than 35 journals in a broad array of categories ranging from architecture to textiles. Its "World News" department retains correspondents throughout the United States and the world. These writers carry press cards, and receive assignments regularly from the home office. They also may generate story ideas on their own, submitting them to World News for consideration by the appropriate editors. There are many such "multiple magazine publishers" in the United States, and a very big one in Canada: Maclean-Hunter, Ltd., with 60 or more publications. (A complete directory of these chains appears in *Bacon's Publicity Checker.*)[1] The title "correspondent" may not guarantee a monthly check. But your queries and articles will receive sympathetic consideration by editors, and (as a rule) a quick response.

+ Trade writing sometimes brings added benefits called "perks" (perquisites). You may occasionally be requested to travel, for example. Or a merchant whom you have interviewed may offer you discounts on his products or services. This is generally not regarded as "payola," unless you are a full-time correspondent working exclusively for a magazine or chain, provided the discount or service does not suborn you into com-

---

[1] *Bacon's Publicity Checker,* issued annually (Chicago: Bacon's Publishing Company).

promising the truth, or into writing mere puffery. If you are guilty of either of these sins, you should be drummed out of the corps.

Now for the Minuses (of which there are several):

– Payment can be miserably low from some of the less-enlightened publishers, who seem to take the position that writing for them is a privilege. Some of these journalistic Scrooges appear unaware of inflation, still offering pre-World War II rates beginning, incredibly enough, as low as a penny a word.

Counterbalancing these penny-pinchers, many trades pay good-to-excellent rates ranging from five to as high as twenty cents a word. The trick is to single out the latter, then to concentrate your fire on such better-paying markets.

– Pay can be slow from the smaller independents with over-worked staffs and marginal bank balances. A few benighted houses cling to the much-detested POP policy (Pay on Publication). Professionals regard POP as a cop-out below contempt. It is as if you were to visit a department store, select a fur coat, agree to buy it, then tell the salesperson you will pay for it once you begin to wear it. Many pros refuse to write for POPs, and the editors of some of these journals are openly embarrassed by their publishers' policies. One such editor wrote to me (on his journal's letterhead!): "I can certainly understand your decision not to work for POP markets. It's a system grossly unfair to writers, and I'm ashamed to work on a magazine that follows that policy. I'm losing writers left to right because of it, and I don't blame them one bit. I'd do the same if I were a free lancer."

– There's little glamour in trade-paper writing. This is essentially no-nonsense, how-to journalism; it is not entertainment. If you are vulnerably thin-skinned, sensitive, and creative (as so many writers are), you may find the rough-tumble world of the trades a bit much. You will get no spiritual highs from interviewing a tire dealer who reveals the techniques which made him regional leader in retread sales and won him a trip to Atlantic City, or the lingerie department supervisor who doubled the store's pantyhose volume through a clever ad campaign.

– If you are not already on speaking terms with a camera, you'll need some on-job training or a night-school course in photography. You may also need to invest several hundred dollars in equipment. "But," you plaintively ask, "can't I team up with a local professional photographer? He could keep all we make on photos." Nope. The pro's rates will—in nearly every case—be much higher than those generally paid by trades. You can't afford to hire the photographer personally on a piece basis, because you'd lose money on every photo. So guess who ends up clicking the shutter?

If, by now, you have not been totally turned off to the idea of exploring the weird and wonderful world of trades, read on.

A VERITABLE SMORGASBORD

If, like a good general reporter on a daily or weekly newspaper, you are interested in anything and everything, the trade-journal field may be your oyster. With your sample-everything curiosity, you may find it challenging to report for a variety of trades on subjects which—only yesterday—you knew nothing about.

During some four decades as a generalist, I have written for trades dealing with dry cleaning, machine shops, aircraft manufacture, canning, woodworking, wooden barrels (no kidding), electrical contracting, precision optics, toys, mortuaries (ugh), oceanography, giftware, lighting fixtures, computers, and I can't remember what else. Yet I am certainly not a dry cleaner, machinist, toymaker, oceanographer, or—but I've always been intensely curious about the world around me, and revel in learning something different every day. If you are endowed, or afflicted, with an insatiable thirst for the new, you could find trade-paper writing a rewarding experience.

NARROW THE FIELD

At the outset, it will prove more profitable for you to search out journals serving fields in which you have special interests, training, or knowledge. In sum, to specialize. The fact that thousands of trades are published in the U.S. is impressive. But remember the realities: you will be able to write for only a relative handful of these. Many journals do not want free-lance material. Many serve fields of specialization which are so alien to your background and capabilities that you could never write for them.

For example, if you were an English or journalism major, or your strength lies in the social sciences or humanities, your chances of writing for *Computer Design*, for example, are miniscule. This journal goes to "digital electronic design engineers" (I don't understand what even *that* means). By the same token, the likelihood is tiny that you could or would write for *American Jewelry Manufacturer*, aimed at producers of supplies and tools for the jewelry industry. And without a crash course in diesel design, you would have little to say that would interest the editor of *Diesel & Gas Turbine Progress*, which wants "technical descriptions of unique diesel or gas turbine engine applications." (But this editor buys 20 manuscripts a year.)

One prolific trade-paper writer, during a 21-year period, sold more than 3,000 features to 200 publications in 50 different fields. During the last ten years he was selling 95 percent of his output, at times averaging 90 sales per month. He owned an airplane for commuting to cities all over his area, a mobile office on wheels, and about $2,500 worth of camera equipment. He dictated every story as he drove or flew between stories, mailed or handed the tapes to a secretary, and never saw the stories again. He never queried ("If it's worth a query, it's worth a story").

Note, however, that, in a generation of writing, he sold to no more than 200 different publications in a marketplace including several *thousand* different journals.

START WITH SIMPLE CONCEPTS

Scores of highly specialized magazines may lie beyond your reach as markets, or may be totally unattractive to you. But do not worry. There are dozens, perhaps scores, of trades for which you are already equipped to some degree to write, thanks to your background and training.

Take one example: the laundry business. Even though you may do most of your own laundry at home, it's no trick to grasp at least the fundamentals of the laundry and dry-cleaning business. What kinds of stories will interest a laundryman as he reads his trades? Read a few sample copies of his magazines, and you are likely to find stories about such subjects as the following:

• Coin-operated Laundries ("coinops"). Laundrymen are interested in how, and why, coinops show a profit. Case in point: a coinop whose owner has landed a contract with a nearby high school or college to launder gym clothing and towels.

• Successful Advertising Campaigns. Some businessmen are more imaginative than others. Those who are less creative look for ideas which have worked for the more imaginative operators, hoping to put these ideas to work for themselves.

• Quality Control. Any business which does not practice good quality control loses customers.

• Handling Customer Complaints. "You tore off all the buttons."

• Uniform and "Career Apparel" Rentals. Career apparel includes those snappy jackets worn by bank tellers and real-estate salespeople; uniforms are worn by nurses, waitresses, busboys, and so forth.

• Office Procedures. Accounting, record-keeping, collection of overdue accounts, and other administrative functions. If you have had accounting or bookkeeping experience, you can write intelligently about such procedures for journals in a wide range of fields.

With a pinch of imagination and a dash of experience, you can extend the list on your own.

Here's another example, which will give you further training in the use of some basic sourcebooks. It's logical to assume that you, like most Americans, spend a good chunk of time in supermarkets, deli's, and convenience stores. Or, perhaps, that you once worked as a bag-boy or checkout cashier in one of these stores. Routine exposure to these enterprises equips you to look for stories which could be written for one of the 60 or more U.S.

publications aimed at people who work in the food-marketing and grocery business. Many of these are regional publications which circulate in small areas of the country; many others are nationwide in scope and circulation. It is probable that some, perhaps many, do not buy free-lance material.

To find out which *do* buy, and—just as important—which do *not*, you may have to write letters of inquiry. *Writer's Market*, which is an absolutely essential tool for writers (see Bibliography), lists someting like 700 trade, business, industrial and professional periodicals. *The Writer's Handbook*, another valuable tool, lists fewer than 200 markets for free lancers under "trade and business." MIMP (Magazine Industry Market Place) includes trade journals in its listing of some 2600 publications in all categories, and in another listing classifies magazines by type (farm, association, house organ, and so on).

There are more than 3500 such journals catalogued in another important source book, *Bacon's Publicity Checker.* And more than 4000 are described in detail in Standard Rate and Data Service's *Business Publications*, which is updated every *30 days.* If you do not find the information you need in *Writer's Market* or *The Writer's Handbook*, search through *MIMP, Bacon's*, or Standard Rate and Data Service's *Business Publications.*[2]

Writer's Market and *The Writer's Handbook* have, of course, already confirmed that the periodicals they list *are* markets for free-lance contributions. Their listings will tell you the names of these periodicals (indexed under broad subject headings), addresses, names of editors, what kinds of articles, fillers, and other items the editors seek and will buy, and for how much. Photo requirements are also indicated.

But for journals not listed in these marketing guides, you will need to ferret out the information on your own by consulting *Bacon's* or *SR&DS*, noting names and addresses, and writing to the editors of the journals which interest you. This is a nuisance, but the exercise will pay off because you will, in this way, build

---

[2]See Bibliography for complete listing of these and other resource materials.

your own private marketing guide, tailored to your specific needs and requirements.

Assuming, then, that you have decided to explore the possibilities of writing for the food-marketing journals, where do you begin? First, get acquainted with the manager of your own favorite market. Tell the manager what you have in mind. Ask if you might examine, or have, several copies of any trades the store may receive. If this market receives none, try another. Chances are you may be given, or shown, periodicals such as *Chain Store Age Supermarkets, Supermarket Management, American Grocer, Convenience Stores, Deli News,* or *Supermarketing.* If your friendly manager is on the subscription list for a regional periodical, he might be reading *Arizona Grocer, Carolina Food Dealer, Gulf Coast Retail Grocer,* or any one of many other regionals.

Note the name, address, and editor's name on the masthead of one or several journals which interest you. Check them out, first, in the two writer's marketing guides mentioned earlier. If a journal is not listed in either or both, write to the editor expressing interest in covering stores in your area, and ask if he encourages free-lance material. Inquire about word and photo rates. Request a sample copy of the magazine, and a copy of any guidelines the editor may have prepared for free lancers. Enclose an SASE for his reply, and offer to pay postage on the sample magazine.

(In time, you should build a library of sample copies. With these at hand, you can quickly check a magazine's editorial style, layout, caption format, article lengths, and other workaday details which will help you prepare pieces for each market.)

HELP FROM EDITORS

Many trade-paper editors will go out of their way to help new writers. Some of them have prepared guidelines which are as good as postgraduate courses in the trade-writing art. Here's an example, from *American Coin-Op,* courtesy of its friendly and cooperative editor, Ben Russell:

AMERICAN COIN-OP'S
GUIDESHEET FOR FREELANCE WRITERS.

AMERICAN COIN-OP is a monthly magazine read by some 23,000 owners of coin-operated laundry and dry-cleaning stores. Our editorial purpose is to show each operator how he can be more successful. In short, we try to tell the reader how he can make more money, or reduce his expenses.

We do this by providing staff-researched-and-written articles on subjects of interest and by presenting case-history stories on successful operations. For the case-histories, we depend mainly upon the freelance writer. Case histories can be obtained and written quickly, thus making it unnecessary for you to waste your valuable time with phone work and correspondence. Usually an interview and a photo session can be accomplished within a couple of hours and the story written in another six or so hours, maybe less.

Stories We Want

Stories on coin-ops that are successful in any one or a combination of the following areas are desirable:

1. Good store appearance, both exterior and interior.
2. Successful promotional activities.
3. Successful advertising campaigns.
4. Successful customer relations activities.
5. Energy-saving methods, including solar energy installations.
6. Store security. (Methods for deterring thieves and vandals.)
7. Diversification. (Offering customer services other than the standard laundry and drycleaning. Examples: rug cleaning, car wash, garment repair.)
8. Maintenance of equipment and building.

How to Find Leads

Finding a suitable story lead is fairly easy in this field. In almost all cases, an attractive, well-maintained store will turn out to be a good story possibility. Those two qualities generally indicate that the owner is progressive, aware of customer's needs and wants, and is actively involved in the management of his store. Other methods:

*Keep an eye open for advertisements in your local newspaper, or for promotional pieces that you might receive in the mail. (Again, these are indicators of good management.)

*Check your *Yellow Pages* for names of local distributors of laundry machinery. These companies are very aware of the best stores in the area and can be extremely helpful in offering suggestions and ideas, and even acting as a liaison between you and the store owner.

Query

If you find a story possibility, *please* query before proceeding to write it. There's always a possibility that we or our competitors have run it. In addition, we can offer suggestions on how to slant a story, what to emphasize, photos to take, etc.

Photos

Black-and-white only. To save you some photographic printing costs, we'll be happy to accept a contact sheet and negatives. We'll then select the photos and do the printing here. If you prefer to submit prints, send a variety of five or six, full negative on 8 x 10 glossy paper. Photos should include: An exterior shot; two or three over-all interior shots (taken from different angles); several medium-length shots of various sections of the store—the washers, dryers, vending machines, drycleaning machines, lounge, and the owner. In all cases, show customers using the facilities, but don't let them dominate the photos. Our readers like to see the machines and the general layout of the store. Remember: The better your photos, the more of them we'll use.

Length

Story length depends strictly on the subject. We'll purchase anything from a paragraph to 3000 words or more, but the average story runs about 1500-1800 words. And we're more interested in thoroughness and accuracy than in writing style. Don't bother writing headlines, decks or photo captions.

Payment

Payment rates start at 5¢ per published word and $5 per published photo. Checks are mailed about two weeks prior to publication of the story.

Ben Russell, Editor
AMERICAN COIN-OP
500 North Dearborn St.
Chicago, Illinois 60610

Ph: 312/337-7700

You will probably receive some negative replies ("We are 100 percent staff-written," or "We buy no free-lance material"). Some editors may not even reply, even though you have enclosed an SASE. If they are that inefficient, you wouldn't want to write for them anyhow, so small loss. On your own master list, you can cross off the indifferent journals to avoid wasting time later with futile queries or submissions. What you are looking for is the encouraging reply ("Yes, we buy free-lance stuff," or "I'd like to see some of your copy"). You have lined up another potential customer.

If the marketing guides don't list a periodical you have in mind, visit any well-stocked public library and ask for the latest edition of the *Business Publications* volume published by Standard Rate & Data Service. If your library does not subscribe to *SR&DS*, visit any prosperous advertising agency, and ask if you might consult their copy. (They may even have some back issues, and will part with a recent one as a gift.) You might also ask, on the same trip, to see a copy of *Bacon's Publicity Checker* if they are subscribers. These two source-books perform different services. *Bacon's* lists periodicals by category, title, address, name of publisher and editor, current circulation, and phone. *Bacon's* also includes a code which indicates whether the magazine is interested in by-line articles. This could be a tip, in many instances, that the journal *does* purchase non-staff material, but you will need to verify this in each case.

Listings in the *SR&DS Business Publications* offer a veritable gold mine of information for writers (although the service is aimed primarily at the advertising fraternity). Once you have examined a magazine's listing in *SR&DS,* you will know:

- o the name and address of the editor;
- o the audience at which the periodical is aimed, described in detail in the "publisher's profile statement";
- o the journal's circulation, in some cases broken down by regions of the country, and by types of readers;
- o in many cases, the percentage of space occupied in each issue by any of several types of information.

This penetrating "biography" of a journal will give you keen insights into the editor's needs and requirements.

Continuing with the hypothetical example, let's assume you have singled out a journal called *Snack Food* as a possible market. You happen to be in the public library, so you look up *Snack Food* in *SR&DS Business Publications.* You find that, according to the publisher's statement, the magazine is edited "to provide executives in the packaged cookie, cracker, potato chip and snack food industry with information on successful methods of management, production, engineering, packaging, flavoring and ingredients, delivery and distribution, merchandising and labor relations."

You also note that *Snack Food* is one of the Harcourt, Brace, Jovanovich family of trades, which includes 24 other journals in a broad range of specialties.

You learn further that *Snack Food* gives the following weight in each issue to these categories of editorial matter:

- o production and technical, 30%
- o management and sales promotion, 20%
- o packaging, 15%
- o news and new products, 20%
- o other topics, 15%

This tells you that your chances may be strongest if you offer

Snack Food something related, first, to "production and technical," and second, to "management and sales promotion."

But there's more. Farther down, you find that *Snack Food's* circulation is mostly non-paid (a standard practice in the trades). Then there's a breakdown of the total circulation by geographical regions, which tells you that the biggest concentrations of readers are located east of the Mississippi—yet another clue to the editor's needs and requirements.

Nor is that all. There is a table which reveals that most of *Snack Food's* readers are in the manufacturing and processing end of the business, primarily in cookie and potato chip lines. The majority of the subscribers are top-level people: owners, presidents, vice presidents, managers, research and development people, sales executives, and purchasing personnel.

You now know more about the snack-food industry than most writers will ever know (or even care to know). But you may find all these oddments of intelligence strangely useful when you talk or correspond with the magazine's editors, and write for the journal's columns.

Throughout this exercise, you may have been wondering: Does *Snack Food* buy free-lance material? Because if it doesn't, all this research has been pointless. For an answer, we turn to *Writer's Market. Snack Food* does indeed want your stories from the field. We find in the market listing that between 10 and 15 percent of each issue is free-lance written. Smugly, we also note that our analysis of the *SR&DS Business Publications* entry is correct: *Snack Food*, says the *Writer's Market* entry (submitted by the journal's editors) is "for manufacturers and distributors." We find, further, that the journal contains 60 pages, and are surprised to discover that *Snack Food* was established in 1912. We are pleased to see that the magazine pays on acceptance (no POP here). It buys all rights, but may reassign these to the writer following publication (usually on the writer's request). We are saddened to observe that *Snack Food* gives no bylines, because pros in the writing business consider bylines part of their income, their "free advertising" in the industry. We note further that the editor will listen to phone queries (an exception to the rule), and we remind ourselves not to phone the editor *collect* unless invited to do so.

Finally, we are pleased to read this direct quote from the editor:

> We are looking for regional correspondents who will be able to move quickly on leads furnished as well as develop articles on their own. A directory of processors in their areas will be furnished upon making working agreement.

Snack Food's pay rates, we note, are inviting: for "mini" features of 300 to 600 words, and longer pieces from 1000 to 1500 words, pay ranges from $50 to $300. This averages out to between ten and twenty cents a word—a very respectable rate indeed. Some of the smaller "consumer magazines" pay less.

In sum, by consulting these source books you may obtain a well-rounded picture of any journal. This should prepare you to search for story leads and to communicate intelligently with editors.

If you own the latest edition of a marketing guide (and you should; the annual investment will pay off many-fold), you may ask why you should ever consult *Bacon's* or the *SR&DS* publication. Answer: you may elect to consult a marketing guide exclusively. If you do not supplement its information with the more detailed descriptions found in *SR&DS*, you may miss many interesting nuances about a given journal. And if you stick exclusively with a marketing guide (which may list only 200 to 700 journals), you will be unaware of the much larger community (more than 3500) of these journals which is continually pumping information to U.S. readers.

Where, and how, do you find story leads? They are everywhere—in newspaper advertisements and news items, window and floor displays, sales promotions, snatches of conversation heard on streets or in elevators, in the shop-talk of those involved in buying, selling, producing, and distributing merchandise and services. As you become acquainted with people who work in various fields, you will almost effortlessly pick up leads to potential stories.

If your eyes are keen and your ears fine-tuned, you cannot *escape* the clues and hints which will bombard you from all sides. Your problem, in time, will *not* be to find marketable ideas. It will be, rather, to concentrate on those ideas which show the most potential, and to bypass the marginal ones.

Here are three examples of ideas which came from newspaper stories or ads, and which I recently exploited and sold to trades:

- In a community already well-supplied with lighting-fixture stores, a new store announces its opening. Why does its owner believe he can compete successfully with the many outlets—some members of chains—already established in his field? What does he plan to offer to contractors and retail customers that is not already available? The answers I obtained and prepared in article form were sold, with photos, to *Home Lighting & Accessories.*

- A bank in my community installed a number of 24-hour automatic-teller machines in branches throughout the city and county. How was the public responding to these novel devices? Was the idea successful enough to encourage the bank to install more machines? What problems did the automatic tellers pose, and how were they overcome? This one sold—with photos—to *Banking*, the journal of the American Bankers Association.

- A major city in my area decided to computerize air conditioning and heating controls in a sprawling complex of city buildings. Were cost savings truly realized? Were employees in these buildings satisfied with the new system? Is it practical and economically feasible to automate such a system in existing buildings? The answer was "yes," on all counts. This one went to *Industrial Research/Development*, with photos.

In each case, someone did something everyone else was doing—or contemplating—and did it well enough to make (or save) money. There was no sleight of hand or necromancy involved in the finding, writing, and selling of these trade pieces (and scores of others). The keynote was common sense: identify a problem, find out how it was solved, and tell the story.

One very quick way to lose your shirt or chemise is to write for journals paying one or two cents a word. A bit of simple arithmetic will explain why. Let's assume you have spotted a market for something called *The Dingbat Digest* (pure fantasy). It goes (let's say) to operators of car-body repair shops. You were recently an unwilling participant in a fender-bender on a local highway, so you take your car to Joe's Automobile Beauty Salon. You selected Joe's because you were impressed with his clever advertising in local papers.

While there, you think you see a story idea for *Dingbat*. Joe agrees—if you get the go-ahead—to an interview. You carefully work up a query to *Dingbat* (which you find listed in a writer's market guide), and drop it in the mailbox.

Investment thus far:

Time: 1 hour
Out-of-pocket: 30¢ (postage, stationery)

Days (or maybe weeks) later, a reply comes from *Dingbat*: "Joe's story sounds good. Go ahead, on spec. Keep it under 1200 words, and I'll need four or five good 8 x 10 glossy photos to illustrate it."

Elated, you phone Joe and make a date. You show up at the appointed hour with camera strapped over one shoulder, tape recorder over the other. You also carry a stenographer's notebook, just in case.

As the interview begins, you snap off the recorder because the din of air hammers, sanders, and buffers would give you nothing but 600 bars of Verdi's *Anvil Chorus*. Shouting, you and Joe talk shop for about an hour. Joe takes off three times to answer the phone, and twice to talk with customers, while you cool your heels. His two assistants eye you as if you were some sort of exotic bug.

Photo time comes. The lighting is O.K. for Kodak Tri-X Pan. You shoot several work situations, trying to make them look natural and making sure Joe is included in some of them. You get the full names of all three people in the photos, and make notes to remind you which is which so you'll get them right in the captions. Joe asks if he can have a copy of one or two photos, and you agree (an added expense). You ask Joe and his two workers to sign model releases, knowing the editor may ask you for these (see sample Model Release in Appendix).

You wrap it up, thank Joe, and head for home. Investment to this point:

Time:

Travel to-from Joe's	40 min.
Interview time	1 hr. 20 min.
Time previously entered	1 hr.
	3 hrs.

Out-of-pocket:

Mileage, 30 mi. @ 20¢	$6.00
Tri-X Pan, 1 roll (20ex)	1.25
Previously entered	.30
	$7.55

En route home, you drop off your films at a photo shop. If you are a very active writer who shoots a lot of film, you may have your own darkroom. You save money on processing, and can crop photos to suit your own tastes. You also may save time, because you aren't at the mercy of the photo shop's schedule. However, you must buy paper and chemicals (expensive, and they must be kept fresh), and all the darkroom paraphernalia. Also, you must have room for a darkroom (a closet or bathroom may work in a pinch). Finally, you must spend many hours in the dark-room, and these hours must be included in your cost accounting.

If you dropped off your films for processing, you return in a day or so to inspect the negatives and a proof sheet, and to order the enlargements. The bill for development plus a proof sheet may come to $4.00. (Obviously these can be only estimates.) You order six 8 x 10 glossies (including one for Joe) at $1.75 apiece, which is a real bargain these days.

Investment to this point:

Time:

Round-trip to photo shop	45 min.
Time previously calculated	3 hrs.
Total to this point	**3 hrs. 45 min.**

Out-of-pocket:

Mileage, round-trip photo shop,		
15 miles @ 20¢		$3.00
Film processing, proof sheet		4.00
Glossy enlargements, 6 @$1.75		10.50
Previously calculated		7.55
Total to this point		**$25.05**

You still haven't written word one. So now you transcribe your notes. This should be done as soon as possible after an interview. Notes—whether handwritten or taped—grow "cold." Allow two hours of transcribing time for every hour of tape, slightly less if you work from handwritten notes which are legible and make sense, slightly more if you are a slow typist.

It takes you an hour to decipher and type up your notes from the scratchpad. (Many pros work directly from handwritten or taped notes, bypassing the transcription time. You may learn to do this, but don't count on it at the start.) In the course of transcribing, you have decided on the lead you'll use on your story.

So now you begin the *real* work—the writing. With remarkable courage, you resist all the temptations to do something else— sharpen your pencils, mow the lawn, go to the store for your wife, jog, walk the dog, read a novel, and so on *ad nauseum.*

Two hours and three false starts later, you have finished a 1,000-word draft which you are happy with. You call Joe for an appointment to review it (an inviolable rule).

You now have 5 hours and 45 minutes invested in this project.

Joe initials every page of your draft, after making a couple of minor corrections (which he also initials). You return home via the photo shop, picking up your glossies and negatives. The latter are carefully identified and filed for possible later use. You type a clean final draft, if necessary, write the photo captions, and stuff everything in a large kraft envelope with cardboard stiffeners to protect the photos. Heaving a sigh of relief, you weigh the envelope, affix the necessary postage, and drop the story in the slot. Because the editor has encouraged you to go ahead, you do not enclose an SASE (as you would have had it been unsolicited).

The arithmetic now looks something like this:

Time:

Writing time, including final retype	2 hrs.
Trip to Joe's for final check	40 min.
Trip to post office and back	20 min.
Previously calculated	3 hrs. 45 min.
Total time invested in story	**6 hrs. 45 min.**

Out-of-pocket expense:

Misc. paper, kraft envelope	$ .50
Mileage to-from Joe's, 2nd trip	6.00
Postage	1.25
Previously calculated	25.05
Total cash invested in story	**$32.80**

In time, you receive a check from *Dingbat,* which pays two cents a word. Here's the final cost accounting:

Check from *Dingbat*:	
1,000 words @.02¢	$20.00
4 photos @$5.00	20.00
Total from *Dingbat*	$40.00
Out-of-pocket expense	−32.80
Difference	$ 7.20

You have 6 hours and 45 minutes invested. This means you have been paid about $1.06 an hour for your labor. You have lost your shirt, or chemise.

Let's see how the math works out if *Dingbat* pays five cents a word (which today is more likely):

Check from *Dingbat*:

1,000 words @.05¢	$50.00
4 photos @$5.00	20.00
Total from *Dingbat*	$70.00
Less your out-of-pocket expenses	−32.80
	$37.20

Net profit (or your labor at $5.50 per hour) **$37.20**

This is still not much, considering that plumbers and electricians these days may draw $25 an hour or more. But it's a start. And it's $37.20 you might not have had otherwise.

Experienced writers know that a one-time sale of "raw material" may do little more than underwrite the cost of acquiring the basic material. So they are constantly alert to ways to sell the same raw-stuff to several markets. They also know that the time and money expended in getting to and from assignments should be shared, whenever possible, by several writing projects instead of being absorbed totally by one.

Assume, for example, that you sell a trade editor on a story about the electrical contracting on a new building. Be alert, as well, to other potential articles on the roofing, flooring, architecture, general contracting, concrete work, plumbing, air conditioning, and other facets of the job. Query every possible lead. Much of the basic raw material you gather for story number one can be worked into stories two and three and so on. This way you "milk" the story for every possible advantage.

Here are some additional trade-writing tips, synthesized from the experiences of many old-timers in the field:

- Remember the KISS rule: *Keep It Short and Simple.*
- Build your article around one single, clear-cut idea. Don't try to write the encyclopedia. Focus your piece *very tightly* on one simple angle. Save all the others for later pieces because (1) you may need them, (2) readers don't like to be confused, and (3) neither do editors.

• The best information source, and the most cooperative, is usually the owner of a business who built the enterprise from scratch. The owner is justifiably proud of his or her success, and usually eager to talk. The worst, most inhibited sources are likely to be lower- and middle-echelon management types (especially buyers for some reason), who are afraid they will reveal a trade secret, or offend the boss, or lose their jobs. Whenever possible, go to the top for your story.

• Always submit your final draft to your source for a personal O.K. Get the source's initials on every page, and on every change. If possible, hand-carry the draft to the source, and sit there while it is reviewed. If you mail the manuscript to the source, it can easily (a) get lost, (b) be pigeonholed, (c) be routed around to several other management types, each of whom will want to make changes, or (d) the story may be killed. You can readily understand the implications of (d).

• Learn to be a fanatical scissor-wielder. Clip every possible lead from every available source (always noting the date and publication). Toss these clips into a "pending" file. During drought periods, ransack the file and pick out a batch of new leads to work on.

• Build a "background" clip file, especially in your areas of specialization. If someone writes a long feature for your local daily or weekly on (say) the automobile business in your community, clip and file it. One day you may write, or be asked to write, a piece about some local car dealer. You can dip into that "backgrounder" (which someone spent a lot of hours on) for information with which to flesh out your own story.

• Don't be a mailbox-watcher. Write your story, mail it, and forget it. Go on to a new project. Flood the mail with queries and manuscripts—that's the only way you'll ever send Junior or Sissy to college, and pay off the mortgage. So long as you keep your typewriter warm, there's a good chance you can afford your own Keogh Plan.

Finally, enjoy. "I like what a young California writer told me when I called and asked if he'd be interested in doing a story on a laundry," Ben Russell once told me. 'I'm interested in doing a story on any tupe of business or organization,' he replied. 'It's the way I learn things. It fascinates me to go into different types of business and see how they operate.' "

For this young fellow, there was more involved than just another laundry, just another writing chore. There was adventure, and a chance to stretch his mind.

IV

THE GREAT
MISCELLANY

chapter 13

*To call working for newspapers a way
of life instead of simply a career goes to
the heart of what journalism is all about.*
JOHN TEBBEL
OPPORTUNITIES IN JOURNALISM[1]

WORKING IN BROADCAST & NEWSPAPER JOURNALISM

In terms of sheer numbers, journalism in all its forms employs more writers than any other branch of writing. As a job market, journalism is enormous. Yet paradoxically, for most newcomers it is a painfully difficult market to penetrate.

By recent count, there were more than 1,750 daily English-language newspapers in the United States and about 8,000 weeklies. The total circulation of the dailies alone averaged, in a given year, just under 62 million copies every day—about one newspaper for every four persons in the United States. Something like 400,000 men and women were employed on newspapers and television and

---

[1] John Tebbel, *Opportunities in Journalism* (Louisville, Ky.: Vocational Guidance Manuals, a Division of Data Courier, Inc., 1977).

radio stations in the writing and reporting of news. Of these, nearly 35,000 were members of the national society of professional journalists, Sigma Delta Chi.

Despite the impressive number of writing positions in the newspaper and broadcasting industries, job seekers may find it difficult to obtain a toehold. Evaluating "the best—and worst—careers for the 1980s," *Money*[2] magazine predicted that prospects would be "poor" in journalism for qualified job seekers. Of some 40 career activities assessed in a *Money* survey, only four showed poorer prospects than those for newspaper reporters: forester, Protestant clergyman, librarian, and schoolteacher.

Why this abysmal showing for journalism? "The worst combination," said *Money*, "is little or no growth (in the number of new jobs) together with a flood of applicants—the situation affecting teaching and journalism."

By contrast, said the magazine, "the need for plumbers, for instance, is expected to grow 39% by 1985 . . . After four or five years (a plumber) can go to work on a union construction job for an average of $20,000 a year." *Money* pointed out, however, that there was little upward mobility in such crafts as plumbing, with workers generally peaking at certain levels and staying there. In the professional activities, the chance for upward movement remains with the individual throughout his or her career.

Despite the grim outlook for employment in journalism, every daily, weekly, and broadcast news department of any consequence is beleaguered by applicants anxious to work for the Fourth Estate. The reasons are many and varied, but *money* is not a primary motivator. Even though news-writing pays better today than it did three or four decades ago (I started in 1939 at $90 a month!), journalism is not—except for the superstars—the place to accumulate wealth.

The lines remain long at the personnel office principally (I think) because the profession attracts romantics and idealists. The romantics are attracted by the alleged glamour of newspapering. They may have read *Front Page*, or *All the President's Men*, or

---

[2]Jeremy Main, "Careers for the 1980s: 10 of the Best—and 10 of the Worst," *Money*, 6, no. 11 (November 1977), 62–69. Reprinted by permission.

watched Ed Asner and Mary Tyler Moore on television. They have accepted the fictionalized versions of newspeople so skillfully portrayed on the screen, and assume that these stage-play characters depict life as it really is in the news room.

Then there are the idealists (who may also be romantics) who sincerely believe—not entirely without reason—that one way to make the world a better place may be found through journalism. They remember Vietnam, Watergate, Korea, and Iran, plus any number of other debacles, and would like to do their bit to stave off repeat performances of such disasters.

There are also the realists who take the position that writing for newspapers, news services, news magazines, radio, or TV is essentially a way of making a living, like teaching, or law, or medicine. They also may be attracted initially by glamour and idealism, but they are basically realists—and they survive to become the hard-nosed investigative reporters, the cigar-chomping editors, and the empire-building publishers.

Oddly enough, many newspeople after years in the business shift from one premise to another, or to a mix. Romantics may become hardened (and sometimes pessimistic) realists; the realists may turn idealistic. And the idealists—well, they may simply become discouraged.

But in the manifestation of one human quality, all of them— if they truly are newspeople—are united: They are curious and have an insatiable thirst for answers to the questions which vex us all. If you do not have an overriding curiosity about life and people, you will find yourself out of place in the news business.

A WAY TO THE TOP

Many writers whose names are now household words began their careers in the city rooms of newspapers. Ernest Hemingway, Paul Gallico, Ring Lardner, James Branch Cabell, Theodore Dreiser, Sinclair Lewis, and Sherwood Anderson are but a few of those who went from news-writing to a kind of immortality. Many who have achieved international stature in journalism began their careers as reporters, among them James Reston, the *New York*

Times pundit whose writings are widely read and respected (and who started as a sports reporter for the Associated Press). Television also has its share of celebrities who cut their editorial teeth in the news room, including John Chancellor, Walter Cronkite, and David Brinkley.

Journalism is also an open sesame to the world of politics. At least two presidents—John F. Kennedy and Warren G. Harding—learned some fundamental lessons in news rooms before advancing to the White House. Adlai Stevenson also served a term as a newsman. And many present-day senators and representatives in Congress, and in state legislatures throughout the nation, came to their posts after working as reporters.

The news room also provides invaluable training for other careers which are allied, one way or another, to newsgathering. The ranks of advertising and public relations are filled with ex-reporters. (A snide comment sometimes heard in news rooms is that a public-relations person is an unemployed reporter. There may be a bit of envy in this assessment, as public-relations people, if they are good at their calling, may make much more money than newspeople do.)

Other editors and reporters may leave the news room for the schoolroom, to teach journalism at high school or university levels (see "Teaching," Chapter 21).

SOME OF THE REALITIES

Whatever the glamour, whatever the appeal to idealism, there are minuses in this, as in any work. Working schedules can at times be insane. If you are employed on a morning paper (of the 1,756 dailies in a recent year, 355 were a.m.'s and 1,391 were afternoons), you may begin work after lunch and rarely see your family in the evenings except on weekends. If your berth is on a p.m., you may start for the office before sunup. Overtime is common, as reporters must be where the news is when it *is* news, not after the fact. There are few holidays, because the news takes no holidays. The same demanding schedules prevail in broadcast journalism as in the print media.

Reporters cannot be shy or reticent by nature. At times they must be aggressive and brassy, even offensively so, if they hope to "get the story." There exists, therefore, a widely shared hostility toward newspeople, especially among those whose careers and activities keep them constantly in the spotlight. In their attitude toward the press, news sources may vary from fawning to openly unfriendly and uncooperative. A source who might be wide open one day may turn clam-tight the next.

News writers are, perforce, cast in a kind of adversary role by the nature of their profession. Dale Carnegie did not have members of the Fourth Estate in mind for his classic model. It may not be the job of reporters to win friends, but it most assuredly is their lot to influence people, wittingly or not. In the case of certain categories of journalists—editorial writers, columnists, and cartoonists—their job is overtly to influence readers, and to win them over to a position fostered by the publisher.

It is fair to say, I believe, that most newspaper and broadcast journalists regard their work as important and useful, if not vital. Newspeople who do not share this view may eventually suffer from depression or demoralization. These—if they stay— sometimes become embittered hacks, relegated to writing obituaries or to other uninspiring tasks.

GETTING STARTED

The royal road to employment for many in the news business is the graduate school of journalism. There are many of these throughout the nation, some of them linked to prestigious universities such as Columbia, Northwestern, Iowa, and Missouri. "J-school" graduates seem to fare better than walk-ins who lack special training. A survey in one recent year by the Newspaper Fund of Princeton, New Jersey, revealed that two out of three journalism-school graduates in that year found work in the media within two months of graduation. One in four of these went to work on a daily, and one in ten found a job on a weekly. An appreciable percentage of these graduates had already lined up jobs before receiving their diplomas.

This is not to say that a J-school diploma is mandatory. It is not. Time was, in fact, when many old-timers in the business would not hire a journalism-school product, regarding a J-school education as unnecessary and a waste of time. This bias appears to be disappearing, although there are still pockets of resistance.

Many editors—and reporters—will advise the hopeful to skip journalism courses, and instead to major in the humanities and social sciences. Journalistic techniques, they argue, can be learned quickly on the job. What reporters really need, according to this line of reasoning, is a broad, solid background in the arts, history, sociology, psychology—and English. Most schools of journalism, recognizing the validity of this viewpoint, have long since cast off their "vocational school" aura, and now require all their students to acquire the kind of broad, general preparation their critics insist is essential.

Every candidate for a job in the news-writing business, whatever his or her other qualifications, must demonstrate at least modest mastery of the English language. Without this skill, a candidate simply cannot obtain employment in the first place or (if someone slips and hires such a candidate anyhow) survive more than a few days.

Another requisite skill—this one mechanical—is the ability to type. All newsmen have it, to one degree or another. Some (especially the old-timers) still use the hunt-and-peck, two-finger system (also dubbed the "Columbus" system: discover and land). But most contemporary newspeople can touch-type rapidly and accurately.

If you hope to carve out a career as a specialist, you should also include courses in your special area during your collegiate training. This is the age of specialization, and news writers with preparation in certain fields may advance more rapidly than a general reporter. The latter may be assigned to cover events which require little or no special expertise. But if a story lies in a special field—medicine, space science, oceanography, finance, politics, education, international affairs (where language skills may be helpful), and others—an editor will naturally select the man or woman best qualified by training and experience to handle the story. On many large papers, specialists work exclusively within their fields.

Writers also are needed as reporters and editors in the many special departments operated by most newspapers, including sports, business and finance, travel, real estate, music, books, society, gardening, automotive, and others.

"START LITTLE"

Classic counsel in the profession, given to most newcomers anxious to break in, is to "start little." This is especially applicable to those who are starting from scratch, without impressive J-school credentials, but who feel they are destined for journalism. Seek employment, first, in the smaller, less glamorous markets where the turnover is greatest—the small-town dailies, the neighborhood weeklies, the minor-league radio and TV stations. There is greater mobility at these lower levels because writers—having gained experience which makes them more valuable—move out and upward to higher-paying jobs, usually in bigger cities. The voids they leave will be filled by applicants with lesser qualifications who have favorably impressed the hiring officer (usually the editor), and whose names come easily to mind. Hence the value of making periodic calls on the prospective employer: If he or she has your name (and face) in mind when an opening occurs, you may get that long-awaited phone call or letter. There may be other applicants with even better qualifications than yours, but it is *your* name and face the editor remembers.

DESK JOBS IN JOURNALISM

You may find, as time goes on, that you will want to abandon the rough-and-tumble arena of reporting to move into a desk job as copy editor, rewrite person, or departmental specialist. Writers who tend to be introverted, who love words and writing but do not especially relish daily contact with the public, often become excellent editors or in-house writers (including editorial writers). In these jobs, you are just as much a newsperson as are your newsgathering colleagues on the outside.

THE CHANGING AMERICAN NEWSPAPER

The classical world of the chain-smoking, tough-guy reporter with a press card stuck in his hatband (who wears hats?), immortalized by Ben Hecht, is long gone. So is the city room of yesterday, with frantic reporters crying "Copy!" as deadline nears.

Today's metropolitan news room may look more like the control center at Cape Canaveral, with reporters and editors seated before Video Display Terminals (VDTs) as they produce their stories. Typewriters linked to these VDTs produce a tape, which can then display the story on the video screen. The operator edits the story on the screen, correcting a misspelled word here, moving a sentence or paragraph there. The edited tape goes into a memory bank, to be called on later to set type automatically.

The day is nearly here when, for example, a West Coast reporter may be assigned to cover a major event in Chicago. With his or her story ready, the reporter will sit down at a computer punchboard in Chicago, and transmit the story directly onto a tape in the paper's newsroom. That tape will then be decoded, and the story displayed on an editing screen, where an editor will make any changes necessary with an "electronic pencil." The tape is then ready to be "translated" into type.

The day also may come when a reporter may dictate his story by phone (perhaps via satellite) to a device in his home office which will "listen" to his voice and convert the soundwaves into type.

As for the subscriber at the other end, the day may be near when the daily newspaper will come to him, or her, via a television set. The subscriber may tune to a certain channel, and receive page 1 of the paper. To turn the page, the viewer simply punches a button on a remote-control gadget attached to the TV. If the viewer wants a copy of a given page (to cut out the food coupon?) he or she may punch another button on a "slave" machine linked to the TV set, and a computer-style printout of the desired page will be produced by the slave. All pages of this TV-version newspaper would be constantly updated with the latest bulletins.

So a new and exciting dimension is being added to a field of writing which already offers innumerable attractions.

chapter 14

*One of Dr. Seuss's immortal writings was
an advertising slogan of four words:
Quick Henry, the Flit!*
                    WRITER'S DIGEST

WRITING JOBS IN ADVERTISING, PUBLICITY, & PUBLIC RELATIONS

Now and then, when martinis flow on Madison Avenue, someone will recall an old tale which goes like this:

An enterprising fellow dropped in one day at an agency handling Lucky Strike cigarettes. He made them a simple proposition: He had created a four-word slogan which would reap untold millions for Lucky Strike, which he would part with for $200,000. (The dollar figure varies in direct proportion to the volume of martinis consumed.) If the agency used his slogan, they would pay. Otherwise, no deal.

What could they lose? The admen agreed, and a contract was signed. O.K., genius, what are those four $50,000 words?

Be happy, go Lucky.

The agency allegedly paid, fixing what must have been—

until then—a world's record on word rates. And, the legend concludes, everyone lived happily, if not ever after, at least for many years while Lucky Strike did indeed make millions traceable to the slogan.

Perhaps the yarn is apocryphal. True or not, the story illustrates a central point about writing and advertising: the welcome mat is always out, and big money is waiting, for creative minds who can put words together in compelling patterns that will move people to buy . . . and buy . . . and buy.

It is no pushover to break into this supercharged industry, which in one recent year funnelled some $37 *billion* advertising dollars into the newspapers, magazines, and television and radio stations of America. It's an ultra-high-pressure calling, with ulcers and migraines virtually guaranteed. But for those who can deliver what it demands, advertising can yield much more handsome returns (fiscal, at least) than perhaps any other occupation based on skill with words.

Not all the men and women who work in advertising are employed in agencies. In virtually every business and industry of any size in the nation, someone functions as advertising manager. In a small firm, one person may handle the entire load; in a major corporation, the advertising department may be headed by a senior vice president who oversees a large staff. Some of these staffers may be directly involved in working with the corporation's ad agency on the conceptualizing, design, and execution of advertising programs in the various media. Others may be charged with generating publicity through press releases and other forms of propaganda. Still others may handle "public relations."

The ultimate aim of them all is generally the same: to create and sustain a positive image of their firm or client. If the client is in business to sell products or services, the objective is to generate sales and to show the highest possible profit. If the client is an association, foundation, council, or other non-commercial (and perhaps non-profit) body, the raison d'etre of their work is to project a positive image for the sponsor, and to counter any assault on that image from whatever quarter.

Writers on the staffs of advertising agencies are among the most creative and fertile in the whole writing fraternity. They are not only exceptionally gifted in the use of the mother tongue, they are (or should be) also experts in the workings of the human mind, and how people react to stimuli.

If you are gifted with an exceptional ability to conceptualize, an unfettered imagination, and a natural gift for tongues, you may wish to explore the world of advertising as an outlet for your talents. Many writers whose names—as authors—were to become legendary began their careers in the advertising business. They learned there how to harness their imaginations, and to work under pressure—assets which served them well in later life when they became novelists.

"PUBLICITY" VERSUS "PUBLIC RELATIONS"

The terms "publicity" and "public relations" often are confused, or used interchangeably. They are related, but distinct.

Publicity, says one widely respected dictionary, is

> "public notice resulting from mention in the press, on the radio, or through any other medium or means of communication, including word of mouth . . . (and) information, articles, etc., issued to secure public notice or attention."

Public relations is defined in the same source as

> "the actions of a corporation, store, government, individual, etc., in promoting good will between itself and the public, the community, employees, etc. . . . the art or technique of promoting such good will."[1]

Publicity, then, is an arm or instrument of public relations (assuming that its aim is positive, that is, to create good will). Public relations is the art or technique of creating good will through the use of many instruments, devices, and strategies, including publicity, advertising, and imaginative stunts of one kind or another (flying a dirigible over the Rose Bowl during the New Year's game, sending petitions bearing thousands of signatures to key government officials, and the like).

---

[1] *Random House Dictionary of the English Language* (New York: Random House, 1967), p. 1162.

Writers form the backbone of all publicity and public relations enterprises and endeavors. Sometimes the men and women who head public relations and publicity agencies are themselves outstanding writers; sometimes they are stronger in sales and psychology than in word manipulation. In any event, a public relations or publicity firm without strong writers cannot survive long.

Many of today's best-known publicity, advertising, and publicity agencies began as one-man or one-woman operations, with little more than a desk, chair and typewriter as furnishings. The achievements of these individuals soon attracted other clients until finally some of them blossomed into enterprises billing millions of dollars every year.

Similar challenges and opportunities are still open to capable and courageous writers, especially in market areas not already saturated with this kind of talent.

PUBLICITY WRITING ON RETAINER

Many free lancers who find it difficult to generate enough sales from their book and magazine writings alone have supplemented their incomes with "retainer" accounts. A writer, for example, may prepare news releases and other publicity for a local charity, hospital, trade association, professional society, club, or other organization on a retainer or fee basis. An organization which cannot afford to hire a full-time publicist (a $20 word for press agent) may be able to budget a more modest sum every month to retain a part-time publicity writer.

For a free lancer, the knowledge that he or she can rely on retainer stipends on a regular basis may make the difference between survival as a free lancer, or returning to a salaried job.

One writer prepared news releases for many years for the Community Chest in his area, even after be began to sell regularly to major magazines. His monthly retainer gave him the confidence, and the financial security, to continue with his free-lance career.

Anyone with the basic skills needed for straight news reporting can write publicity copy. Most news releases are built around some activity or event in which the client has been, is, or will be involved—the opening of a new facility, an important policy statement by an official, a report on services rendered to the community, and so forth. The client and the writer consider the information newsworthy, and hope that newspaper and broadcast news editors will share their conviction.

To establish a fair retainer fee, explain to a potential client that you base your fee on an hourly rate of (X) dollars. Before this conference, you have predetermined the rate prevailing in your area for comparable services, and decided what your own rate will be (above, at par with, or below the market). The rate must be fair to both yourself and the client, otherwise the arrangement will not work. If you overcharge, the client will come to know this and will cancel. If you undercharge, you will be robbing yourself. It may be wise to insert a provision in your agreement that allows for periodic review of your retainer by both parties.

Whatever you charge, you should build in an allowance for non-writing time, that is, time you will spend on the client's behalf but which will not be devoted to writing. For example, if you invest a full day doing legwork and research required for a story, but only three hours actually writing the piece, you should charge the client for legwork and research time as well as for the hours spent at your typewriter.

If you are just beginning, you may find it expedient to shave your rates to below the prevailing market in light of your experience. The important thing is to establish yourself with one or more clients on steady retainers. You can then, at least, buy hamburgers and pay the room rent. This will give you the freedom—fiscal as well as philosophical—to do the writing which really has meaning for you.

Warning: if you overdo the retainer business, you may end up running a full-time publicity and public-relations agency. Because, if you are good at your job, word-of-mouth advertising will guarantee your expansion.

If that's what you really want, fine. If not, *verbum sap.*

chapter 15

*. . . it is a necessity to me to be always
learning something, and I am possessed by
an insatiable desire for books.*
VINCENT VAN GOGH

THE JOYS OF BOOK REVIEWING

For the highly literate, bookish person who revels in reading, book reviewing can be one pleasant way to make money with words. Not a lot of money, it is true. But then, there are always those free books, which one may enjoy for a day or for a lifetime.

Most dailies of any appreciable circulation, and many larger weeklies, regularly receive review copies from publishing houses. According to one reviewer, even a moderate-sized daily may be shipped more than 3,000 books a year. Yet there are many dailies that do not have a book editor, and which farm out all reviews to staff members or outsiders anxious to write them in exchange for free books.

On many papers, book reviewing is taken seriously. Some of these papers publish special book sections each week (conventionally on Sunday), with their own editors who fill the sections with news and reviews from the world of books. In such cases, an editor normally has more work than he or she can handle, and must rely on a "stable" of contributing reviewers who will read and critique new titles on demand. Some of the great dailies (*The New York Times* and the *Los Angeles Times* among them) are famed among publishers, authors, and literate people everywhere for their erudite reviews. These appear in special sections which also contain advertisements from publishing enterprises and are, therefore, money-making departments. For contributions to such sections, reviewers customarily are paid for their work, in some cases generously ($300 or more for a single review).

So great is the flood of new titles that not even the most specialized publications can cope with the deluge. *Library Journal,* the book-review bible of the library world, which probably prints more reviews per year than any other publication, was able to review only about 6,000 titles of the total 24,000 published in one recent year. The same year, *The New York Times* found space to report on fewer than 3,000.

Reviewers who stay with it generally manage to build formidable private libraries, unless they sell their copies to book dealers to supplement their meager income from the reviews. One writer who averaged ten to twelve reviews a month confessed that "I soon had books coming out of my ears." His collection ran the gamut of subject matter from spy stories to reference books, and from science fiction to politics.

This writer also enjoyed many fringe benefits stemming from his reviews. Hostesses invited him to cocktail parties to mingle with the guests and chat knowledgeably about books. Amateur writers sought his counsel. Published authors cursed him—at least some of them. He didn't mind, because he had attained "a quantum of fame, a negligible amount of fortune, and a copious quantity of printed matter." What's more, he noted, he enjoyed it.

Still another reviewer, assigned a quota of four to five books plus an 800-word author interview every week, said he'd read the books for pleasure in any event, so why not be paid for something he enjoyed doing and would do anyhow.

As a reviewer you will be in distinguished company. Erskine

Caldwell—among many famed writers who also reviewed books—wrote scores of reviews for Southern papers, and was paid in books. Unfortunately he could not eat these, so he sold many of them (at twenty-five cents a copy) to keep from starving. After reviewing for the *Atlanta Journal* for about a year, Caldwell had accumulated nearly 2,000 volumes. He packed them up and carried them with him with each move. Once, while living in Maine and writing around the clock, Caldwell recalled:

> When money was needed, the only thing to do was to pack two suitcases with copies of books I had received for review, take a bus to Boston, and visit the second-hand bookshops. I may not have originated the twenty-five cent book business in America, but I believe I helped it to get off to a good start in Boston.[1]

To break into reviewing, make contact with the book editor of your local daily or weekly, or of a newspaper in the nearest big city. If the editor is not identified through a byline or listing on a book page or in a book section, you may find his or her name or title in the latest copy of the *Editor & Publisher Yearbook*. This source book is usually available in the reference department of any well-stocked library.

Write the editor, stating that you would like to review books for the paper. Set forth your qualifications. If you have special credentials (you teach literature, or are yourself a published author, and so forth) be sure to mention these. State your areas of special interest and preparation, if any. Ask for an appointment.

Should the appointment be granted, go prepared to tell the editor what service you think you might render. If the editor is swamped with unreviewed books, you may be invited to select one for review from the pile on the editor's desk. Take just one, and do a thorough job on it. Ask the editor for word lengths and other requirements (deadlines, how manuscripts should be prepared, and other details), and rigidly adhere to these. If the editor says 500 words, don't write 900 or 750. Keep it to 500 words or fewer, because the editor knows (you do not) what the paper's space

---

[1] Erskine Caldwell, "Call It Experience," in *The Creative Writer*, Aron Mathieu, ed. (Cincinnati: Writer's Digest Publications, 1968), p. 225.

limitations are. Write clean, crisp copy—no spelling errors, no sloppy grammar, no messy erasures, no interlineations or x-outs. Put your best editorial foot forward, because you may not get a second chance if you muff the first one.

If the editor likes your maiden effort, you may well be on your way toward "a quantum of fame" and a large free library, if not a copious measure of pure enjoyment.

chapter 16

If Columbus had given up and turned back when the going got tough, no one would have blamed him. No one would have remembered him, either.

H. JOSEPH CHADWICK[1]

WRITING JOBS IN LOCAL, STATE, & FEDERAL GOVERNMENT

To render an accounting to the tax-paying public, government units at all levels (city, county, state and federal) retain "public information" personnel who serve as liaison between the media and government officials. These personnel also may be charged with various writing tasks, including the preparation of news releases, brochures, reports, and speeches.

The influence and authority exercised by some of these staff officers often go far beyond the duties and responsibilities set forth in their job descriptions. Witness, for example, the enormous power exerted by the press secretary of the President of the United States.

Government units at all levels also retain writers and editors

---

[1] Onetime director of *Writer's Digest* correspondence school. Quoted by permission of *Writer's Digest*, Cincinnati, Ohio.

for a wide range of editorial tasks. There are an estimated 4,000 writer and editor positions scattered throughout federal government agencies in Washington and overseas. About 100 new writers are hired in Washington every year at the entry level (lowest on the totem pole in terms of pay and responsibilities). Occasional openings occur in top-level positions, but most of these probably are filled by advancements in rank.

The great majority of federal posts are located in sprawling bureaucracies which carpet the nation's capital wall-to-wall. Some jobs are, of course, located in government outposts in states throughout the nation, and overseas in U.S. embassies and consulates.

"Competition for mid-level positions is extremely keen," cautions a bulletin from the Office of Personnel Management (OPM) in Washington. "Unless your experience and/or education is significant, your chances for referral to an agency are very poor. You will be competing for a limited number of jobs mainly against highly qualified candidates."

Some idea of the wide variety of these writing opportunities may be seen in the following lists of "mid-level" occupations, prepared by the OPM. Numbers in the left-hand column are the "code" numbers of these positions. Candidates interested in a given post may request information by citing the code number in writing to the OPM.

WRITING AND EDITING

Experience/Education in:

310	Writing Popular Printed Matter (Newspaper or Magazine)
311	Writing Popular Printed Matter (Book Length)
312	Editing Newspapers or Magazine Articles (Non-Technical)
313	Editing Book Length Works
316	Technical Writing/Editing (ADP)
317	Technical Writing/Editing (Agriculture)
318	Technical Writing/Editing (Biology)
319	Technical Writing/Editing (Consumer Affairs)
320	Technical Writing/Editing (Economics)
321	Technical Writing/Editing (Education)
322	Technical Writing/Editing (EEO)
323	Technical Writing/Editing (Engineering)

324	Technical Writing/Editing (Foreign Affairs)
325	Technical Writing/Editing (Finance)
326	Technical Writing/Editing (Fine Arts)
327	Technical Writing/Editing (Law)
328	Technical Writing/Editing (Legislative Liaison)
329	Technical Writing/Editing (Medicine)
330	Technical Writing/Editing (Military History)
331	Technical Writing/Editing (Physical Science)
332	Technical Writing/Editing (Social Science)

The "Experience/Education in" reference at the head of the list is OPM's notice to interested persons that either experience or education, or both, are required to qualify for these positions. For writer and editor posts, the educational requirement is usually a minimum of four years of college education. For positions in scientific and technical writing, education should include at least 15 semester hours of study in the appropriate subject matter.

As for duties assigned to writers working for the government, the OPM explains:

> The Federal service employs writers and editors to produce articles, press releases, periodicals, pamphlets and brochures, speeches, and radio, television or motion picture scripts. These employees occupy key positions in maintaining and facilitating avenues of communications between American citizens and their government. The writer must usually research the subject to be presented, select information to be used, and write and edit the final manuscripts. This includes determining a style and manner of presentation consistent with the interests of the audience. Writers may also specialize in technical fields such as engineering or social science. Persons who have talent for writing in clear and readable style are offered numerous opportunities for advancement in this field.

Bulletins issued by the OPM to interested candidates spell out the requirements and duties of the various posts in detail.

Pay scales for federal government writing jobs range from modest to king-sized. A writer or editor with six years of experience, three of them in specialized writing work, might qualify for a rating as high as GS-14, which carries a beginning salary in the $35,000 range. A writer with three years of general experience might be offered a GS-5 grade, beginning in the $11,000 to $12,000 range.

(Federal jobs generally are rated on a "GS" scale from one through 18, with steps within each grade.)

WRITING FOR STATE GOVERNMENTS

Many states of the Union also offer writing positions in a wide range of types, salaries, and duties. Here, for example, is the description of a "research writer" post in the State of California:

> Under direction, to do interpretive writing of technical material for news releases and publications of state agencies. . . . Summarizes and interprets facts and trends shown in technical studies and reports; writes articles which are adapted to the needs and interests of diverse groups such as commercial, industrial, agricultural, and labor organizations, planning commissions, and chambers of commerce; assists in the writing of releases and publications and of addresses to be given by other staff members.

To qualify for such a post, the candidate must have had at least three years of full-time paid experience in feature writing for newspapers, trade journals, magazines, or for radio broadcast, or in the writing of technical reports. He or she also must have an education "equivalent to graduation from college. Additional qualifying experience may be substituted for the required education on a year-for-year basis."

The pay range in this post was $1782 to $2149 per month.

A lower-level post for an "editorial aide" in California's state government calls for the same degree of work experience, but the educational requirement is lower: "Equivalent to completion of the twelfth grade, preferably with course work in journalism, public relations, or English." With higher education, the candidate may qualify for a better classification and pay grade.

This employee "reads, edits, and checks for style, grammar, punctuation, and clarity of expression articles prepared by staff members for publication in departmental, trade, or association journals; makes up pages and prepares dummies of departmental journals; writes captions," and performs other related chores. The pay range was $1030 to $1232 per month.

There are many other classifications for writers in state service in California, including information officer, editorial technician, and editorial assistant in various departments (education, health and science, and so forth).

Information about writing posts at the federal, state, county, and municipal levels may be obtained by writing or visiting the appropriate personnel or employment office in each case. For federal jobs, write the Office of Personnel Management, Washington D.C. 20415.

GOVERNMENT PUBLIC-RELATIONS WORK

Most federal, state, and local agencies employ public-relations personnel to explain how these agencies are using taxpayers' money and—at times—to answer public outcries against the agency's work (or lack of it).

In government, a public relations or publicity person is often (if not usually) termed a "public information officer," or PIO. In some institutions, notably universities, the "public relations practitioner" (as professionals sometimes rather pompously dub themselves) may rate an even more lofty designation: public affairs officer (or director, or manager). No one seems able to define precisely what a "public affair" is, although there have been several ribald attempts at a definition.

In Washington, the Office of Personnel Management listed the following public information occupations (at the so-called "mid-level") in a recent bulletin:

PUBLIC INFORMATION

Experience/Education in:

299	Public Information Program Administration
300	Public Information Dissemination (Press)
301	Public Information Dissemination (Radio)
302	Public Information Dissemination (Television)
303	Public Information Dissemination (Magazine)
304	Speech Writing
305	News Gathering and Reporting
306	Publicity Campaign Development or Product Promotion

All U.S. embassies abroad, and many of the nation's larger consulates, retain public information officers on their staffs. As a rule, these officers are career employees of the United States International Communication Agency (USICA) who have diplomatic status while serving abroad. They are charged with, among other tasks, relations with the media in the host countries, and with disseminating news and features to the foreign press which portray the United States, its policies, and its people in a favorable light.

State governments, as well as city and county administrations, also retain public information writers and specialists. In a large metropolitan community, the mayor, police chief, fire chief, and other top officers may have "p.r." people on their staffs to provide liaison with the media, prepare press releases, write speeches, and perform other image-making chores.

In some cases, enterprising free lancers have approached a unit of government in their localities—city, county, or departmental— to offer their services on a fee basis. This approach has worked well in areas where governmental units do not collect sufficient tax revenues to support full-time staffers for this kind of work.

One Southern writer lived in a small community which was the center of a region embracing ten counties. He had worked on a weekly newspaper and a radio station in his area, and had observed that the public really did not understand its own local government. He had also noted that the coverage given by local media to governmental matters was inadequate.

This writer lined up three retainer jobs: one for a city, one for a county, and a third for a public agency. In each case, his fee was based on a given number of hours of service per month, with an allowance for additional fees for all work performed in excess of the hours contracted for. With these three retainers as his economic base, he was able to continue his chosen work as a free-lance magazine writer.

A typical California "information officer" job description (level II) reads like this:

> Under administrative direction, to develop, organize, direct, and evaluate a comprehensive program to inform the public of the activities and objectives of a State agency; to consult with and advise top management

of the agency on public relations implications of the agency's activities...
analyzes the extent of public understanding of the program administered
by the agency and determines the need for further public information
and education activity; establishes the objectives of the agency's information program ... directs a staff in the conduct of the program ...
meets with top management level as a regular participating member ...
makes speeches before various groups; promotes the knowledge and use
of the agency's services.

To qualify for this post, which pays in the $2000–2500 a
month range, the candidate must have had either two years of
experience in California state service performing information-
officer duties, or "broad and successful experience which has
demonstrated the ability to plan and direct a comprehensive
public information program. This must have included at least five
years professional experience in preparing and disseminating
information, a substantial part of which also included supervising
the writing of others. Writing experience, while an integral part of
the above, will not be considered qualifying in itself ..."

The candidate also must have the equivalent of a college
education, certain special knowledge and abilities, and "special
personal characteristics" including "appreciation of news value"
and "emotional stability under stress."

Obviously, this job is not for amateurs. Nor, indeed, are
most of the better-paying writing jobs in government. There are,
however, entry-level openings from time to time, through which
beginning writers may gain the experience which will qualify them
for more enviable posts.

chapter 17

LET'S GET TECHNICAL

Technical writing has much in common with newspaper and broadcast journalism. The writer—or reporter—must elicit information from one or more sources (which often are reluctant if not downright hostile), and convert this raw data into clearly understandable prose.

Thousands of technical writers are employed by American businesses and industries. Even more thousands are on the payroll of the federal government. The calling attracts men and women alike, and pay scales range from modest to munificent.

Certain qualities are shared by writers who succeed in this specialized branch of the craft. Better-paid technical writers are exceptionally good communicators. They have learned how to filter out essential information from masses of undigested (and indigestible) data, then to present this information in terms that a person using a given piece of equipment or a process can grasp quickly and follow easily.

A competent tech writer also must be something of a diplomat, for the work calls at times for close collaboration with scientists, engineers, lab technicians and others whose knowledge of their subject is profound but whose patience with "outsiders" is limited. It is the writer's responsibility to extract information as painlessly as possible from reticent sources, then to clear the final product with these sources to the satisfaction of all concerned. This is not easy when the source may be a Nobel laureate in physics or chemistry, and the subject is so abstruse that not even the laureate's colleagues understand it.

If you are considering a career in technical writing, measure yourself against this checklist of qualifications:

1. You should be—potentially or actually—a good reporter, preferably one who already has cut his or her teeth in the city room of a daily or weekly newspaper. This is not to say that newspaper or broadcast journalism is a mandatory prerequisite; it is not. But the experience would help.
2. You are one who enjoys research, who revels in probing the mysteries of subject matter about which you know little or nothing today so that you may know a great deal about it tomorrow. If you are not, by nature if not by experience, an investigative reporter, forget technical writing.
3. You should know enough about human relations and popular psychology to be able to tell someone to go to hell but make him or her enjoy the trip. You will deal at times with two types of geniuses: (a) those who really are, and (b) those who think they are, and both can be difficult.
4. Your memory should be elephantine.
5. Logic should be a strong suit with you.

If you can meet all or most of these measurements, and if thinking in scientific terms comes naturally to you, technical writing could well be your metier. If a certain branch of science interests you more than any other, it will help insure your success if you seek employment within that branch. The range and variety of specialties are sufficiently diversified to accommodate virtually everyone's interests. There are tech writers in aerospace, pharmaceuticals, electronics, food technology, oceanography, and medicine, to cite but a few areas of specialization.

The federal government is the biggest user of technical-writing talent. Thousands of tech writers are employed directly in government jobs, while other thousands work for industries which have contracts with federal agencies, and are thus indirectly employed by the government. The armed forces, through Department of Defense contracts, are the biggest users of all. Other heavy employers are the National Aeronautics and Space Administration, the Department of Agriculture, and the Atomic Energy Commission.

In the private sector, tech writers are retained to perform a variety of tasks including the preparation of reports, manuals, technical papers (either for publication or for oral presentation), documentation required for patent applications, and many other chores. Writers employed by trade journals also can be considered as tech writers, as their job is to digest and refine complicated data and to serve it up in a form which can be readily understood by non-technicians.

Special training for technical writers is available at many institutions throughout the nation. Prominent among these is the Rensselaer Polytechnic Institute in Troy, New York, where a four-year curriculum is offered for tech writers.

Many writers who have begun their careers in other areas have eventually succumbed to the lure of technical writing. Well-known among these is Isaac Asimov, himself a scientist with a Ph.D. in chemistry, who has proved that a facile, inquiring mind may write about nearly everything, and write exceedingly well. Though many of Asimov's more than 200 books are centered on scientific matters, he has also written books on such non-scientific subjects as the Holy Bible and the Bard of Avon. Truly, Asimov has made the world his personal oyster.

Apart from the money—which can be very good—there are fringe benefits enjoyed by technical writers. Those who work in the "break-through" areas of government and industry—space, oceanography, and medicine among them—live and work with the men and women who make the news of today and the history of tomorrow. On a day-to-day basis, tech writers work alongside these people in the vanguard, sharing with them a one-to-one relationship which is denied to lesser mortals.

Though most technical-writing assignments are normal nine-to-five jobs, there are also numerous opportunities for free-lance tech writers. Known in industry and government as "job shoppers," such writers follow work from site to site, just as itinerant farm workers follow the harvests.

No one in industry or government who hires tech writers looks down his or her nose at a job shopper, because the term is not viewed as derogatory in this context. Job shoppers are, rather, men and women who prefer—for reasons of their own—to work for brief stretches at higher rates than they would earn in full-time employment. They know that industries, especially those with government contracts, go through peak periods when they urgently need all the help they can hire, and slack periods when they must cut back on personnel. The job shopper can work intensely to help fill this peak-time need and, in slack months, enjoy the luxury of doing what he or she pleases. This mobile work force is vital to American industry and to the national defense.

Tech writing is not, of course, for everyone. But for those who can meet its exacting qualifications, this branch of writing offers a highly fulfilling, remunerative, and stimulating form of useful employment.

chapter 18

Of all those arts in which the wise excel,
Nature's chief masterpiece is writing well.

JOHN SHEFFIELD
DUKE OF BUCKINGHAMSHIRE
(1682)

SPINOFF WRITING: USING WHAT YOU ALREADY KNOW

In your present job, you may do little if any writing beyond an occasional memo, letter, or report. Yet your occupation may be loaded with inherent possibilities for magazine and even for book-length manuscripts. In short, for spinoff writing opportunities. Witness these examples:

- A Colorado real-estate broker developed some unusual ideas about selling residential properties. He had long dreamed of writing articles as a sideline. As a spinoff of what he already knew, he began to write articles for trade papers serving the real-estate field.
- A high school teacher, anxious to try her wings as a writer, found an opportunity to serve as a consultant in her subject matter, for a group which was developing new instructional

materials. From there it was a short jump into writing about curriculum development—a spinoff.

• A personnel manager believed he had developed some useful answers to problems related to personnel supervision. He worked up his ideas in the form of an article, and sold the piece—his first—to a management journal. Spinoff.

• A woman working in the advertising department of a large radio station (in a non-writing capacity) became intrigued with the advertisements being aired on her station, and decided to try her hand at writing copy. Somewhat shyly, she submitted a few of her ideas to the advertising manager. To her surprise, the manager liked them very much. Soon she was able to leave her non-writing job to concentrate full-time on ad copy. Spinoff.

In many cases, these spinoff writing experiences were incidental to the writer's full-time work. They served to supplement the writer's income, and to give him or her the satisfaction of recognition. In other instances, spinoff writing has led to full-time employment as a writer.

The point should be clear: examine your potential. Make an inventory of your capabilities, your special knowledge, your expertise. Then move to capitalize on these.

You do this by, first, identifying the subjects or fields about which you believe you can write because of your special background. You then survey the potential outlets for articles, books, or other written materials for your special information. You meld the two—your know-how and the need for it—and the result is publication.

There's an old story in the writing trade—probably true—about the short-story editor who received two manuscripts "over the transom" in the same day's mail. One, from Brooklyn, came from a fledgling writer who had never been west of Jersey City. His was a cowboy yarn complete with spurs, saddles, and a shoot-out at high noon. It was also complete with a lot of misinformation about the Old West.

The other manuscript hailed from Wyoming: a tough-guy tale about Mafia hoodlums gunning down one another in mid-Manhattan. Its author had never been east of Laramie—and he was a cowhand!

For some reason best known to psychologists, people who dream of writing seem to believe that the only way into print is to write about something exotic: a place they've never been, a lifestyle they've never experienced, an object they've never seen. If they would draw from their immediate environment, their chances for publication would be heightened enormously.

Spinoff writing can stem from other aspects of one's life and lifestyle. From one's hobbies, for example. You may be enjoying one or more hobbies without the slightest thought of ever writing about them. Yet the possibility is always there, waiting to be capitalized upon. Consider these examples:

• An Arizona salesman makes kachina dolls—a very exacting and unusual hobby. He also studies sand-painting, an ancient art practiced for centuries by certain Indians of the American Southwest. He did not adopt these hobbies with the thought of writing about them, but the spinoff possibility occurred to him. Now he writes for craft magazines about both subjects, and finds he has added another hobby—writing—to his inventory of pleasures.

• A California secretary collects and presses wildflowers as a hobby. She found a way to use pressed flowers to make charming greeting cards. As a spinoff, she wrote an article about this unique hobby for a craft magazine.

• A Wisconsin farmer has been a life-long handgun aficionado. He decided to write about his hobby—shooting, and reloading his own ammunition—and has made several sales to shooting and gun magazines.

If you are strictly a homebody, but you have a real knack for cooking, sewing, or gardening, or creative housekeeping, you can "spinoff" these skills into words, and sell them. Articles on these subjects are what keep the women's magazines in business.

If you are a weekend carpenter, plumber, or electrician around the house, with a capacity for inventive thinking and problem-solving, the whole panoply of do-it-yourself magazines is waiting for your spinoff contributions. In one instance a weekend handyman was asked by his wife to figure out how to use an awkward corner of a floor-to-ceiling cupboard. Conventional, fixed shelves wouldn't do—his wife couldn't see the stuff at the back, or reach anything there. So, how to capitalize on this potentially useful space?

He devised a "Christmas tree" of circular shelves, mounted on a length of galvanized pipe, each shelf "floating" loose so it could be revolved. By turning these "lazy Susan" shelves, his wife could instantly inspect their contents, and bring desired items to the front. As a spinoff, the handyman took pictures of his project and wrote a short article describing how to make a "lazy Susan Christmas tree" shelving system. He sold it to a well-known handyman magazine for $150—enough to repay all his construction costs, finance some fishing tackle—and inflate his ego!

Truly, in the matter of spinoffs, the sky is the limit. Put your imagination to work, then harness it to your typewriter—and spin.

chapter 19

It is better to keep still and be thought a
fool, than to speak and remove all doubt.
ADLAI STEVENSON

WRITING
INSTRUCTIONAL
MATERIALS

Just as surely as $E=mc^2$, there is money to be made in writing
instructional materials. Throughout the history of education in
America, starting perhaps with William Holmes McGuffey and his
Eclectic Readers, teachers at all levels have written texts and other
materials which—in numerous cases—have created more income for
their authors than they earned in the classroom. In a few instances,
royalties have made these teacher-authors independently wealthy.

Of course, opportunities to write for this special field are not
limited to academicians. Administrators, executives, workers in
many trades and professions—anyone with depth of knowledge in
his or her line of activity—can combine expertise with a flair for
communications and succeed in this market.

Though textbooks comprise a vital sector of the instructional
materials field, they are by no means the only important category.

Nor, in terms of opportunity, do they offer the primary challenge to the average writer. Here are a few of the other categories, all of which require writers for their production:

- filmstrips
- audio cassettes
- video cassettes and tapes
- curriculum guides
- instructors' manuals
- operators' manuals
- educational films
- self-instruction materials
- technical bulletins
- field service bulletins
- job orientation materials

and many others. The range is enormous, embracing every aspect of education whether it be public or private, industrial or commercial, governmental, institutional, organizational. In every conceivable form of human activity, there is someone who needs to learn something. And a writer must be employed to put that something into printed, spoken, or audiovisual format.

The field has been vastly extended in recent years through advancements in technology, notably in the audio and video areas. And other innovations just around the corner will add even more exciting dimensions: TV superstations which will cover an entire nation or even the world from one site by bouncing signals from satellites; expanded coverage by cable TV, which may one day relegate the familiar rooftop antenna to the status of the dodo; video discs, and other space-age advances which will bring more information to more people, faster and at lower costs.

Most major corporations, and many smaller ones, retain staffs whose job it is to produce training manuals and films, audiovisual aids, and other filmed, taped or printed matter designed to instruct or motivate company personnel. Employment opportunities open on these staffs from time to time. Companies and organizations which do not have their own in-house writers and producers for such materials turn to independent companies which specialize in the production of instructional materials. Many of these companies retain their own writers, while others rely on the help of free lancers.

In sum, writing opportunities exist for both full-time staff writers and for part-time free lancers in the instructional materials field. To break in, one needs to examine the available options, and to decide which he or she wishes to explore first, which second, and so on.

In terms of recognition and professional advancement—though not necessarily in terms of money—textbook writing ranks very high. However, this can be a most difficult field to penetrate. Competition is fierce, and politics may play a role in whether or not a textbook succeeds.

Within a school system, one place to start is with a curriculum development department. By working first in a consultative or advisory capacity, a teacher or administrator may work up to a writing assignment. One assignment then leads to another, until the writer finds that he or she has work lined up for months or years ahead.

In the audiovisual field, a person with special experience and knowledge can turn these assets into money by writing scripts for independent producers, or through staff employment. For free lancers, the same rules apply as those which pertain to breaking into the motion-picture and TV markets (see Chapter 5). AV producers generally do not read finished scripts, or synopses, submitted by unknowns. The general procedure is to submit a query, telling the producer who you are, what you know, and why you consider yourself competent to write for his or her productions. If you have earlier writing credits, cite these. If you have a sample of your work, or can produce one for this purpose, include it with the query (but not a complete script).

Here are some examples of the kinds of materials AV producers are looking for:

- A Champaign, Illinois, company wants material for both business and general audiences.
- An Oakdale, New York, firm seeks AV ideas for elementary-high school language arts students.
- A Pasadena, California, organization produces educational

materials for all levels, kindergarten through college, and for the public-library market for both school-age and adult audiences. It also serves the business and industry markets.

• An Overland Park, Kansas, company specializes in materials for junior and senior high school and college students, and for technical-minded adults. "We need writers who can research a given area and create a script," says their market note.

• A firm in Anacortes, Washington, is interested in "all subjects that schools will buy." It will work with people who can design filmstrips, take photos, and produce the required artwork, write the scripts, and send them the total package ready for production.

• A Stanford, California, outfit produces materials for elementary and secondary grades in social studies—history, biography, economics, anthropology, archeology.

The names, addresses, officers, and editorial needs and requirements of some 150 AV markets are listed in *Writer's Market* and in *Audiovisual Market Place*, both of which are revised annually.

In the textbook and supplementary reader fields, many of the nation's leading publishing houses either are built around this enormous market, or have special divisions to serve it. Departments of education in the various states also produce their own texts, prepared by writers assigned by the departments and printed at state expense.

There are also a number of smaller publishing houses which specialize in instructional materials for a wide range of target audiences. These are listed and described in the various writers' marketing guides cited in the reading list in the Appendix.

chapter 20

LYRICS, LIMERICKS, & OTHER EPHEMERA

In the beginning was the word. . . .

Frank Sinatra said it, and so did St. John. But Ol' Blue Eyes (who phrased it somewhat differently and with a lower-case "w") had something else in mind: song writing.

However, two Oscar-winning tunesmiths disagree: Al Kasha and Joel Hirschhorn argue that either can come first—lyrics or melody. Whichever comes first, the fact remains that all popular tunes require a writer. And it is musical history that some of these writers have achieved world-wide fame, along with fortunes the likes of which have accrued to very few writers of fiction or nonfiction.

But for every songsmith who makes it to the top, there are countless thousands who never even make it to the basement. Nobody knows how many thousands of tunes are written every year, but their number must be staggering. Untold numbers of hopefuls have their musical offspring recorded—some at great expense—and ship them off to one or more of the 16,000 or so music publishers said to be operating in the United States. Most of those offspring bounce right back. And just as there are vanity presses in the prose field (see Chapter 22), there are we-publish-your-song-for-a-fee operators in the music business. Song writers who seriously contemplate underwriting the publication of their own tunes should look very skeptically at this form of publishing before taking the leap.

Writing a song can be a challenge like no other ever faced by a writer. A song, according to Kasha and Hirschhorn, is essentially a short-short story to be set to music. The writer has from 50 to 80 words, no more, in which to set the stage, introduce the characters, unfold the drama, reach a crisis and resolution, and bring the whole thing to a climax that will leave the listener gasping, crying, laughing, sighing or otherwise emoting. A lot of writers can't do that kind of job in 10,000 words, and you have to do it in fewer words than are contained in the paragraph which ends here.

Most music publishers, like their kin in the book and magazine business, prefer queries to the finished product. This is a highly specialized business, so anyone planning to write a query should bone up on the ground rules before writing word one. There are many sources for such information, and some of them are listed at the close of this chapter.

HAPPY BIRTHDAY, DEAR WHOEVER

Creative writers with a flair for making the banal sound bright and witty can collect an occasional check (usually modest) in the greeting-card marketplace. The trick lies in saying what's already been said a trillion times (*Get well, Uncle Zeb*) in a way it's never been said before, which isn't likely. And to say it not only on greeting cards, but on buttons, or bumper stickers, or place mats, or wall plaques, or bathtowels, or beer mugs, or T-shirts, or . . .

In this marketplace, variety is the keynote. There are seasonal cards for every conceivable holiday or special event and for a few inconceivable ones (Be Kind to Your Neighborhood Blacksmith Week). There are topical cards which ride the crest of some current event (Happy Watergate). There are mechanical cards which pop up, pop out, or otherwise contort when opened by the delighted recipient (Well-endowed Maiden Emerges from Birthday Cake). There are sight-joke or visual message cards where the message lies in the artwork and the writer writes nothing (although he or she may contribute the idea, and be paid for it). And of course there are perennial inspirational cards, which may quote profound thoughts from Edgar Guest, Joyce Kilmer, or Senator Sam Erwin designed to make the ill feel well or vice versa.

More than 25 outlets for the greeting-card writer's output are listed in *Writer's Market* alone. Most of these appear to be actively seeking new material, which puts them in refreshing contrast to most of the markets listed under other headings. Phrases such as "we never get enough" and "we are in special need of" are found sprinkled through these market notes. Pay is generally on acceptance, and may range from $1 a line for verse to $50 or more for a concept.

WAIT'LL YOU HEAR THIS ONE!

And then there are gags.

Even cartoonists, it seems, run dry. So they turn for help to writers who take being funny very seriously. Most of the cartoonists who invite free-lance gags appear to pay the writer a 25 percent commission on sales of ideas contributed by the writer.

Here again, as in the song-writing business, certain ground rules must be observed. These rules, and the markets open to gag writers, are detailed in sources included in the reading list in the Appendix.

MISCELLANEA

Finally, there are markets for such ephemera as limericks, advertising slogans, puzzles, contests, and ghosted love letters.

But we must stop somewhere.

V

NON-WRITING
WORK IN THE
WRITING WORLD

chapter 21

The two most beautiful words in the English language are: "Check enclosed."
DOROTHY PARKER

MAKING MONEY WITH WORDS WITHOUT WRITING THEM

Writers can be remarkable people.

But without the help of a lot of non-writers, no writer would ever amount to anything.

Behind every author who ever publishes anything is a small army of men and women who have never written anything—editors, assistant editors, copyeditors, copy readers, researchers, indexers, permissions editors, reprint editors, literary scouts, publishers' representatives, literary agents, translators, and a legion of others. Any one, or all of these, can play an indispensable role in the success of a writer and his or her book, article, play, poem, or other work.

Together, the writer and these "support people" form a wondrous example of literary symbiosis. Without support troops, the writer might as well abandon his or her craft; without the writer, those armies of support troops would become unemployed overnight.

The moral is: If you love the world of words and of books, you don't need to be a writer to live in that world and enjoy its manifold pleasures. Without writing one word for publication, you can become involved in publishing by adapting your talents and your experience to the industry's needs and requirements in any one of a hundred ways.

Here are some of those ways.

IN BOOK PUBLISHING

This nation's book publishers produce every year something in the neighborhood of 30,000 new titles. Thousands of editorial personnel are required to perform a variety of services for an estimated 6,000 or so publishing houses spread from coast to coast.

The key figures in the publishing hierarchy (setting aside the publishers themselves, who sometimes are not book people) are the editors. As a beginner, you will not as a rule start as an editor. Indeed, you may begin in a very humble station, serving an apprenticeship as—perhaps—a secretary, mail clerk, or receptionist. From such modest beginnings you may advance, if you have the qualifications, to other steps on the ladder which can lead to editorships. You may, for example, be given an opportunity to read unsolicited manuscripts which have come in over the transom, and accumulated in the slush pile. If you are good at this work, you may be promoted to editorial-assistant, and eventually move into the upper echelons.

If your forte lies in grammar and syntax, you may be put to work as a copy editor, checking authors' manuscripts for spelling, punctuation, construction, and consistency of style. Persons with strength in this field may seek employment as staff workers, or they may elect to free lance.

The editor with whom an author makes his or her first contact is usually a senior person, known perhaps as a "subject" or "acquisitions" editor, who is charged with coming to terms with the writer on a project favored for publication. This editor acts for the publisher in contracting the writer for work, and oversees negotiations until the manuscript is finally accepted.

At this point, the manuscript passes to a production editor. His or her job (usually her, since the majority of these posts are filled by women) is to shepherd the manuscript through the long and involved production process: design of the book, editing of the manuscript, reading of galley proofs, preparation of illustrations (if any), indexing, transmitting galley proofs to the author, liaison with others engaged in the project, and so forth. This editor also maintains contact with the author during the months of gestation—a demanding and often taxing assignment.

Other editors also may become involved. All of these staff persons may be working on several book projects simultaneously.

EDITORIAL FREE LANCING

Those who prefer to work on their own may elect to free lance for publishing houses and others who may need their special services. Free lancers will also find that many of the smaller houses, and even some of the larger ones, prefer to assign certain types of work to outsiders. It is more economical to contract this work out than to retain year-around employees to do it.

Free lancing is, naturally, more precarious than · salaried employment. But it also has its obvious advantages and fringe benefits, among them a degree of freedom and independence never enjoyed by staffers.

Prerequisites are, in general, the same as those for staff employment, including:

1. At least an undergraduate college degree.
2. A long-standing love affair with the English language, coupled with a fascination for tracking down such editorial miscreants as dangling participles, tautologies, and the abuse of "hopefully."
3. A life-long and irreversible addiction to reading books and any other printed matter which passes within eyesight.

If you lack any or all of these characteristics, you would probably be well advised to seek other employment.

You should also boast a marked capacity for self-discipline, because your hours will be your own and no one will hold you to them. If you succumb to the temptation to procrastinate, or watch television, or walk the dog when you should be editing a manuscript or reading proof (with the deadline noon tomorrow), this work may not be for you.

To get some feel for this kind of activity, sit down with a copy of the publishing industry's "bible," a fat, heavy paperback called *Literary Market Place.*[1] Known informally in the profession as *LMP*, this invaluable guide—revised and published annually—contains a section titled "Free Lance Editorial Work," in which are listed scores of individuals and firms which offer a wide range of services to publishers and others. Here are some samples:

- ○ Editing, writing, rewriting. Educational materials & nonfiction adult & juvenile; specializing in history and social studies.
- ○ Copy editing & production, manuscript analysis & revision, indexing, research, rewrite. Medical, technical & business.

Some may offer simply "indexing," or "proofreading." Others may advertise such specialties as "photo & picture research," or "mathematical & scientific editing." Whatever the specialty, it appears that there will be a call for it sometime, by somebody.

Though the majority of these free lancers have historically been concentrated on the eastern seaboard, notably in the New York metropolitan area, there are many free lancers listed from coast to coast. If you find such a person listed near you, you may wish to write or phone for a word of counsel from a veteran to a newcomer.

When the time comes to offer your services, either as a staff employee or as a free lancer, check *LMP*'s detailed listing of publishing houses for the addresses of those nearest you. Either visit their offices, résumé in hand, or send your résumé with a

---

[1] *Literary Market Place*, issued annually (New York: R.R. Bowker).

well-phrased letter. (Samples of résumés and letters may be seen in a valuable source book which is highly recommended, *The Complete Guide to Editorial Freelancing.*[2])

Nor are publishers your only prospective clients. Free-lance editorial services are needed by advertising agencies, magazines, writers, and printers, to cite a few possibilities. Make the rounds of printers in your area, leaving a résumé and a list of services you offer. Many of these firms print newsletters, brochures, and even full-length books for private clients. Few printers have in-house editing capabilities, and must job out this kind of work. They may be interested especially in indexers, as this is a very specialized activity which requires considerable training and experience. Professors at nearby universities and colleges who are in the process of writing books or learned papers also are potential clients.

Some free lancers have wedged a foot in the door of this marketplace by typing manuscripts at the start. This can be tedious and fatiguing work, but it can lead to more responsible and remunerative assignments.

EDUCATION FOR EDITORIAL WORK

In recent years, publishers have shown an increasing awareness of the need for training people for their industry. The Association of American Publishers, giving formal expression to this concern, has an "Education for Publishing" program with its own full-time director. The program is charged with working with universities on the development of book-publishing courses, and with encouraging publishers to develop their own in-house training programs.

Several noted universities and colleges have been involved in such courses for many years, among them Harvard and Radcliffe (which offer summer curricula), Stanford, Sarah Lawrence, City University of New York, and Hunter College. For further information, consult the *Guide to Book Publishing Courses.*[3]

[2] Carol L. O'Neill and Avima Ruder, *The Complete Guide to Editorial Freelancing* (New York: Dodd, Mead, 1974).
[3] *Guide to Book Publishing Courses* (Princeton, N.J.: Peterson's Guides, 1978).

MAGAZINE PUBLISHING

This branch of publishing also relies heavily on people with special editorial qualifications—men and women who may not themselves be writers, but who are attracted to and understand the world of writers and writing.

Most major magazines, and many smaller ones, will have several key personnel listed as editors. There may be an editor-in-chief, executive editor, managing editor, articles editor, fiction editor, and others assigned to such special departments as food, fashions, sports, fillers, and so forth.

Under these are editorial assistants who research, check facts, and perform other tasks related to manuscript preparation. These personnel often are advanced to the editor positions as openings occur.

There are also copy readers, who check material scheduled for a given issue, watching for grammatical errors and other details. On smaller magazines, the editors themselves may perform these chores. These, or other personnel, may also do the proofreading.

Persons with skills developed in the magazine field will find their talents and experience transferable to other branches of publishing, and even to newspapering.

NEWSPAPERS

Opportunities in this field have been discussed in some detail in Chapter 13. It is obvious that an editor's job in the newspaper business differs radically from his counterpart's work in book publishing, or even in the magazine world. Entirely different qualifications are involved, and these qualifications may not be transferable from the Fourth Estate to the book and magazine industries.

TEACHING

Many of the nation's leading teachers of journalism were once active as full-time reporters, editors, or free-lance nonfiction

writers. Many writers carry a part-time teaching load while continuing to free lance for magazines.

For obvious reasons, people with actual writing experience
are preferred for teaching posts. In the case of magazine writers,
those who have actually sold articles to leading periodicals are
selected over those who know the subject theoretically rather
than empirically.

Except at the high school and junior college level, teachers
without actual writing and selling experience are not, as a rule,
prime candidates for teaching positions. The best way to attract
the attention of a college or university—either for full-time faculty
appointments, or for part-time assignments in extension departments—is to publish.

Assignments also may be obtained by non-writers to teach
such subjects as editing and indexing.

AGENTING

Though most agents are non-writers, all of them are (or should be)
well informed about the world of writers and writing. Many agents
are ex-editors. However, it is probably safe to say that most agents
will not function as editors for the writers on their lists.

An agent's primary asset (and qualification for the job) is
his or her marketing sense—a special "feel" for the right magazine
or book publisher for a given manuscript. Obviously, this is not
a field for amateurs.

TRANSLATING

If you speak and write one or more foreign languages fluently,
you may wish to investigate the opportunities open to translators.
Generally, this is free-lance work.

A helpful resource is the *Education for Publishing Program,* Association of
American Publishers, 1 Park Avenue, New York, N.Y., 10016.

VI

BEING YOUR
OWN PUBLISHER

chapter 22

*It is always the little books, packed with
emotions, aflame with passion, that do the
business.*

VOLTAIRE

SELF-PUBLISHING
& ECCLESIASTES 12:8

For any of a variety of reasons, you may fail to convince a publisher to produce your book. Despair not. Thousands of writers before you—some of them all-time "greats"—have faced the same ugly dilemma, and prevailed.

If publishers scorn your book, you have at least two options before burning your manuscript:

You can become your own publisher—you can self-publish.
or
You can sign up with a "vanity press" that—for an arm and a leg—will publish it for you.

If you join the ranks of the self-published, you will find yourself in such illustrious company as:

• William Caxton, printer, who self-published the first book ever printed in English: *The Recuyell of the Historyes of Troye*, in 1475.

• Thomas Paine, who in 1776 published a 47-page pamphlet called *Common Sense*. Paine priced it at two shillings, and sold 120,000 copies in 90 days. Total sales eventually passed half a million copies—a remarkable feat even today, but phenomenal in those colonial times. This thin work was to exert such enormous influence that the Continental Congress, six months later, proclaimed the independence of the United States of America.

(Paine was following common practice in taking his work to a printer for publication. Before the establishment of commercial publishing houses in the 19th century, this was standard procedure.)

• Washington Irving, who self-published his two-volume *History of New York*, and later his *Sketchbook*.

• Edgar Allen Poe, who in 1827 arranged with a printer to produce 40 copies of a slim volume containing 406 lines of poetry. He called it *Tamerlane and Other Poems*, signed it "A Bostonian," and set the price at 12½ cents. One copy of this exceedingly rare work recently brought $123,000 at an auction.[1]

• John Bartlett's *Familiar Quotations* was published by himself until 1863, when Little, Brown contracted to publish the fourth edition.

The roll call is long and notable, including Walt Whitman (who set type himself for the first edition of *Leaves of Grass*); Edward Fitzgerald, who found no takers for his translation of something called *The Rubaiyat* by an obscure Persian poet named Omar Khayyam; Mary Baker Eddy, who sought the help of friends to publish *Science and Health* after commercial houses saw no market for it; Henry George (*Progress and Poverty*); Kate Douglas Wiggin (her first book, *The Story of Patsy*); Mark Twain (*Huckleberry Finn*); Upton Sinclair (*The Jungle*); Zane Grey (his first novel, *Betty Zane*); Ezra Pound (his first book of poems, *A Lume Spento*); D.H. Lawrence (*Lady Chatterley's Lover*); Anais Nin (*Winter of Artifice* and *Under a Glass Bell*, printed on an old foot-powered press by Ms. Nin herself, with the help of a friend),

---

[1] Robert A. Wilson, *Modern Book Collecting* (New York: Knopf, 1980), p. 97.

and countless others. These were some of the self-published works which gained fame, and deserved it. Others flopped, and deserved to.

And for dramatic relief, this entry: a slim little volume of outhouse ribaldry which shocked—and titillated—America in its more innocent days was self-published by Chic Sale. He called it *The Specialist*, and it sold mightily.

After warning would-be authors about self-publishing ("don't do it"), Ralph Daigh, in his *Maybe You Should Write a Book*, recounts how Rod McKuen published his own book of poems and sold 40,000 copies. When the late Bennett Cerf of Random House heard about this fantastic sales record, he immediately signed McKuen. Random House (among others) still publishes McKuen's work.

Stimulated in recent years by waves of libertarian, protest, off-beat, feminist, alternative and other non-establishment manuscripts, self-publishing has become firmly rooted in literary America. "Small presses" also have proliferated in response to the need for outlets for works of special, limited appeal. Their contribution to American letters is regarded highly by The National Endowment for the Arts, which makes grants to some of these presses to help them survive. The Ford Foundation, through The Coordinating Council of Literary Magazines, also has financed projects in behalf of small presses.

So popular has the subject become that persons contemplating a self-publishing enterprise may now attend seminars, workshops, and courses on self-publishing, offered by individuals and at colleges and universities throughout the nation.

UTOPIA FOR ECOTOPIA

One dramatic success story concerns a contemporary self-publishing enterprise built around the novel *Ecotopia*, by Ernest Callenbach. More than 20 major New York publishers turned down *Ecotopia*. So Callenbach sold shares at $350 each to a dozen friends, and published the book himself. In 1975, he hired two Oregon firms to print and bind the book. Total run: 3,000 copies—2,500 paperbound, 500 hardcover. A firm in Berkeley, California, agreed to distribute the books.

Two years later, after 27,000 copies of *Ecotopia* had been sold and the novel was in its fourth printing, a light went on at Bantam Books—one of the 20 majors which had earlier turned the book down. Bantam made a deal with the shareholders to publish a Bantam edition.

The total investment in *Ecotopia* was "not great," said Callenbach—only $3500. But the 500 hardcovers were "a sad mistake," he noted. These were sent out to "Establishment" reviewers, and netted only one review—in *American Forest*!

TOP MAN ON THE TOTEM

How would you react if you were a publisher, and someone proposed a book on how to carve totem poles? You're right—that's the way they all reacted.

On December 8, 1977, newspapers throughout the country carried the following Associated Press item:

> Anacortes, Wash. (AP)—How could 23 publishers turn down a do-it-yourself guide to totem-pole carving, written by an Italian immigrant grocer?
>
> Undaunted, the author, Paul Luvera, 79, published his book himself. He and his wife of 51 years, Mary, invested $19,000 to have 5,000 copies printed. Mrs. Luvera, who paints totem poles, wrote part of the book.
>
> "It's the one and only book in the United States and Canada on how to carve a totem pole," Luvera said "It should be in great demand.
>
> "We invested all the money we saved, and we knew we could get stuck," said the former miner, grocer and state senator. "We knew we might have to eat a lot of spaghetti."

A year later, I wrote to Mr. Luvera. Did he get stuck? Were he and Mary eating a lot of spaghetti—or maybe books?

Mr. Luvera replied:

> Yes, my book is a huge success. We have sold our 5,000 books in four months, and we are at the end of the second printing and negotiating

for a third. I have an excellent book, and that is not self praise but an actuality. BUT, if Mike Royko of the *Chicago Daily News* (now folded) had not given me such a plug, I don't know what could have happened. Of course, our National Wood Carvers Association (15,000 members) . . . has been very helpful, and so has The Mallet . . . the National Carvers' Museum of Monument, Colorado, and the Associated Press. So you see, I have had some outstanding publicity to help me market the book. Also, word of mouth by people who see the book and the buyers who praise it . . . I feel that my book will be a steady seller, not phenomenal but steady, as more retirees will be buying it. I was 79 years old when Mary and I decided to invest most of our life savings and spent $20,000 to have 5,000 books printed. God must have been our protector.

BIG DIVIDENDS FROM
SMALL VOLUMES

One of the nation's truly unique self-publishing enterprises is the Mosaic Press, owned and operated (virtually single-handedly) by Ms. Miriam Owen Irwin. Ms. Irwin loves and *writes* miniature books, and decided to publish her own writings along with those of others.

These books are the result of months of preparation, hours of conferences, mountains of correspondence, continuous problem-solving, and great, great pleasure in knowing that what we are doing we do very, very well.

At last reports, Editor-Writer-Publisher Irwin's Mosaic Press, in Cincinnati, had published more than 20 of these tiny volumes, some of them no bigger than a man's thumbnail. Many of the titles are intriguing—*Itty Bitty Bottles, Turquoise, Seventeen Haunted Houses, Arachnids, Forty Is Fine,* and *Betsy Ross* among them.

Our bookbinder found some hundred-year-old end paper, and I designed an elegant little book in my mind—paper over boards with a maroon leather spine. It took a year to find the right manuscript for this beautiful binding, and almost two years to find leather thin enough that was just the right color. The subject of this new book is folk medicine![2]

[2] From a letter to the author.

Ms. Irwin admits she has administrative and financial problems . . . but they don't really bother her.

"I am absolutely in love with what I am doing," she says.

And that's what counts.

BEGINNING THE BEGAT

Three old school chums made self-publishing history when they wrote *The Begatting of a President*, mostly for fun. The book is a spoof on the presidency, couched in pseudo-Biblical style. But poor timing doomed their efforts to find a commercial publisher—they sent it around to a dozen houses just as Senator Robert Kennedy was assassinated.

Undaunted, the three authors—Lincoln Hayes, Myron Roberts, and Sasha Gilian—decided to proceed on their own. They briefly considered vanity publishing, but finally decided self-publishing was cheaper.

Fresh from the presses, the first thousand copies of their book were loaded into the trunk of a car, and the authors began the rounds of the booksellers. Buyers were reluctant at first, but then the buyer for UCLA's student bookstore took 10 copies on consignment. The 10 sold out the next day, and the buyer re-ordered. The book then got favorable reviews—one of them by long-time humorist Richard Armour—and gradually caught on.

As sales mounted, the authors decided to take another crack at Publishers' Row. They sent copies, with sales reports, to 45 New York houses. The box score: 44 rejections—and one acceptance, and that's all it takes. The 45th—Ballantine Books—offered a contract, and a healthy advance.

The writers later sold recording rights (narrated by Orson Welles, no less), the book was optioned for film and television, United Feature Syndicate distributed a condensed version to newspapers nation-wide.

In short, *Begatting* begot for its courageous authors.

WEIRD AND WONDERFUL

Further encouragement for prospective self-publishers comes from George Mair. A nationally syndicated columnist (Los Angeles Times Syndicate) and author of eight published books, Mair decided that no one was capitalizing on the wealth of strange and wacky anecdotal material floating around the nation's Capital. So he wrote *The Weird and Wonderful World of Washington.* New York publishers looked at his short manuscript, and told Mair it was too regional. The following is reprinted from a personal letter.

> Some thought it wasn't even a book but, rather, a souvenir shop item. But the most important aspect of my decision to self-publish was time. Big publishers are very slow . . . and my *Weird and Wonderful* little books idea was perishable. . . . Also, most big publishers would not market such a small book with small profit vigorously.[4]

Mair went ahead. Writing and researching took him three months, editing and artwork another 60 days, and printing two weeks. His initial run was 10,000. Cost: $4,700. Mair reports that profit on this first of a series of *Weird and Wonderful* books was not as attractive as he hopes it will be on later volumes, primarily because he "gave book stores a better than normal break to encourage their handling the book at the start."

Others in the series, planned for early release, will cover the White House, Congress, and the Supreme Court (*The Weird and Wonderful Brethren?*).

NUTS AND BOLTS

To self-publish successfully, you will need to become well informed on an astonishing variety of technical questions, such as printing processes (letterpress versus offset), book design (hardcover or paperback), book size (which sizes sell best, and offer the fewest production problems), typefaces (there are scores of these), printing runs (how many copies for your first edition), prices (retail versus the discount price to booksellers), book jackets

[4] From a letter to the author.

(also called dust jackets or covers), distribution (if you print in Peoria, how do you get books to Spokane or Montpelier?), International Standard Book Numbers (ever heard of these?), fulfillment, remaindering unsold copies, and a host of other details.

You will need to select a printer and a binder (getting comparative bids from several). You may need to locate and retain a layout person, an illustrator, and perhaps even an editor to read down your manuscript before type is set, and to ready galley to insure that no errors creep into the printing run.

All these challenges are formidable enough. But the big one lies ahead: marketing. It will do you no good to wind up with a barn full of books. So you'll need to become knowledgeable about selling to the retail trade, to libraries, and to wholesalers. Will you retain commission sales representatives to sell your books, or visit the bookstores yourself (as Walt Whitman did)? Can you make a deal with a commercial publisher who already has a sales network (with maybe 200 or more salespersons in the field) to distribute your books? The answer: Maybe, if you have an item which the commercial publisher recognizes as highly marketable.

These and other technical and business details of self-publishing are discussed in depth in many books and manuals now in print on the subject—some of them self-published. (See Bibliography, pp. 250-51.)

For now, it is sufficient that you realize that the self-publishing route is open. Whether you have the will, the skill, the fortitude—and the cash—to follow this route, you alone can answer.

"Vanity of Vanities, saith the preacher; all is vanity." Ecclesiastes 12:8

Vanity presses, sometimes more charitably dubbed subsidy presses, are almost universally despised and maligned by commercial publishers and professional writers. Most of this antipathy is well deserved, as there are countless recorded cases involving the fleecing of gullible and unsophisticated writers by vanity presses.

It is strictly a case of caveat emptor. Vanity presses offer a commodity on the open market. Their merchandise: a way to turn a manuscript into a book, for a price. Customers always seem to exist who want this commodity, and are willing to pay for it. So buyer and seller get together, and a book is born. In some cases, the customer ends up satisfied, and in a few cases he or she may even sell some books and make a little money. But don't count on it.

The argument is sometimes advanced that vanity presses offer a legitimate service to those who have a book to produce, and cannot bring it into being any other way. The argument has some merit. If the writer goes into the deal with eyes wide open, knowing full well all the ground rules, that is one thing. If that writer then finds himself or herself with X hundreds of copies on hand even after gifts have been made to every conceivable friend and relative and library, that is the writer's problem.

The question of morality arises when an innocent (gullible) writer, unaware of the wolf lurking behind those sheepskins, falls victim to the blandishments of the vanity presses and confuses them with full-fledged commercial publishing enterprises. As one ex-editor for a vanity press put it: "Vanity publishing is to legitimate publishing as loansharking is to banking."

Witness a typical vanity-press advertisement, of the variety often seen in newspapers and heard (in rewritten form) on radio:

> Authors Wanted by New York Publisher. Leading book publisher seeks manuscripts of all types: fiction, poetry, scholarly and juvenile works, etc. New authors welcomed.

That one, complete with name and address of the press, appeared in (among other media) the prestigious *Chronicle of Higher Education*.

Here's another.

> Have You Written a Book? A publisher's editorial representative will be in (name of city) in (month). He will be interviewing local authors in a quest for finished manuscripts suitable for book publication by (name of press), well-known New York publishing firm. All subjects will be considered including fiction and non-fiction, poetry, drama, religion, philosophy, etc. If you have completed a book-length manuscript (or nearly so) on any subject, and would like a professional appraisal (without cost or obligation), please write immediately describing your work and stating which part of the day (a.m. or p.m.) you would prefer for an appointment and kindly mention your phone number. You will promptly receive confirmation for a definite time and place.

Note carefully the wording of these announcements. "Leading book publisher" is the advertiser's own somewhat biased assessment of his status in the publishing community. "Leading" what? (Leading astray?) The adjective also implies that the "publisher" is a member of the same community which includes such prestigious members as Harper & Row, Simon & Schuster, Prentice-Hall, McGraw-Hill, and Little, Brown, which it is not.

The advertiser "seeks" manuscripts of all kinds, including poetry. Anyone who knows anything at all about the realities of publishing will attest that poetry is rarely if ever "sought" by publishers, and that the publication of poetry is virtually always an invitation to lose money. No publisher in his or her right mind would "seek" poetry from unknown, unpublished writers—the deluge of responses would drown Manhattan Island!

The second advertisement contains several dead giveaways which should put even the most gullible prospect on guard. The house, says the ad, is "well-known." By whom? Certainly not by the reader of the ad. Second, there is (again) a bid for poetry. Third, the reader is offered a "professional appraisal (without cost or obligation)." There is no reputable publishing house in the entire industry which will offer a professional appraisal of any manuscript to an unknown writer, and no reputable critic or agent would make such an appraisal "without cost or obligation." These are patently obvious come-ons designed to attract the innocent.

Unfortunately, ads such as these do draw clients, to the ultimate regret of many writers who—year after year—are separated from their money. One West Coast vanity press filed for bankruptcy after fleecing customers from California, Washington, Arizona, Minnesota, Michigan, and as far away as Saudi Arabia. A California author put nearly $60,000 into subsidies with this press for a lavishly printed and illustrated book of poetry. At last report, copies of this book and of the books of many other victims were languishing in a warehouse, while lawyers wrangled over suits and countersuits involving the press's previous owners and the impending bankruptcy.

The sorry world of vanity presses has been subject to multimedia investigations. What it all boils down to is this: Vanity presses really are nothing more than printers. They are not publishers. Any writer may have his book produced by a printer, virtually any printer. But this is not publishing, in the true sense. Publishing involves not only the physical act of printing and binding a book. It also involves, before and after the act of printing, a myriad of other services—editing, layout, book design, illustration, sales, promotion, the obtaining of reviews, issuance of re-runs, inventorying the product, negotiations with foreign publishers for overseas rights, negotiations with film and television studios for movie and broadcast rights, deals with book clubs, translations, and so forth.

The most important function performed by publishers—apart from the physical act of producing the book—is marketing. A major publishing house may have scores, if not hundreds, of salespeople on the road, contacting libraries, bookstores, schools and other potential purchasers. A vanity publisher simply cannot afford to maintain a large marketing staff. Printers simply are not in the business of selling and promoting books. So, if you are tempted by the siren-song of a vanity-press advertisement, quickly put plugs in your ears.

If you are determined to get your work into type, no matter what, go to a reliable printer. In other words, self-publish.

I hear, and I forget.
I see, and I remember.
I do, and I understand.

Chinese proverb

THE APPENDICES

TIPS AND HINTS FOR WRITING
(OR REWRITING) ARTICLES
FOR THE MOTHER EARTH NEWS[1]

1. KNOW WHAT YOU'RE WRITING ABOUT. It's amazing how many "how-to" articles we receive from people who don't know "how to". Articles full of misinformation, hazy instructions that evade salient points, and cop-outs such as "I think it would have worked better if we'd mixed the concrete a little richer, but we never tried it."

SO RESEARCH YOUR SUBJECT. Know it inside out *before* you try to tell someone else about it. It's not enough to inform our readers that you've raised ducks and you think they're groovy. Get specific. And exhaustive (without being a bore). Tell 'em quickly how successful you've been with ducks and then give 'em *everything* they'll need to duplicate that success. Or surpass it. Tell *THE* reader (and always remember that you're communicating directly to *ONE* single individual who is exactly as intelligent as you are) how to go about locating ducks or eggs of his or her own . . . how to pick the best breed for him or her to raise . . . how to make a suitable home for the birds . . . what to feed them . . . how to protect the flock from predators . . . how to protect your garden or sidewalks or children from the flock . . . how to sex and mate the birds . . . how to hatch duck eggs in an incubator, under a duck, under a hen, and in other ways (if there are any) . . . what particular quirks that ducks have that might not have been expected . . . how to kill and pluck a duck . . . how to cook one of the birds (with recipes) . . . how to raise the web-footed fowl as a small or large cash crop . . . how to use feathers and down in pillows, comforters, and outdoor clothes . . . etc., etc., etc.

Since we like firsthand reports and "down home" flavor, it's very probable that you'll want to tie your article together by basing it—at least in part—on your own personal experiences. And that's fine. Still, it's highly unlikely that you've personally experienced everything there is to know about ducks simply because you've raised 15 or 20 or 2,000

[1] Excerpts and form letter reprinted with permission from *THE MOTHER EARTH NEWS*, copyright © 1977 by *The Mother Earth News*, Inc., PO Box 70, Hendersonville, N.C. 28739. One-year subscription, $15.00.

of them. So ask, read, inquire about the subject. *Delve* into it. Flesh out your own experiences with the experiences of others who've kept ducks. Talk to such people in your own area. Stop and exchange information with others when you're on vacation. Read the trade journals that cover the field. Check out every book that your library carries on the subject. Order catalogues from dealers in ducks and duck eggs. Track down state and federal pamphlets about raising the birds. Look over the ducks being shown at the state fair. USE YOUR IMAGINATION, BUT FIND OUT EVERY DAMN THING THERE IS TO KNOW ABOUT DUCKS. *Before* you begin to parade your knowledge in front of our readers.

This, of course, is *not* to say that every dreary fact that you dredge up will go into the final article. But until you have a genuine and near-exhaustive working knowledge of what ducks are actually all about, you're only kidding yourself when you think you know what to leave in and what to drop from that finished and polished piece. SO DO YOUR HOMEWORK BEFORE YOU EVER TOUCH TYPEWRITER TO PAPER. Our readers expect you to write with authority . . . not to guess at the facts.

2. MAKE SURE, BEFORE YOU BEGIN, THAT YOU KNOW WHAT WRITING IS ALL ABOUT. Few people do, you know. Most beginning authors foolishly think that their work is "good" or "bad" because of "style" (whatever that is) . . . when the real question is whether or not they have anything worthwhile or interesting to communicate. Most beginners, in short, approach the whole problem wrong-end-to.

IDEAS AND *EMOTIONS*. That's what writing and editing are really all about. *Not* words. *Not* punctuation. *Not* syntax. *Not* grammar. *Not* "style". What you're really trying to do, if you want to be an effective writer or editor, is get a *pure* idea out of your head or a *pure* emotion out of your heart . . . and put that idea (intact!) or that emotion (intact!) into the head or the heart of your reader. That's what it's all about. Period.

6. IT'S AWFULLY HARD TO BEAT A TIME SEQUENCE WHEN YOU'RE ORGANIZING A HOW-TO ARTICLE. We are constantly dumbfounded, here at THE MOTHER EARTH NEWS, by manuscripts that contain such catchy little phrases as, "Next you put the bearings

back into the case, but I'll get to that later," or "And I forgot to tell you back when you were setting the generator on the tower that if you don't bolt it down right then it'll probably slip off and kill you."

If you can't tell your reader how to do something in a step-by-step sequence (with each step fully and completely explained at the time it's introduced), you have no business trying to write a how-to article. Skipping blithely back and forth from one spot to another may be a winning tactic in hopscotch . . . but it has absolutely no place in the construction of an article that aspires to teach anyone anything. Bear in mind that your poor reader (who obviously has been attracted to your piece because he or she wants to learn something that he or she doesn't already know) has a big enough job on his or her hands already. Don't complicate your transfer of information with sloppy, slipshod, and slovenly organization.

Break your total lump of information down into bite-sized bits and then put your arm around the reader's shoulder and spoon-feed that nourishment to him or her *starting* with the appetizer, and *proceeding* (without backtracking) through the soup and salad to the main course, and *closing* with the dessert.

8. ALWAYS STRIVE TO WRITE WITH ABSOLUTE CLARITY. Bear in mind *constantly* that the English language (*any* language, for that matter) is a very imperfect carrier of ideas and emotions . . . especially when frozen to a piece of paper and sent hundreds of miles away for final consumption by an individual who has tastes, prejudices, priorities, pressures, goals, and a background that is considerably different from your own. An individual who, to boot, may well try to read your masterpiece under a poor light while distracted by a shoot-'em-up on TV, a dog fight in the back room, and a wet baby in his or her lap. Under such circumstances, there are an almost infinite number of ways for the reader to miss some, most, or all of your article . . . or misinterpret major or minor points in the piece . . . or, while reading the whole thing and understanding it, fail to catch the spark of enthusiasm that you wanted him or her to catch.

What I'm saying is that the odds are overwhelmingly *against* you when you sit down behind a typewriter with the intention of informing and inspiring people. You're playing with one hell of a stacked deck . . .

and, if you expect to win the game, you'd better be able to handle the cards with utterly professional shrewdness and dexterity. Muddy thoughts and copy fumbles don't make it. THINK CLEAN. WRITE CLEAN. THINK AND WRITE WITH ABSOLUTE PRECISION AND CLARITY. Because if you don't, you're licked before you start.

25. WATCH YOUR LANGUAGE, PART II. Please don't try to write for MOTHER (or any other magazine) unless you know the rudiments of the English language.

Don't—in other words—say, "We're not sure we can but, hopefully, we'll get the job done"... when you *really* mean, "We're not sure we can but we hope we'll get the job done." (The first version of the foregoing sentence is such a complete bastardization of the King's English that any writer guilty of the crime should be immediately drawn and quartered and dragged to the four points of the compass by wild horses.)

Don't, in other words, say something is decimated (cut by one-tenth) when you mean "devastated" (wiped out completely).

Don't say that someone told you verbally ... when you mean "orally" or "vocally".

Don't tell me you're nauseous (because you certainly *are*) ... when you mean "nauseated".

26. KNOW THE LIMITATIONS OF THE WRITTEN WORD. Sometimes a sketch, a drawing, or a photograph can transmit an idea or an emotion much better and with much greater impact and economy than the most adroit copy. To coin a maxim: "One picture is (frequently) worth 10,000 words."

27. AND NOW THAT YOU KNOW DAMN NEAR EVERYTHING WE DO, *WRITE BRIGHT*! I didn't *have* to tell you to "use every possible rule of civilized *word*fare" back in (8), you know. Nor did I *have* to talk about communicating "starbursts" of feeling. And maybe I shouldn't have.

Then again, I know of no law that requires an author to limit him or her self to the same dull, dead, gray boilerplate that most of the rest of today's "writers" deal in. Have we all turned into IBM machines? Does no one now know how to sprinkle flecks of silver and gold into his or her copy? Are all the magical wordsmiths who once used nothing but paper and ink to conjure up misty moors, melodious chimes, and shimmering sunsets in the minds of their readers . . . all . . . gone. . . .?

I think not. I hope not. I prefer to believe that such crafts men and women have only temporarily been forced to hide up in the cool, green hills . . . while the brutish mutants who identify everything by social security numbers and view the world through 18-inch screens and who lurch back and forth across the valley floor on clangorous trail bikes and snowmobiles and converse with such depthy expressions as "wow" and "you know" have their day. A short one.

And soon, those who value the texture and the color and the emotion and the feel and the nuances of the language will once again be able to practice and strengthen their craft. And today's stainless steel computerese will once again give way to living, breathing words that soothe and cradle grown people's hearts in the mysterious and marvelous worlds that language can create.

In the meantime, the least you can do is try to brighten and focus and intensify every part of every sentence you write for THE MOTHER EARTH NEWS. I expect nothing less.

John Shuttleworth
Editor-Publisher
The Mother Earth News

Author's Note: **Excerpts** from the preceding guidelines are issued free to interested writers by *The Mother Earth News*, explaining what the magazine's editors want, and how they want it written. The editors have gone to considerable trouble—13 single-spaced pages of it—to help writers. Free lancers interested in working for *Mother* should write for a copy, enclosing a SASE.

To answer free lancers who send queries or manuscripts, *The Mother Earth News* uses the following form letter. It is a one-stop education in (1) why editors reject manuscripts or ideas, and (2) why they accept them. Study the form carefully—it contains more information than many textbooks on article writing.

224

DEAR CONTRIBUTOR:

☐ Please forgive this printed letter. It's the only way we can keep up with the mail.

☐ Here's a report on your ☐ query,_____ ☐ article,_____

☐ Thanks for the query, but we just aren't interested in this subject at this time. ☐ Your query _sounds_ good. We'd like to see the article.

☐ Please study the enclosed slant sheet and 14-page mini-manual. They'll help you zero in on our audience and our current needs.

☐ This one just isn't for us. See our enclosed slant sheet.

☐ We feel that this article is of only marginal interest to our readers.

☐ This isn't really up to our standards. Please study the enclosed 14-page manual.

☐ Our readers don't appreciate that much philosophy.

☐ This is a Sunday supplement piece . . . not the how-to material our readers want.

☐ Your treatment is too academic for us.

☐ The treatment is too light for our readers. They demand more meat.

☐ There's not enough involvement for our readers here.

☐ Your treatment is too brief,_____, for this subject.

☐ Your treatment is too long,_____, for this subject.

☐ The writing is too personal.

☐ Our audience doesn't want to be preached at.

☐ We're just too overstocked to consider this one at this time.

☐ We've got other treatments of this subject in our files.

☐ Nice, but we've got articles on this subject running out our ears.

☐ Sorry, but we've done this subject ☐ recently. ☐ to death.

☐ This piece would probably be of more interest to _____

☐ We like your subject, but _____

☐ You seem to write well but you haven't picked a subject of primary interest to our readers. Study the enclosed slant sheet and try us again.

☐ Your material is better than most of the submissions we see. We hope you'll try us again. ☐ You're close, but not quite there.

☐ Although we can't yet promise we'll buy it, we'd like to see this piece again . . . but rewritten as noted elsewhere on this sheet.

☐ See Point Number(s) _____ in the enclosed 14-page manual.

☐ We're not interested in seeing a rewrite of this piece at this time. ☐ Would you like to try us again with this one in about_____ ?

☐ We like this material but wonder if you'd like to ☐ rewrite ☐ update it before we give it further consideration?

☐ We like it! Our check is enclosed for_____ (_____of this is for the article and_____is for ☐ photographs ☐ artwork.) Please remember that we buy any use we might ever want to make of this material while, at the same time, leaving you free to resell it as many times as you like.

☐ We'll publish your material in an upcoming issue of THE MOTHER EARTH NEWS®, one of our books, and/or wherever else we find a spot for it. At that time, you'll receive complimentary copies of "your" issue of the magazine, book, or whatever. But be patient: We draw from an enormous file of material and it may be some time before this submission appears in print.

☐ The enclosed check for_____is a holding fee. We're sorry we kept your submission so long.

☐ The enclosed check for_____is a resubmission fee. We still can't use this material, but we _did_ ask to see it again, so . . . .

☐ Here's an additional payment of_____for your article_____. The piece ☐ ran longer ☐ worked up better than we expected and we feel that you're entitled to the extra payment. The complimentary copies of "your" issue of the magazine and/or book and/or other publication that this article appears in are being sent to you under separate cover. Enjoy! Enjoy!

☐ Remember that a picture is worth 10,000 words. How about a ☐ drawing ☐ floor plan ☐ schematic that explains what you're talking about?

☐ We like the piece, but we'll need some good ☐ black and white glossy photographs ☐ color slides or transparencies to illustrate it. If you can supply them (try a local newspaper photographer if you can't take the pictures yourself), send the article back to us—rewritten, if necessary, as noted on this sheet—accompanied by the photos and/or slides. (And send us a bill for the photos and/or slides.)

☐ This piece would have received more consideration if accompanied by good, clear photos. ☐ What about color transparencies or color slides?

☐ Do you have any ☐ additional ☐ better photographs or illustrations to add to this submission? ☐ The photos are better than the copy!

☐ Editors' eyes receive a tremendous amount of wear. All manuscripts should be typed, double-spaced, with a black ribbon on white 8-1/2 X 11 paper.

☐ PLEASE RETURN THIS SHEET WITH ANY QUERY/QUESTION/RESUBMISSION/UPDATE/ADDITIONAL INFORMATION HAVING TO DO WITH THIS SUBMISSION.

☐ Please address all queries/questions/resubmissions having to do with this submission to _____

☐ All other submissions/queries/questions should be directed to Submissions Editor, THE MOTHER EARTH NEWS®, P.O. Box 70, Hendersonville, N.C. 28739.

PHOTOS:
THEY'RE MORE IMPORTANT THAN YOU THINK!

We hope this book will help you to get better photographs for OGF. We are happy that many of our contributors have improved the quality of the photos they send in within the last few years, but there is still plenty of room for improvement.

If you keep these two thoughts in mind, it may help:

A. Try to get pictures that will arouse the interest of the reader in what you are saying.

B. Get pictures that will force the reader to understand your subject. (If you say in your article that John Jones' tomatoes are bigger than those his neighbor grows next door, get a picture of the two groups of tomatoes side by side.)

If you are not a photographer, or if you feel that your own photos may not be suitable, please scout around the vicinity of your subject to find the names of one or more commercial photographers whom we could commission to take the necessary pictures. We do this quite often, and with good results. It makes *your* articles look better, and makes our readers happier, too.

When you submit an article which you feel could be illustrated better, you might include a list of picture opportunities and angles which would be helpful to a commercial photographer whom we send to the site.

Here is another important point: Please send us the negatives of the pictures you take as well as the prints—unless you are sure that your prints are of top quality. Very often, prints made by photofinishers are not reproduction calibre, and we can achieve better printing results by making our own prints from your negatives.

If you have your local photofinisher make 5" x 7" or 8" by 10" *custom* enlargements of your pictures, you are likely to get quality suitable for reproduction, and you will save us the trouble and the time of making the prints ourselves.

Occasionally, a contributor asks us to recommend camera equipment that he should use. We feel that a 2¼ x 2¼ inch twin lens reflex is best, because it will focus easily and you can see what you are getting. However, you can take good pictures with many types of cameras. If you have specific questions about your own camera equipment or photographic problem relating to our magazine, we will be glad to try to answer them.

Author's Note: Photos that help to illustrate your stories are always welcomed. Here are some tips for amateur or professional photographers.

*Author's Note: The inspirational or self-help magazines are constantly searching for competent writers with something useful to say. The editors of *Home Life* describe their editorial needs as follows in their guidelines.

Preparing Your Manuscript

1. Give approximate word count.

2. Give full name, address, and Social Security number in top left-hand corner of first page.

3. Begin first page with title and by-line centered halfway down page.

4. Manuscript should be typewritten, double-spaced, with at least 1½-inch margins on white bond paper.

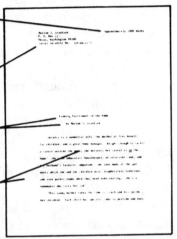

5. Document all quotes, statistical information, and unusual facts. Provide photocopies of sources if possible.

6. Use *Webster's New Collegiate Dictionary*, eighth edition, for spelling and hyphenation of words.

7. Include self-addressed, stamped envelope for return.

8. Mail to:
   Editor
   Home Life
   127 Ninth Avenue, North
   Nashville, Tennessee 37234

In General...

Since *Home Life* is a Christian family magazine, all materials submitted should be (1) Christian in tone and theme and (2) related to family life. We prefer first-person, experience-centered material, but the case study approach is acceptable. This means that all materials must have a strong, human interest angle.

We prefer articles (actual experiences and case studies) which are 1200-1400 words, but longer ones are occasionally acceptable. Short stories (fiction) should fall within the 2,000-2,500 word range, and shorter ones are always welcome. We also need poetry — metric and free verse, humorous and serious. We prefer 4-16 lines.

Fillers (500 words or less) should be family-oriented or devotional in nature. Brief accounts of humorous or meaningful incidents in your own family are always welcome.

Our payment rates are as follows: (1) articles and short stories, 2½¢ per word; (2) poetry, from $5.00 to $10.00 per poem, depending on length; (3) cartoons, $15.00 each.

For Instance...

Anything that concerns the Christian family is possible subject matter for *Home Life*. Here are some topics which have appeared in *Home Life* articles in past issues:

Husband-wife Relationships
Adoption
Foster Parents
Aging Parents
Parent-teen Communication
Family Crises
Society's Influence on the Family
The Family and the Church

Art Guidelines
Cartoonists and Photographers

All photographs and illustrations in *Home Life* are done on assignment by professional photographers and illustrators. However, we are in the market for free-lance cartoons with a family orientation. Please send all your cartoons with acetate overlays marked clearly for a second color. Please sign your work, since *Home Life* does not give type-set credits.

Professional Free-lance Illustrators

Home Life requires the highest quality in its illustrations. If you are interested in doing illustrations for *Home Life*, send us several sample pieces that represent your various styles. Formal assignments are made by the artist-designer, who will specify the style of art he wants from you. Send samples of your work to him at 127 Ninth Avenue, North, Nashville, Tennessee 37234.

Author's Note: The following guidelines for writers describe the needs and requirements of *Bride's* magazine. Much of the advice given here would apply with equal relevance to writing for any consumer magazine. Note the distinction between material generated by free-lance contributors and staff writers.

SUGGESTIONS FOR WRITERS[3]

When you choose the topic of a feature article for BRIDE'S, think of a current sociological or psychological issue, then link it to the ongoing concerns of marriage in a constantly changing world. Zero in on a narrow aspect of something significant, something salient. But, of course, choose a subject that's universal enough to give almost every happy but anxious young woman the sense that you're talking to her alone. Avoid elevating a string of cute anecdotes to feature proportions or settling on a topic that relates best to the wife with children. Also, don't duplicate the work of our staff, who thoroughly cover wedding planning and customs, decorating, fashion, beauty, travel. And forget about poetry and fiction, too.

When you test the viability of your idea, ask yourself, "How will this help a bride adjust to her new role?" Consider it your mission to explain and to guide—even at the expense of journalistic balance, news value, and amusement. At the same time, remind yourself that every couple deserve to choose their own lifestyle free from any stereotypes, traditional or modern.

When you gather your material, do background reading, if necessary. But plan to incorporate the knowledge you thus gain in presenting your own sensitively worded generalizations. For emphasizing those important specifics, rely on primary research—interviews with young couples and with marriage experts, like psychologists, physicians, social workers, and so on. And if you've ever been married, don't overlook yourself as a special source. In the process, take no photographs or make no sketches with the intent of their being published.

When you write the piece, address yourself to a first-time bride in her early twenties, who grew up as the girl-next-door. Choose a format that not only suits the material and your style but also conveys warm implications to her. You might try a first or second person narrative, maybe divided into sections by sub-topic; accompanied with instructive interpretations; a quiz, designed for a couple to take together; a series of questions and answers, geared to teach technical matters; a chart, drawn up to present related facts economically. Organize your article carefully, giving it a sparkling introduction, a tight body, and an optimistic conclusion. Remember that such simple, concrete organization as well as short sentences, consistent voice, clear definitions, and precise logic make intangible or difficult concepts easy to understand. Use direct and indirect quotations liberally. And include plenty of real-life case histories (especially the gently humorous) as brighteners and illustrations, but avoid any sad tales that admit of no solutions. Keep in mind, too, that on occasion our suggestions can be ignored beautifully. In any case, limit your piece to 1,500 to 2,500 words.

When you submit your story, type it double-spaced on heavy, white paper. Attach a cover letter and self-addressed, stamped envelope, then mail it to BRIDE'S, Copy and Features Department, Condé Nast Building, 350 Madison Avenue, New York, New York 10017. Look for a response from us in three–four weeks. Should you succeed in selling us the piece (plus all rights), expect a check for $350 to $550 two–three weeks later. However, if you are asked to make any changes by one of our editors, don't plan on payment until you've completed your revision. To save yourself time and energy, you may send us a detailed outline of your proposed piece before going ahead. But remember, unless we see your article in finished form, we can't promise to buy it. If you need more specific examples of what we print, pick up any issue of BRIDE'S for $2 per copy at your newsstand. Finally, don't trust that we'll claim all responsibility for your unsolicited manuscript. But do trust that we'll read it with sincere and hopeful interest.

---

[3] Reprinted by Permission of *Bride's* Magazine, a Condé Nast publication.

Author's Note: Alfred Hitchcock's Mystery Magazine and its companion publication, *Ellery Queen's Mystery Magazine,* now in its fortieth year, read all "over the transom" submissions, and take pride in publishing newcomers. Many of today's mystery-writing "greats" began their careers in one or both of these magazines.

ALFRED HITCHCOCK'S MYSTERY MAGAZINE

380 LEXINGTON AVENUE
NEW YORK, N.Y. 10017

In reply to your query regarding the requirements for manuscripts submitted to *Alfred Hitchcock's Mystery Magazine,* we hope the following will help you and wish you good luck as a future contributor. This information should help you decide if your story conforms to our editorial needs. We do, in any event, give all stories received full consideration.

We use new stories ranging from 1,000 to 10,000 words in length and, as this is a mystery-suspense-crime-fiction magazine, subject matter should fit into this category. Originality, good writing, ingenious plotting and plausible characterizations will determine acceptance or rejection.

Any manuscripts submitted to AHMM are also read, for the author's convenience, as possibilities for *Ellery Queen's Mystery Magazine.* Our rates are basically the same as those paid by EQMM, with payment made on acceptance.

All manuscripts must be typewritten, double-spaced on plain white bond paper, and accompanied by a self-addressed stamped envelope of suitable size. Your name and address should appear on the title page. It will benefit you to study a copy of *Alfred Hitchcock's Mystery Magazine* before submitting material to the magazine so as to familiarize yourself with the range and quality of fiction we publish.

ELLERY QUEEN'S
Mystery Magazine
A DAVIS PUBLICATION

380 LEXINGTON AVENUE · NEW YORK, N.Y. 10017 · 212-557-9100

Ellery Queen, Editor
Eleanor Sullivan, Managing Editor

Ellery Queen's Mystery Magazine is always in the market for the best detective, crime, and mystery stories being written today -- by new writers as well as by "name" writers. We have no editorial taboos except those of bad taste. We publish every type of mystery: the suspense story, the psychological study, the deductive puzzle -- the gamut of crime and detection from the realistic (including the policeman's lot and stories of police procedure) to the more imaginative (including "locked rooms" and "impossible crimes"). We need private-eye stories, but do not want sex, sadism, or sensationalism-for-the-sake-of-sensationalism. We especially are interested in "first stories" -- by authors who have never published fiction professionally before -- and have published more than 500 first stories since EQMM's inception.

Ellery Queen's Mystery Magazine is now in its 38th year of publication, and critics agree it is the world's leading mystery magazine. From the beginning there have been three criteria: quality of writing, originality of plot, and professional craftsmanship. These criteria still hold and always will. The most practical way to find out what EQMM wants is to read EQMM: every issue will tell you all you need to know of our standards, and of our diversified approach.

We use stories of almost every length. 4,000-6,000 is the preferred range, but we occasionally use stories of 10,000 words. Short-shorts of 1,500-2,000 words are also welcome. Manuscripts submitted to EQMM are considered alternatively, for the author's convenience, for Alfred Hitchcock's Mystery Magazine. Authors retain all subsidiary and supplementary rights, including movies and television (a remarkable number of stories from EQMM have appeared and are still appearing on TV). Our rates for original stories are from 3¢ to 8¢ a word.

We are also looking for fine reprints -- any type of crime, detective, or mystery story, no matter where it has been published before (providing the author owns and controls the reprint rights), and no matter how long ago the story first appeared.

We urge you to support the high standards of EQMM by writing the best mystery stories of our time, and by giving EQMM first chance to publish them. Note to beginners: It is not necessary to query us as to subject matter or to write asking for permission to submit a story. We do not want fact-detective cases or true stories; this is a fiction magazine. All manuscripts should be typed on one side of the paper and double-spaced. Please enclose a self-addressed stamped envelope of suitable size in case the manuscript must be returned; if outside the U.S., use International Postal Reply coupons for return postage. Please do not ask for criticism of stories; we receive too many submissions to make this possible.

Author's Note: An example of a model release form used by magazines to protect photographers and the publication itself. Reprinted by permission of Volkswagen of America, Inc.

MODEL RELEASE

FORM FOR A MINOR

I, _____, hereby consent

to the following use of _____

(Minor's name)

name, portrait, picture and photograph by Volks-

wagen of America, Inc. in its publication Small

World, or any of its other publications, together

with the following biographical materials con-

cerning _____:

(Minor's name)

_____

_____

_____

(Description of material)

I hereby certify that I am the parent (or

guardian) of _____.

(Minor's name)

Date: _____

_____

(Signature)

234

MODEL RELEASE
Form for an Adult

In return for _____ and other considerations, I, _____, hereby consent to the use of my name, portrait, picture and photograph by Volkswagen of America, Inc. in its publication Small World, or in any other publication, together with any biographical materials concerning me.

_____

_____

_____
(Description of material)

Furthermore, I hereby release Volkswagen of America, Inc. from any and all claims for damages for libel, slander, invasion of the right of privacy or any other claim based upon the use of said material.

Date: _____

Signature: _____

Address: _____

City, State, Zip: _____

Author's Note: The guidelines for *Organic Gardening and Farming* are another example of the methods used by magazine editors to help potential contributors write salable articles appropriate for a specific publication. Reprinted by permission.

HOW TO GET GOOD ARTICLE IDEAS

Many people who would like to write articles for OGF (or for any magazine) are puzzled as to how to get good ideas for articles. They know how to write clear prose and they know how an article should be constructed, but they don't have exciting and colorful things to write about. One way to get good article ideas is to find interesting people to write about. A large percentage of good magazine articles are centered about people. But you have to find the right person. There are people who have done important things and who have a worthwhile story to tell—but they are unable to tell it themselves. Many of the most successful writers know how to seek out and associate with people who have stories that are asking to be told. Nothing will breathe new life into your writing like a half-day visit with a person who has a story worth telling.

How do you find the "right" people? You have to know their haunts. Here are some places to look for them:

Meetings of the specialist plant societies and organic gardening group meetings.

Or visit a college and just walk in on the horticulture, botany or agriculture department and start talking to the professors.

Talk to garden editors of newspapers. You will find them challenging people and they will be acquainted with gardeners who are worth visiting.

Visit your county agent.

And there are plenty of other places to find the kind of people we are talking about.

You can also get good article ideas by reading the right books, magazines and newspapers, but we think that the articles inspired by *people* are the easiest to write.

SCIENCE AS A SOURCE OF ARTICLE IDEAS

OGF does not agree with some of the beliefs of modern technology, but that is not to say that we are in any basic conflict with science. Science is classified knowledge, and we feel that the more man learns about his world the more appreciation he has of the value of a life as close to nature as possible. Some of the technological methods we are opposed to, such as the widespread use of poisonous sprays, can be best debunked by a revelation of the scientific facts concerning their areas of use.

So don't overlook science as a source of article ideas for us. Look through the technical and scientific journals in your library—especially the ones relating to the life sciences—and you may be surprised how much challenging article potential you find.

The basic purpose of any magazine in a specialized field is to keep its readers aware of all information available in that field. A specialized magazine like OGF must report the new developments in plant breeding, horticulture, soil science, biology, botany and many other disciplines. And it must relate that information to the practical techniques its readers use.

HOW ARE ARTICLES JUDGED?

Each manuscript submitted to ORGANIC GARDENING AND FARMING is read and considered by a group of editors. Here are the qualities they look for in deciding on the use of any material:

1. Does the article present new information that will be of value to readers?

2. Does it hold interest from beginning to end?

3. Is it written in clear, readable language?

4. Does it represent adequate (or more-than-adequate) research and preparation?

5. How much response will it elicit from readers?

These qualities are not necessarily listed in their order of importance, but keep in mind that each one is a factor in selecting good articles.

Measure your writing and each story you send to us for consideration up to these criteria. Remember, we are proud of the *quality* of the editorial material we have been providing OGF subscribers with—now numbering well over 800,000, by the way, and we are proud of *you,* the people creating that material.

BIBLIOGRAPHY

ADVERTISING AND PUBLIC RELATIONS

American Association of Advertising Agencies, *The Advertising Business and Its Career Opportunities*. (Free Booklet) American Association of Advertising Agencies, 200 Park Avenue, New York, New York 10017.

Center, Allen H., *Public Relations Practices: Case Studies*. Englewood Cliffs, N.J.: Prentice-Hall, 1975.

Kleppner, Otto and Irving Settel, *Exploring Advertising*. Englewood Cliffs, N.J.: Prentice-Hall, 1969.

Lesly, Phillip, *Lesly's Public Relations Handbook*, 2nd ed. Englewood Cliffs, N.J.: Prentice-Hall, 1978.

BOOK REVIEWING

Kamerman, Sylvia E., *Book Reviewing*. Boston: The Writer, 1978.

EDUCATION (WRITING FOR)

Association of American University Presses, *One Book—Five Ways: The Publishing Procedures of Five University Presses*. Los Altos, California: W. Kaufmann, 1978.

Barnes, James, (ed.), *Audiovisual Market Place: A Multimedia Guide*. New York: Bowker, issued annually.

Beedon, Laurel and Joseph Heinmiller, *Writing for Educational Journals*. Bloomington, Indiana: Phi Delta Kappa, 1979.

Cross, Peter R., *Write a Teacher-Aid Book: An Author's Guide*. Belmont, California: Fearon, 1978.

Edmonds, Robert, *Script Writing for the Audio-Visual Media*. New York: Teachers College, 1978.

Linton, Marigold, *A Simplified Style Manual: For the Preparation of Journal Articles in Psychology, Social Sciences, Education & Literature*. Englewood Cliffs, N.J.: Prentice-Hall, 1972.

Pickett, Nell and Ann A. Laster, *Writing for Occupational Education*. New York: Harper & Row, Pub., 1974.

Zenger, Weldon F. and Sharon K. Zenger, *Writing and Evaluating Curriculum Guides*. Belmont, California: Fearon, 1973.

FICTION (CONFESSIONS)

Feldhake, Susan C., *Writing Confessions*. Boston: The Writer, 1980.

Palmer, Florence K., *The Confession Writer's Handbook*. Cincinnati: Writer's Digest, 1975.

FICTION (GENERAL)

Cassill, R.V., *Writing Fiction*. Englewood Cliffs, N.J.: Prentice-Hall, 1975.

Kirkland, James W. and Paul W. Dowell, *Fiction: The Narrative Art*. Englewood Cliffs, N.J.: Prentice-Hall, 1977.

Knott, William C., *The Craft of Fiction*. Reston, Virginia: Reston, 1977.
Koontz, Dean R., *Writing Popular Fiction*. Cincinnati: Writer's Digest, 1972.
Owen, Jean Z., *Professional Fiction Writing*. Boston: The Writer, 1974.
Rockwell, F.A., *How To Write Plots That Sell*. Boston: The Writer, 1975.
Rockwell, F.A., *Modern Fiction Techniques*. Boston: The Writer, 1969.

FICTION (MYSTERY, SUSPENSE)

Burack, A.S. (ed.), *Writing Suspense and Mystery Fiction*. Boston: The Writer, 1977.
Highsmith, Patricia, *Plotting and Writing Suspense Fiction*. Boston: The Writer, 1972.
Treat, Lawrence, *The Mystery Writer's Handbook*. Cincinnati: Writer's Digest, 1976.

FICTION (THE NOVEL)

Burack, A.S. (ed.), *Techniques of Novel Writing*. Boston: The Writer, 1973.
Perry, Dick, *One Way To Write Your Novel*. Cincinnati: Writer's Digest, 1975.
Wallace, Irving, *The Writing of One Novel*. New York: Simon & Schuster, 1968.

FICTION (SCIENCE FICTION)

Science Fiction Writers of America, *Writing and Selling Science Fiction*. Cincinnati: Writer's Digest, 1976.
Asimov, Isaac (ed.), *Hugo Winners* (annual). Garden City, N.Y.: Annually issued. (Best science fiction of the year, voted by delegates to the annual World Science Fiction Convention.)

FICTION (SHORT STORY)

Dickson, Frank and Sandra Smythe (eds.), *Writer's Digest Handbook of Short Story Writing*. Cincinnati: Writer's Digest, 1970.

FILLERS

Burack, A.S. (ed.), *How To Write and Sell Fillers, Light Verse and Short Humor*. Boston: The Writer, 1977.

Boggess, Louise, *Writing Fillers That Sell*. Scranton, Pennsylvania: Funk & Wagnalls, 1978.

GAG WRITING

Markow, Jack, *The Cartoonist's and Gag Writer's Handbook*. Cincinnati: Writer's Digest, 1967.

GENERAL

Barzun, Jacques, *On Writing, Editing, and Publishing: Essays Explicative and Hortatory*. Chicago: University of Chicago Press, 1971.

Bernstein, Theodore M., *The Careful Writer: A Modern Guide to English Usage*. New York: Atheneum, 1965.

Brandt, W. and others, *The Craft of Writing*. Englewood Cliffs, N.J.: Prentice-Hall, 1969.

Casewit, Curtis, *Freelance Writing: Advice from the Pros*. New York: Macmillan, 1974.

Duncan, Lois, *How To Write and Sell Your Personal Experiences*. Cincinnati: Writer's Digest, 1979.

Fowler, Henry W., *Dictionary of Modern English Usage*. New York: Oxford University Press, 1965.

Mathieu, Aron, ed., *The Creative Writer*. Cincinnati: Writer's Digest, 1972.

Newman, Edwin, *A Civil Tongue*. New York: Bobbs-Merrill, 1976.

Polking, Kirk and Jean Chimsky, eds., *The Beginning Writer's Answer Book*. Cincinnati: Writer's Digest, 1977.

Renshaw, E. and D. Hacker, *A Practical Guide for Writers*. Englewood Cliffs, N.J.: Prentice-Hall, 1979.

Rivers, William L., *Writing: Craft and Art*. Englewood Cliffs, N.J.: Prentice-Hall, 1975.

Shenker, Israel, *Words and Their Masters*. Garden City, N.Y.: Doubleday, 1974.

Skillin, Marjorie E. and R. Gay, *Words Into Type.* Englewood Cliffs, N.J.: Prentice-Hall, 1974.

Steward, Hal D., *Successful Writer's Guide.* Englewood Cliffs, N.J.: Prentice-Hall, 1971.

Strunk, Wilbur, Jr. and E.B. White, *The Elements of Style.* New York: Macmillan, 1972.

Swain, Dwight V., *Techniques of the Selling Writer.* Norman, Oklahoma: University of Oklahoma Press, 1974.

University of Chicago Press, *A Manual of Style.* Chicago: University of Chicago Press, 1969.

Weisbord, Marvin, ed., *A Treasury of Tips for Writers.* Cincinnati: Writer's Digest, 1975.

Zinsser, William, *On Writing Well: An Informal Guide to Writing Non-fiction.* New York: Harper & Row, Pub., 1976.

GREETING CARDS

Chadwick, H. Joseph, *The Greeting Card Writer's Handbook.* Cincinnati: Writer's Digest, 1975.

Hardt, Lorraine, *How To Make Money Writing Greeting Cards.* New York: Fell, 1968.

HISTORY

Higham, John, *Writing American History: Essays on Modern Scholarship.* Bloomington, Indiana: Indiana University Press, 1970.

Marston, Doris, *A Guide to Writing History.* Cincinnati: Writer's Digest, 1975.

JOURNALISM (COURSES)

Editor & Publisher, *Editor & Publisher Yearbook* (issued annually). New York: Editor & Publisher. Lists more than 280 Schools and Departments of Journalism.

Association for Education in Journalism, *Journalism Educator* (annual directory issue). Minneapolis: University of Minnesota.

JOURNALISM (BROADCAST AND PRINT MEDIA)

American Newspaper Publishers Association Foundation, *Your Future in Daily Newspapers.* Washington, D.C.: ANPA Foundation.

Bittner, D. and J. Bittner, *Radio Journalism.* Englewood Cliffs, N.J.: Prentice-Hall, 1977.

Brady, John, *The Craft of Interviewing.* New York: Random House, 1977.

Chester, Giraud and others, *Television and Radio.* Englewood Cliffs, N.J.: Prentice-Hall, 1978.

Dygert, James H., *Investigative Journalist: Folk Heroes of a New Era.* Englewood Cliffs, N.J.: Prentice-Hall, 1976.

Hulteng, John L., *The News Media: What Makes Them Tick?* Englewood Cliffs, N.J.: Prentice-Hall, 1979.

——, *The Opinion Function: Editorial and Interpretive Writing for the News Media.* Hayden Lake, Idaho: Ridge House, 1977.

Jackson, Gregory, *Getting into Broadcast Journalism.* New York: Hawthorne Books, 1975.

Metz, W., *Newswriting: From Lead to "30."* Englewood Cliffs, N.J.: Prentice-Hall, 1979.

Metzler, K., *Newsgathering.* Englewood Cliffs, N.J.: Prentice-Hall, 1979.

——, *Creative Interviewing: The Writer's Guide to Gathering Information by Asking Questions.* Englewood Cliffs, N.J.: Prentice-Hall, 1977.

National Association of Broadcasters, *Careers in Radio and Careers in Television.* (Booklets.) Washington, D.C.: National Association of Broadcasters.

National Newspaper Association, *There Is a Career Waiting for You with America's Community Press.* Washington, D.C.: National Newspaper Association.

Rosenfeld, Megan, *Careers in Journalism for the New Woman.* New York: Franklin Watts, 1977.

Ruehlmann, William, *Stalking the Feature Story.* Cincinnati: Writer's Digest, 1978.

Stein, M.L., *Your Career in Journalism.* New York: Julian Messner, 1978.

Tebbel, John, *Opportunities in Journalism.* Louisville, Kentucky: Vocational Guidance Manuals, a Division of Data Courier, Inc., 1977.

Williams, P., *Investigative Reporting and Editing.* Englewood Cliffs, N.J.: Prentice-Hall, 1978.

Wolfe, Thomas and E.W. Johnson, *The New Journalism.* New York: Harper & Row, Pub., 1973.

JUVENILES

Nixon, Joan Lowery, *Writing Mysteries for Young People*. Boston: The Writer, 1977.

Whitney, Phyllis A., *Writing Juvenile Stories and Novels*. Boston: The Writer, 1976.

Wyndham, Lee, *Writing for Children and Teenagers*. Cincinnati: Writer's Digest, 1972.

Yolen, Jane, *Writing Books for Children*. Boston: The Writer, 1976.

LAW FOR WRITERS

Crawford, Tad, *Writer's Legal Guide*. New York: Hawthorne, 1979.

Polking, Kirk and Leonard S. Meranus, *Law and the Writer*. Cincinnati: Writer's Digest, 1978.

Wittenberg, Philip, *The Protection of Literary Property*. Boston: The Writer, 1978.

MAGAZINE PUBLISHING/EDITING

Click, J.W. and Russell Baird, *Magazine Editing and Production*. Dubuque, Iowa: William C. Brown, 1974.

May, Charles Paul, *Publishing Careers/Magazines and Books*. New York: Franklin Watts, 1978.

Mogel, L., *The Magazine: Everything You Need To Know To Make It in the Magazine Business*. Englewood Cliffs, N.J.: Prentice-Hall, 1979.

Peterson, Theodore, *Magazines in the Twentieth Century*. Urbana, Illinois: University of Illinois Press, 1964.

Rivers, William L., *The Free Lancer and the Staff Writer*. Belmont, California: Wadsworth, 1976.

MARKETING (GENERAL)

Gearing, P. and E. Brunson, *Breaking Into Print: How To Get Your Work Published*. Englewood Cliffs, N.J.: Prentice-Hall, 1977.

Reynolds, Paul R., *A Professional Guide to Marketing Manuscripts.* Boston: The Writer, 1968.

MARKETING (DIRECTORIES AND GUIDES)

Ayer Press Staff, *Ayer Directory of Publications.* Philadelphia: Ayer Press (revised annually). Guide to newspapers and periodicals printed in the United States, Canada, and certain other areas. Useful as a directory, but contains no marketing data on the newspapers and general-circulation magazines listed.

Bacon's Publicity Checker (issued annually). Chicago: Bacon's Publishing Company. Volume I of this service lists some 4,000 U.S. and Canadian magazines and newspapers in the following categories (magazines): business, industrial, trade and professional; consumer, and farm journals. Listings include brief descriptions of publicity requirements, which indicate whether or not a given magazine accepts and runs news and feature articles. This handy guide includes scores, if not hundreds, of publications not found in the standard marketing guides, especially in the area of trade journals.

Editor & Publisher Staff, *Editor & Publisher Yearbook.* New York: Editor & Publisher, (issued annually). Lists newspapers published in the United States, and principal newspapers of the world. Also lists news and feature syndicates. Does not include descriptions of market requirements.

Fulton, Len and Ellen Ferber, eds., *International Directory of Little Magazines and Small Presses.* Paradise, California: Dustbooks (revised annually). Includes book publishers and periodicals which may not be listed in such standard directories as *Literary Market Place* and *Writer's Market,* together with much useful marketing information. Beginning writers and authors of avant-garde or off-beat material may find outlets for their work listed in this directory.

Literary Market Place (issued annually). New York: R.R. Bowker. The "Yellow Pages" of the publishing industry, *LMP* includes listings of "agents, artists and art services, associations, book clubs, book lists, book manufacturing, book publishers, book reviewers, calendar of trade events, columnists and commentators, courses for the book trade, direct mail and promotion, editorial services, employment agencies, exporters and importers, government agencies, literary prizes and awards, magazines, newspapers and news services, paper mills-suppliers, photographers, public relations services, radio and television, sales representatives, services-typing, shipping, translators, wholesalers, and writers' conferences." Although *LMP* does indicate the broad areas of subject matter in which publishers may be interested, it does not describe editorial needs and requirements in detail.

MIMP–Magazine Industry Market Place. New York: R.R. Bowker (issued annually). A valuable reference tool for writers. The first section lists some 2600 magazines in various categories (consumer, trade, professional, and so forth). Each listing includes names, addresses, phone numbers of principal editors, a description of the periodical's editorial content, and in many instances such guideline information as "accepts unsolicited mss.," "buys freelance fiction, nonfiction, poetry, cartoons, etc.," or "query first." *MIMP* also classifies publications by type (business, farm, association, house organ, journal, etc.) and by subject matter (agriculture, art, fraternal, industry, medical, and so forth). Also included is a useful section titled "Reference Books of the Trade." As in the case of *LMP, MIMP* closes with a directory of names, titles, addresses, and phone numbers of key people in the magazine world.

Greenberg, Howard, *Standard Periodical Directory* (revised annually). New York: Oxbridge. Listing more than 65,000 publications in the United States and Canada, this directory claims to include "four times more titles than any other directory." Under more than 200 categories, it lists consumer magazines, trade journals, newsletters, government publications, house organs, and many other classifications. Does not include marketing information.

Standard Rate & Data Service, *Consumer Magazine and Farm Publication Rates and Data.* Skokie, Illinois: Standard Rate & Data Service, Inc. (revised monthly). Two publications of this service are of special interest and utility to writers: the one cited above, and another titled *Business Publications* (also revised monthly). Though designed primarily for the use of the advertising industry, these listings include "profiles" of publications which give the writer valuable insights into the editorial needs and requirements of the magazines listed. (See Chapter 12 for examples of the ways in which these sources can be used.)

Black, A. & C., eds., *Writers' & Artists' Yearbook.* Boston: The Writer, annual editions. A guide to markets in Great Britain, Ireland, Canada, and other British Commonwealth countries, for writers, playwrights, composers, and photographers. Includes lists of magazines, book publishers, agents, and broadcast companies, with marketing requirements. Also includes a section on foreign rights and international copyright.

National Research Bureau, *Working Press of the Nation.* Burlington, Iowa, periodically revised. This five-volume set includes the following titles: (1) *Newspaper Directory*—information on some 6,600 dailies and weeklies; (2) *Magazine Directory*—data on approximately 5,000 U.S. and Canadian periodicals, categorized into 200 different classifications; (3) *TV and Radio Directory*—listing 2,200 television and 6,900 radio stations; (4) *Feature Writer, Syndicate, and Photographer Directory*—lists some 1,770 free-lance writers and photographers alphabetically and by areas of specialization, plus information on feature syndicates, and (5) *Internal Publications Directory*—describing some 4,200 house organs and internal publications in the United States and Canada.

The Writer, *The Writer's Handbook.* Boston: The Writer, revised annually. More than 60 percent of this volume is devoted to articles on various aspects of writing, with the balance given to market listings. A useful reference source, although not as comprehensive as *Writer's Market* in terms of marketing data.

Brohaugh, William, ed., *Writer's Market.* Cincinnati: Writer's Digest, revised annually. An indispensable reference source for professional writers, this volume contains by far the most complete and useful collection of marketing information available in one book. Lists periodicals by categories, names and addresses of publishing houses and their editorial requirements, names and titles of editors, rates and methods of payment, and other valuable information.

MOTION PICTURES/TELEVISION

Cousin, Michelle, *Writing a Television Play.* Boston: The Writer, 1975.

Herman, Lewis, *Practical Manual of Screen Playwriting for Theater and Television Films.* New York: New American Library.

Nash, Constance and Virginia Oakey, *What To Write, How To Write It, Where To Sell It.* New York: Harper & Row, Pub., 1978.

Nash, Constance and Virginia Oakey, *The Television Writer's Handbook: What To Write, How To Write It, Where To Sell It.* New York: Harper & Row, Pub., 1978.

Simon, Arthur, *The Success Guide to Writing for TV and Motion Pictures: Learn the Business Side of Show Business.* Hollywood: Future Shop, 1978.

Trapnell, Coles, *Teleplay: An Introduction to Television Writing.* New York: Hawthorn, 1974.

Wylie, Max, *Writing for Television.* Chicago: Contemporary Books, 1975.

NONFICTION (ARTICLES)

Arnold, Glenn F., *Writing Award-Winning Articles.* New York: Nelson, 1979.

Boggess, Louise, *Article Techniques That Sell.* San Mateo, California: B&B Press, 1978.

Dillon, Mary T., *Magazine Article Writing.* Boston: The Writer, 1977.

Gunther, Max, *Writing the Modern Magazine Article.* Boston: The Writer, 1977.

Holmes, Marjorie, *Writing the Creative Article.* Boston: The Writer, 1976.

Kelley, Jerome E., *Magazine Writing Today.* Cincinnati: Writer's Digest, 1977.

Newcomb, Duane, *A Complete Guide to Marketing Magazine Articles.* Cincinnati: Writer's Digest, 1975.

Samson, Jack, *Successful Outdoor Writing.* Cincinnati: Writer's Digest, 1979.

NONFICTION (GENERAL)

Jacobs, Hayes B., *Writing and Selling Non-Fiction.* Cincinnati: Writer's Digest, 1975.

Knott, William C., *The Craft of Non-Fiction.* Reston, Virginia: Reston, 1974.

Rockwell, F., *How To Write Non-Fiction That Sells.* Chicago: Contemporary Books, 1975.

Thomas, David S. and Hubert Bermont, *Getting Published: The Complete Guide for the Non-Fiction Writer.* New York: Fleet, 1973.

Zinsser, William, *On Writing Well: An Informal Guide to Writing Non-Fiction.* New York: Harper & Row, Pub., 1976.

NONFICTION (BOOKS)

Daigh, Ralph, *Maybe You Should Write a Book*. Englewood Cliffs, N.J.: Prentice-Hall, 1977.

Doyle, Thomas F., *How To Write a Book about Your Specialty*. Sacramento, California: Creative Book, 1976.

Gunther, Max, *Writing and Selling a Non-Fiction Book*. Boston: The Writer, 1973.

Reynolds, Paul R., *The Non-Fiction Book: How To Write and Sell It*. New York: Morrow, 1970.

PHOTOJOURNALISM

Ahlers, Arvel W., *Where and How To Sell Your Photographs*. Garden City, N.Y.: Amphoto, 1977.

Milton, John, *The Writer-Photographer*. Radnor, Pennsylvania: Chilton, 1972.

POETRY

Armour, Richard, *Writing Light Verse and Prose Humor*. Boston: The Writer, n.d.

Hamilton, Anne, *Seven Principles of Poetry*. Boston: The Writer, n.d.

Hillyer, Robert, *First Principles of Verse*. Boston: The Writer, 1950.

Jerome, Judson, *The Poet and the Poem*. Cincinnati: Writer's Digest, 1974.

Trefethen, Florence, *Writing a Poem*. Boston: The Writer, 1975.

Turco, Lewis, *Poetry: An Introduction through Writing*. Reston, Virginia: Reston, 1973.

PUBLISHING

Bailey, Herbert S., Jr., *The Art and Science of Book Publishing*. New York: Harper & Row, Pub., 1970.

Dessauer, John P., *Book Publishing: What It Is, What It Does*. New York: R.R. Bowker, 1976.

O'Neill, Carol L. and Avima Ruder, *Complete Guide to Editorial Freelancing.* New York: Dodd, Mead, 1974.

Tebbel, John, *Opportunities in Publishing Careers.* Louisville: Vocational Guidance Manuals, 1975.

REFERENCE (GENERAL)

Brohaugh, William, ed., *The Writer's Resource Guide.* Cincinnati: Writer's Digest, 1979. ". . . compendium of research sources for freelance writers and for anyone else who needs a handy one-volume directory of free information on practically any subject."

Books in Print (published annually). New York: R.R. Bowker. Four volumes, listing all books in print in a given year by title and author. Listings include price, publisher, year of publication.

Sterling, Christopher H. and Timothy R. Haight, *The Mass Media.* New York: Praeger, 1978. Detailed statistics on all mass media in the United States, including schedules of salaries paid to reporters in cities throughout the nation.

Subject Guide to Books in Print. New York: Bowker, revised annually. Lists all books in print under subject headings. All subjects are also cross referenced. Another Bowker title performs the same service for children's books in print.

RELIGIOUS PUBLICATIONS

Schell, Mildred, *Wanted: Writers for the Christian Market.* Valley Forge, Pennsylvania: Judson, 1975.

SELF-PUBLISHING

Henderson, Bill, ed., *The Publish-It-Yourself Handbook: Literary Tradition & How-To.* Yonkers, New York: Pushcart, 1973.

Mueller, Lothar W., *How To Publish Your Own Book.* Detroit: Harlo, 1976.

Nicolas, Ted, *How To Publish Your Own Book and Make It a Best Seller.* Enterprise Del., 1978.

Poynter, Dan, *The Self-Publishing Manual.* Santa Barbara: Parachuting Publications, 1979.

Stickter, Jim, *You Can Write, Print, Publish Your Own Book.* Corpus Christi: Hemisphere House, 1976.

Thompson, Paul, *How To Be Your Own Publisher and Get Your Book into Print.* Sacramento, California: Creative Book Co., 1978.

SONG WRITING

Boye, Henry, *How to Make Money Selling the Songs You Write.* New York: Fell, 1975.

Kasha, Al and Joel Hirschhorn, *If They Ask You, You Can Write a Song.* New York: Simon & Schuster, 1979.

Shemel, Sidney and M. William Krasilovsky, *More About This Business of Music.* New York: Watson-Guptill, 1974.

TEACHING OF WRITING

Graham, John, *Craft So Hard To Learn: Conversations with Poets and Novelists About the Teaching of Writing.* Garrett, George, ed. New York: Morrow, 1972.

Murray, Donald M., *Writer Teaches Writing.* Boston: Houghton Mifflin, 1968.

TECHNICAL AND BUSINESS WRITING

American Chemical Society, *Handbook for Authors.* Washington: American Chemical Society, n.d.

Bowen, Mary E. and J.A. Mazzeo, eds., *Writing about Science.* New York: Oxford University Press, 1979.

Blicq, Ronald S., *Technically Write: Communications for the Technical Man.* Englewood Cliffs, N.J.: Prentice-Hall, 1972.

Dagher, Joseph P., *Technical Communication: A Practical Guide.* Englewood Cliffs, N.J.: Prentice-Hall, 1978.

Sherman, Theodore A. and Simon S. Johnson, *Modern Technical Writing.* Englewood Cliffs, N.J.: Prentice-Hall, 1975.

Whalen, Doris H., *Handbook for Business Writers.* New York: Harcourt Brace Jovanovich, 1978.

TRANSLATING

Selver, Paul, *The Art of Translating Poetry.* Boston, The Writer, 1966.

WRITERS' ASSOCIATIONS

Academy of American Poets, 1078 Madison Ave., New York, N.Y. 10028. Publishes newsletter. Conducts workshops, awards prizes.

American Society of Journalists & Authors, Inc., 1501 Broadway, New York, N.Y. 10036. ASJA describes itself as "the nation's foremost organization of professional writers of nonfiction articles and books." Publishes market information and other data useful to members.

Associated Business Writers of America, 1450 S. Havana, Suite 620, Aurora, Colorado 80012. Publishes an annual *Directory of Business Writers* and a monthly *Confidential Bulletin* for members. Purpose: "To improve the image and working conditions of business writers."

The Authors Guild, Inc., 234 W. 44th St., New York, N.Y. 10036. Services to members only, including counsel on business and professional problems. Write for membership requirements.

Authors League of America, Inc., 234 W. 44th St., New York, N.Y., 10036. Membership restricted to authors and dramatists who are members of the Authors Guild, Inc., and the Dramatists Guild, Inc.

Aviation/Space Writers Association, Cliffwood Rd., Chester, N.J. 07930. Publishes brochures, newsletter, and offers other services to members.

Canadian Authors Association, 18 St. Joseph St., Toronto, Ontario, Canada M4Y 1J9. Write for membership requirements and application.

Garden Writers Association of America, 101 Park Ave., New York, N.Y. 10017. Publishes newsletter for members only.

International Association of Business Communicators, 870 Market St., Suite 928, San Francisco, California 94102. Publishes information about internal communications, newsletter, brochures, and other data, for members only.

Mystery Writers of America, 105 E. 19th St., New York, N.Y. 10003. Membership open to writers who have made at least one sale in mystery, crime, or suspense writing. Novices and nonwriters may qualify for associate memberships.

National Association of Science Writers, Box 294, Greenlawn, N.Y. 11740. Publications for members include a newsletter and brochures "to increase the flow of news from scientists" and to improve the general level of science writing and reporting.

The National League of American Pen Women, Inc., 1300 17th St., NW, Washington, D.C. 20036. Sponsors workshops and contests for women writers, artists, and composers. Offers scholarships in the creative arts. Publishes brochures and pamplets.

The National Writers Club, 1450 S. Havana, Suite 620, Aurora, Colorado 80012. Wide range of services to members, including market information, bibliographies, newsletter, special reports.

Outdoor Writers Association of America, Inc., 4141 W. Bradley Rd., Milwaukee, Wisconsin 53209. Members are professional outdoor writers, lecturers, photographers.

Society of Children's Book Writers, Box 296, Los Angeles, California 90066. Publishes market reports, research guides, counsels members on contracts and other professional matters.

Society of Professional Journalists, Sigma Delta Chi, 35 E. Wacker Dr., Chicago, Illinois 60601. Largest and oldest organization serving professional journalists. Student membership category available. Publishes monthly organ *The Quill* and brochure "How To Apply for a Job in Media."

Women in Communications, Inc., Box 9561, Austin, Texas 78766. Offers brochures, bibliographies, information searches, newsletter, career pamphlets and other aids. Members are women engaged in all fields of communication.

The Word Guild, 119 Mt. Aburn St., Cambridge, Massachusetts 02138. Services to free-lance writers. Publishes monthly magazine, holds monthly meetings, offers placement services and help on assignments.

Writers Guild of America, East, 22 West 48th St., New York, N.Y. 10036. "A labor organization representing all screen, television and radio writers." Membership requirements and fees.

Writers Guild of America, West, 8955 Beverly Blvd., Los Angeles, California, 90048. "A labor organization representing all screen, television and radio writers." Membership requirements and fees.

PROFESSIONAL PUBLICATIONS FOR WRITERS

Editor & Publisher, 575 Lexington Avenue, New York, N.Y. 10022.

Folio; The Magazine for Magazine Management, 125 Elm Street, P.O. Box 697, New Canaan, Connecticut 06840.

Publishers Weekly, 1180 Avenue of the Americas, New York, N.Y. 10036.

The Quill, 35 E. Wacker Dr., Chicago, Illinois 60601.

The Writer, 8 Arlington St., Boston, Massachusetts 02116.

Writer's Digest, 9933 Alliance Road, Cincinnati, Ohio 45242.

Writer's Yearbook, 9933 Alliance Road, Cincinnati, Ohio 45242.

INDEX

255